Society and Culture

Society and Culture

S.P. NAGENDRA

Edited by
C. Lakshmanna
Jugendra Sahai

RAWAT PUBLICATIONS
Jaipur • New Delhi • Bangalore • Hyderabad • Guwahati

ISBN 978-81-316-0514-1

Published by
Prem Rawat for **Rawat Publications**
Satyam Apts, Sector 3, Jawahar Nagar, Jaipur 302 004 (India)
Phone: 0141 265 1748 / 7006 Fax: 0141 265 1748
E-mail: info@rawatbooks.com
Website: www.rawatbooks.com

New Delhi Office
4858/24, Ansari Road, Daryaganj, New Delhi 110 002
Phone: 011 2326 3290

Also at *Bangalore, Hyderabad* and *Guwahati*

Typeset by Rawat Computers, Jaipur
Printed at Chaman Enterprises, New Delhi

Contents

Acknowledgement

First of all, we applaud the decision of some of Professor S.P. Nagendra's old students who had assembled in New Delhi to bring out a volume in his honour. The occasion was to participate in a national seminar and luckily all of them were staying with one of the editors, Professor Lakshmanna. It was then decided that Professor C. Lakshmanna and Professor Jugendra Sahai will jointly edit the volume.

We appreciate the effort of Professor R.C. Sarikwal in initiating the correspondence with the assistance of Professor Lakshmanna who was posted at New Delhi as state representative to the centre with cabinet rank. Professor Sarikwal used to visit him whenever required to handle the correspondence. It can be well imagined that in those summer days how difficult it would have been to travel from Ghaziabad to Andhra Bhawan, New Delhi. He never felt disappointed or disgusted even when replies were not coming.

We are grateful to the family of Professor Nagendra for their effort to collect the articles and got loaded in CD available for publication. Mrs Nagendra always kept reminding us of the timely publication of the book as she too is not well. Professor Nagendra's youngest son Professor Srivardhan Pathak deserves special mention as he always remained in touch with us and attended the queries promptly.

We also feel obliged to Professor Shailly Sahai for the hard work done by her in the proofreading and suggested improvements.

We have no adequate words to express our gratitude to Mr Ramesh Chand Tiwari who helped us in so many ways, whether it was a personal reminder to contributors or planning the publication of the book.

We also feel obliged to Mr Kailash Rawat and Mr Pranit Rawat of Rawat Publications for publishing the book in the shortest possible time.

Jugendra Sahai

Prologue

C. Lakshmanna

This commomerative volume in honour of Professor S.P. Nagendra consists of some of his published articles. There are many others but these are significant ones. These articles can be broadly subsumed under the themes, viz., "traditions and their moral and ritual foundations", "culture and its policy implications", "development and its important ramifications", "regional and sectoral developments" and finally, his tributes to his teacher, philosopher and guide, Professor D.P. Mukerji.

Nagendra was an incisive and versatile thinker. An attempt has been made through this volume to address the sociological fraternity in particular and general public in general to make available some of his stimulating and thought-provoking ideas for their consideration. It has been a privilege, as mentioned elsewhere, to be a student of Professor Nagendra and to have been associated with him both in the classrooms and outside which provided me with an opportunity to closely observe and assimilate his thoughts.

Nagendra feels that the ancient Indian society was the nearest approximation to what Rene Guenon calls 'a normal civilization'. He goes on to explain how it rests on principles which guided the hierarchical ordering of the society and also implied application and extension of a pure and metaphysical doctrine underlying a traditional civilization. Nagendra contends that Guenon considered this as correspondence between "men's intimate nature and his particular vocation". He differs with Emile Durkheim who had described a traditional society as mechanical. The theory of hierarchy for him is a natural corollary of the traditional doctrine of the inherence of many and different things. He states that even Christian theology rests on this theory of inherence or inclusions.

The change which takes place in traditional society is from one order to another. These changes are similar to those in the life of an organism. Deviations from the norms are common because of the imperfectability of human nature. However, these are looked after by the traditional methods of socialization and social control. Nagendra is concerned with the model on which the normal societies are based and for delineating this, he looks for Vedic and Upanishadic literatures. In order to derive this mode, he discusses in great detail concepts such as primeval sacrifice of gods, the immortality of gods, *Mukti* or freedom. He further states that "it is not an accident of history that the sacrifice (rite) is the central principle of social organization in traditional (normal) societies". He discusses Shruti or inspirational knowledge (revelation in Hindu and Christian traditions), myths (derivative mythology), and Smritis and Dharma (the moral law of Hindus). He also discusses the paths (marg) of realization, Ashrama scheme of life and Varna Vyavastha, including Gotra and Pravara orders. We can conclude with his own observation that the ancient Indian society was the nearest to normal society.

There are two more articles in this volume which discuss the traditional basis of social life. The article "The Traditional Theory of Caste" discusses the basis for the evolution of caste in India. Modern sociological theory points out that there are two modes of assignment of role and status to the individual in the society, viz., the ascription and achievement systems. The ascription model assigns role and status at birth, adherence to which is mandatory – the traditional theory of caste is an example of this model. In the other model, the individual is trained and achieves the role and status himself. The modern social stratification system represents this latter model. In Nagendra's words, "the texture of the theory is made up of a number of principles, all penetrating into one another and centring around the supreme principle of what the Hindus call Dharma". Thus Dharma is central to the traditional theory of caste. This theory simultaneously represents the law of one's own nature at the micro-cosmic level and the nature's law or the law of the comic being at the macro-cosmic level. It significantly explains the relationship between the whole and the part.

Nagendra contends that the caste system is a naturally determined organization of social functions or, in other words, a given and unalterable system of functional differentiation. He goes on to say that the Indian caste system (Jati Vyavastha), with its characteristic emphasis on hereditary occupation and ritual observance, is the nearest approximation to the model of natural social hierarchy. He also strongly believes that it stands for the individual freedom. The traditional theory of caste combines both metaphysical and mythical aspects which can be understood properly in the context of Moksha which is the ultimate goal of all Hindus. There are two paths or margas open for attainment of Moksha, namely, the Pravrthi and Nivruthi. One explains the way how an individual being part of the worldly order (Ashrama scheme) gradually be detached and attain Mukti while the other is a path of renunciation and complete detachment from the surrounding world. In varying degrees, sacrifice occupies an important place in both the paths. In passing he also recognizes that this traditional theory of caste does not find favour with the modern sociologists.

Among studies on the caste system, Nagendra places Louis Dumont's *Homo Hierarchicus* on a special footing, for according to him, Domont's interest is not in the substantive whole, i.e., caste system, but the hierarchy of parts in the whole or, in other words, the order of orders. *Homo Hierarchicus* has relevance to traditional man as well as his modern counterpart. In his efforts to locate the order of orders, Dumont realizes the same structural principle in every layer of the caste system. "The rank order, the division of labour, marriage regulations, commensal relations, in fact, all the lived in orders are shown to reflect the same structured principle", the exception being power and authority. Because of this, Nagendra points out that Dumont opposes this to "social stratification", the expression used by modern sociologists to describe their own gradation of power and authority. "Gradation", Dumont says, "is implicit in hierarchy too, but it is a gradation of status, and not of power and authority". Commenting on endogamy and hypergamy Nagendra says that they are "the basic features of marriage within the caste system, but as Dumont would argue, they are just applications of the principle of hierarchy. For instance, marriage within the caste is a mechanism by which the castes reproduce themselves, and in so reproducing themselves what they tend to retain and perpetuate is their respective status in the transmission order". Nagendra goes on to state that as regards restrictions on physical contact and eating and drinking it is not different to see how they constitute one of the basic criteria by which the castes separate and distinguish themselves hierarchically from one another. In this context, it is notable to observe that "the preoccupation with status can be seen to be present even among the untouchables some of whom close themselves to others whom they consider as more untouchable". On explanations offered by Dumont on division of labour and the jajmani system, Nagendra is inclined to accept them, rather than explanations offered by others. He sums up his comments on Dumont's *Homo Hierarchicus* thus: We began by remarking that "Dumont's work is of a different kind". It is different because here is an attempt to understand the system in the true spirit of understanding; at no stage does it appear that the experience from which Dumont speaks, he has not re-lived with the hierarchical man in India and it is this re-living of an already lived experience which must inform every comparative sociological enquiry. There is no attempt at all either to belittle the system or to denigrate it. There is yet another merit of this work. Dumont has neatly reassembled all fragments of understanding bearing on the caste system which had been lying scattered in the work of scholars like Blunt, Ghurye, Stevenson, Karve, Gough, Srinivas, Bailey, Mayor etc., and woven them back into the texture of his own structural understanding.

However, we must not forget that Dumont has his own limitations imposed by the sociological perception, which he shares with the modern man. It is this perception which is at the back of his sociocentric view of hierarchy. There is no contradiction in the hierarchical man's mind, between the caste and varna, between birth and function and between status and power. On the basis of separation and complementarity between purity and impurity, the principle of hierarchy accounts for the differentiation of the status among all the varnas or castes. Nagendra further argues that "the structural principle of separation and complementarity cannot be given meaning in secular terms. To say that man is hierarchical is more or less than to say he is religious". Dumont and modern thinkers refuse to see the logic of their own arguments.

In conclusion, we may say that one may or may not fully agree with all that Nagendra or for that matter Dumont and others say about hierarchy and traditional caste system but one cannot but appreciate the logic of their arguments or presentation.

II

Professor Nagendra was greatly concerned with culture in its different aspects as was his teacher Professor D.P. Mukerji. Nagendra borrows "interpretive understanding" – the concept widely used by Wilhelm Dielthey – to adequately comprehend the concept of culture. He distinguishes science from history, for the former studies nature while the latter studies culture. There were, however, different perspectives among thinkers regarding the scope of history. Without getting into the detailed discussion which he presents in this essay, it is sufficient for us to say that Nagendra leans on the perspective which Dielthey and a few others hold on it: "Being the manifestation of the life of mind, culture is an essentially ahistoric reality". He states further that cultures are ahistoric realties, not only because we do not know their origins but also and more especially as their traditions consist of ahistorical material in the form of myths, legends, art forms, fairy tales, songs, customs etc. These represent the oral traditions of the common people. They are not historically dates. Nagendra bemoans that modern industrial society flourished on the destruction of folkways and mores.

Nagendra feels that the conventional historical method is inadequate to have an appropriate understanding of a normal or traditional civilization like India. The best way to understand such societies is interpretive or hermeneutic appreciation of them. Nagendra next discusses thinkers such as Ananda Coomaraswamy, Rene Guenon, Heinreich Zimmer, Joseph Campbell and G.C. Pande. His main object is to present the best interpretations of the understanding of traditional society. Each of them, in their distinct way, attempts to have a comprehensive view of the traditional Indian society. All of them are more for interpretive understanding of the society in terms of myths, archetypes, symbols and primordial manifestations. He emphasizes that opposition between modern civilizations created by the scientific and industrial revolutions and the cultures organized around traditions should not be construed to mean that we point out a fundamental opposition between the truth of science and the truth of religion or metaphysics. The opposition actually is between the scientific world view which has glorified appearances and their scientific representations into truth and traditional thought where even the truth or social world of science is considered the epiphenomenon of the real or ultimate truth. After a detailed discussion of the thought processes of the earlier mentioned thinkers, Nagendra concludes that the reconciliation of the two (tradition and modernity) is possible only if modernity would be willing to test its principles against the primordial norm and correct them accordingly.

Professor Nagendra's concerns on cultural policy are similar to those of Professor D.P. Mukerji who, in his essay on Indian culture, states that the new Indian middle classes are the creation of British rule. The political and administrative exigencies of British rule threw open new liberal professions and to nab them arose the need for English educated Indians. This new middle class was not the carrier of the traditional Indian culture nor was the extension of the alien British culture. Nagendra laments that the Indian national movement and its leaders, except Gandhi, had neither the time nor inclination to mould durable culture because of its very nature and purpose, namely, attaining independence from the British rule. Nationalism, according to Nagendra, which was propped up as a new religion, produced a culture without its corresponding ethics. Under the circumstances, in post-independent India, planning for a new culture and cultural policy becomes a herculean task. He cites the views of Professor Mukerji to strengthen his argument: "In may view", says Professor Mukerji, "culture as such cannot be fully planned. If culture comprehends the whole of life, then, surely a large segment of living formed by the unconscious world have to be recognized, respected and allowed freedom. This is truc of individuals, more true of groups and still more so of strata of people whose living is one long persuasive new to tradition."

Planning of culture involves freedom at different levels, namely, (i) freedom of discussion and opinion, (ii) freedom of association and action, and (iii) freedom for securing distinctive justice by eliminating fear of want and obstacle free situation for enjoying prospects which follow such a situation. Professor Mukerji, Nagendra points out, is highly doubtful about current conditions being conclusive to plan culture effectively. He further says that "in a word, no manner of revivalism is the remedy against the situation. It will be an offence against the law of change". To the extent that culture is an attribute of man, it can neither be controlled nor planned as "man qua man" cannot be controlled or planned. Culture for him is different from economics and politics. It raises the question of difference between the scientific and the artistic view of life. He cites C.P. Snow who says that while scientists have a culture of pragmatic optimism, men of arts and letters have a different view. On the question of culture, in this regard, Nagendra discusses in detail the world view of culture in traditional societies where life was an integrated whole and the modern societies which view various categories as distinct fields of human action. This also raises for him the question of pursuit of knowledge which has been elaborately discussed in the essay. Nagendra concludes that "the human condition of plurality, then, is the sine qua non of culture. Man must enjoy a measure of freedom to reveal what he has to reveal or to become what he has in him to become. Should this freedom be taken away from him, i.e., should action be reduced to labour, man will cease to be man".

Following Karl Jaspers, Nagendra advocates "democratic planning" or planning for freedom, i.e., planning as an alternative to laissez-faire and as an antidote to totalitarian planning. However, Nagendra, following Professor Mukerji, feels that culture cannot be fully planned. However, a liberal state must ensure that its democratic ethos and its pluralist culture ensure each other. It must pressure the distinctiveness of all groups and the pluralist fabric be upheld to present the unity in diversity.

III

For Professor Nagendra, the process of development is part of social change. He holds, however, that a lot of misinformation has gathered around these concepts. The confusion which exists between the natural reality and social reality contributes to this misinformation. For him, social reality is para-natural reality. But, from the time of founding of sociology, the effort of these eminent thinkers has been to highlight the nature-image of human society. The social science methodology used to investigate the social reality has been grounded in scientific method instead of metaphysics. The modern sociological theory of development, however, considers development as a change from lower to higher state of social order, on the assumption that the model of higher state reflects the harmony present in nature. Nagendra goes on to state that "it is interesting to note that the sociological concept of rationality means nothing but adaptability to nature when it comes to man-nature opposition, and social conformity when it comes to individual-society opposition". Thus understood development becomes "synonymous with linear change implying a point of beginning and a point of end of which the former is the lower point and the latter the higher point". But

Nagendra has reservations about this proposition for social reality is perceived as ontological or phenomenological; in a state of being or becoming tradition considers reality as either performance or change of one is a reality, the other is an illusion. But they are complementary. From performance to change and from change to performance is a cyclic process. He states that all living things manifestly undergo cycles of growth and decay and of life and death. In traditional thought development means becoming according to one's own nature. Further of decay and development are processes within time, the question arises as to who can fill the interregnum between the two. It is said that it can be done only by a temporal authority who can stop the drift and start development a fresh. He goes on to say that this agency may be called charismatic personality sociologically or the divine incarnation in terms of living religions.

The end of the Second World War saw the end of the colonialism and the dawn of freedom in many former colonies. Symbolically, the end of colonial power in India and China heralded the freedom movements all over the world and the emergence of sovereign nations in the colonies. During the colonial period, either traditions in these subject nations were ravaged or were subjugated to western world ethos under the regime of modernization. Thus modernity and westernization became the catchwords for development. The emphasis was that the newly liberated societies had to transform their sub-human existence, obviously the relic of colonial oppression, and they must follow the examples of their western counterparts – be those of the rightist modernity or leftist modernity. Sub-divisions of the global society were in terms of the so-called development, namely, the first world, the second world and the third world. The nagging question still is: What is the place of tradition? Nagendra asserts that tradition is simply underdeveloped modernity and modernity, developed tradition. He recalls, in this context, Million Singer's statement that modernization takes the form of traditionalization. In essence, it is the same in M.N. Srinivas' theory of modernization and westernization.

On the attainment of independence for India, two dominant thought processes prevailed in India. One, that the Indian society had been a bad society and hence we have to abandon all the institutions that existed in India and should be replaced by the ones borrowed from the western economy model. Two, that the centralist planning is the model for eliminating poverty and backwardness. Not soon thereafter, we were awakened to a realization that the fruits of this planning are not reaching the common man for whom it was intended. Further, unlike in traditional India, modernizing India found the division between cities and villages as disparate entities. This has been the nemesis of current planning process.

The theory of development followed so far has failed and an alternate theory of development is the urgent necessity. The basic for the new theory must be "cultural action for freedom" which means the creation of an institutional set up suited to the people's own genius. The search for this new identity began during the freedom movement, when Indian leaders strived for a new educational system suited to India. Swadeshi movement of Mahatma Gandhi was the answer to this pressing question. This reflects the basic philosophy that "unity within a culturally plural society cannot be thought of except within the framework primordial human values which constitute the core of all cultural traditions and yet transcend them each individually." Further, "but the compatability of development with tradition is as axiomatic as its incompatability with modernity".

Development a la modernity is a manipulation of man and society according to a set formula devised by a historically successful group. But development a la tradition is growth of man and society according to the law of their being. A theory of development, therefore, presupposes an adequate understanding of tradition and culture whose source is myth and folklore now consigned to the limbo by contemporary sociology. Gandhi's love for Swadeshi, traditional village communities, a need-oriented rather than acquisition-oriented economy organized round the virtues of Asteya and Aparigraha (non-stealing and non-acquisitiveness) can be matched only by this relentless opposition to universalized, abstract and impersonalized systems of education, health and law etc., which could never serve the genuine ends of life. A full discussion of Gandhi's social philosophy, particularly his scheme of social reconstruction, will not be possible here. But let there be no doubt of the fact that there is no better answer, to date, to the challenge of globalized yordism, with all its sinister implications for the so-called developing societies, than Gandhi, with his social philosophy, particularly the scheme of social reconstruction. It is unfortunate indeed that the successor to the traditional civilization of India, the contemporary Indian society, instead of offering a creative response to the challenge of modernity, has been virtually behaving like a hungry body, subsisting upon its own reserves of energy and trying at times, to revive its old traditions without understanding what they stand for, or others to trace the dominant values of modernity to its own traditions.

Apart from the theory of development, Professor Nagendra was also highly concerned with the specific issues confronting the Indian society. This is evident from his essays on "Attacking Rural Poverty: University and NGO Partnership", "The City and Urbanization", "Rethinking Development in Relation to the Scheduled Castes" and "Sociological Perspective on the Development of Eastern Uttar Pradesh". In these essays he brings to bear upon his astute mind to critically examine the issues with a view to find solutions for them. These essays reflect his comprehension of the development needed for improving the living conditions and the welfare of these neglected groups and sections. The last essay of this volume is Professor Nagendra's centenary tribute to his great teacher, Professor D.P. Mukerji, highlighting his seminal and thought-provoking contributions of DP to theoretical sociology for which Lucknow School of Sociology is justifiably famous in Indian sociological world.

Tributes to an Outstanding Teacher

C. Lakshmanna

Professor Sheetala Prasad Nagendra, Bhai Saheb for me, was a rare intellectual and a rarer person. He had several 'firsts' to his credit in his long, illustrious career. He stood tall in any gathering with his outstanding and sterling qualities. He endeared himself to one and all, with whom he interacted, both with his mind and heart. Endowed with an amiable nature and personality, Nagendra struck an empathetic chord with all who surrounded him in personal and intellectual endeavours. He was a unique person who trod this world in his seven decades of life. One comes across like him rarely. He loved his family immensely, and family for him was not merely the biological one but extensive with his students and friends, indeed one spread throughout the length and breadth of the country.

Born and brought up in the village Nawapaar of a humble town area of Peepeganj, Nagendra hailed from a middle class family. Born on 11th day of January 1930, he had his early primary education in his village. He acquired his matriculation and intermediate qualifications from Gorakhpur with perceptibly outstanding merit. He was a brilliant student, having cornered all the honours in all the merit lists. He moved to Lucknow University for his further studies and brimmed with brilliance in his undergraduate studies. He achieved a meritorious first class in the University, with a gold medal for English. It was only a prelude to greater heights in his pursuance of postgraduate studies in sociology, in Lucknow University. Lucknow University, at that time, was one of the two outstanding centres in sociological studies in the country. The other was Bombay University. Here, Nagendra was exposed to the best of intellectual traditions in sociology, more particularly in theoretical pursuits. He stood first with distinction and merit amongst all the successful students. With excellent record to his credit in his postgraduate programme, he attracted the attention of the entire University, right from the Vice-Chancellor to downwards. He had the rare and unique distinction of being appointed as an Assistant Professor on the very same day when his results were announced, through a selection committee (1953).* Thus started a purposeful and

* There is an interesting episode connected with his appointment as Assistant Professor which came to light when I faced a similar situation in my own professional career. In early 1960, when I was pursuing my PhD programme in sociology in the Department of Sociology and Social Work at Lucknow University, under the supervision of Professor Nagendra, I had two simultaneous offers: one of scholarship (or was it a teaching assistantship) and the other was admission into PhD programme in sociology with specialization in social demography under the guidance of Professor Philip Hauzer of the Department of Sociology of Chicago University in the USA. There was also a possibility of my appointment as an Assistant Professor in the Department of Sociology, Lucknow University. Naturally I sought the advice of Nagendra. He did not choose to advise me in the matter. Instead, he told me that he will narrate an incident in his own life and the decision he had taken, thereof, to enable me to arrive at a decision by myself.

He narrated that he was himself placed in this predicament on the day of the announcement of the results of his Master's programme in sociology and also, incidentally, the day of the meeting of the Selection Committee to appoint an Assistant Professor in Sociology in 1953. He was asked by his teacher, the great Professor D.P. Mukerji, an incisive and outstanding scholar and eminent teacher, who was heading the department then, to meet him in the early morning. D.P. Mukerji then told him that he had two alternatives of Nagendra before him. He could choose a scholarship to pursue Doctoral Programme at the International Institute of Social Sciences at the Hague in the Netherlands or have an opportunity of appointment in the department since the selection committee was meeting the very same day.

Since Nagendra was already a married man, Professor Mukerji felt that Nagendra should prefer the appointment as a teacher. However, he made it clear that the choice was that of Nagendra. That Nagendra made a choice to remain in India and pursue his teaching career is a matter of history. He advised me similarly to take my own decision. Taking his choice as an example and also weighing a few other factors into consideration, I also made a choice to pursue teaching career in Lucknow in India. Neither Professor Nagendra nor I had to regret our decisions in favour of remaining in India and pursing the teaching careers.

brilliant teaching career of Nagendra. He never looked back from there. He was a centre of attraction among all the teachers for his students. They looked upon him for inspiration in their thirst for acquisition of knowledge in sociology. For the next five decades, he was a doyen among teachers of sociology and scholars in the country. He scaled heights in his profession at Lucknow University and later at Gorakhpur University. He became a Reader in 1963 and a Professor in 1968 in Gorakhpur University. For three long decades, he shaped the destiny of the Department of Sociology at Gorakhpur. Through his efforts, he raised the status of the department at Gorakhpur with munificent grants from the University Grants Commission at New Delhi. Vast bodies of faculty and students were the beneficiaries of these programmes.

Nagendra was the pivot around whom the student community in all the places he taught – be it the Department of Economic and Sociology, later the Department of Sociology and Social Work at Lucknow University, the Department of Sociology at Gorakhpur University or even the inter-faculty students at G.B. Pant Institute of Social Sciences at Allahabad – revolves. He was an outstanding teacher everywhere whatever position he held. He took classes to fulfil his inner urge to interact with student community. Inspired by great teachers of his time, Professor Radhakamal Mukherjee, Professor D.P. Mukerji, Professor D.N. Mazumdar and Professor G.S. Ghurye (Bombay University), he continued to teach throughout his life. He did so while he was the Vice-Chancellor of Lucknow University as well. At this place, he was following in the illustrious footsteps of renowned Vice-Chancellors, Acharya Narendra Dev and Radhakamal Mukherjee who had enlivened the students with their erudition while they had the top administrative position. While in class, he was an embodiment of knowledge and always encouraged his students to come out and share their ideas in discussion with him and other fellow students. His classrooms mirrored lively debates and academic exchange between him and the students and among the students themselves. He was simply a marvellous teacher. His memory is etched in all those who have been left behind him. His influence pervades even long after his death.

While he was the Vice-Chancellor or the Pro-Vice-Chancellor or the Director, he put the institutions on the map of the country with his administrative acumen. They became the excellent centres for pursuit of knowledge and erudition. He was adept in establishing contacts and exchanges with the funding institutions. He pursued academic and intellectual exchanges with the institutions in India and abroad. He worked relentlessly for the well-being of the students and faculty. Under his astuate leadership, the disciplines and academic programmes wore new looks for the benefit of all. He was a born leader. Inspired by socialist thoughts of Dr Ram Manohar Lohia, he was in the thick of student movements in his student days, particularly by his intellectual and academic inputs in such activities. Thus, he always rendered a new focus and purpose to such movements. His leadership qualities were even evident throughout his life. His idealism, vivacity and faith in himself remained undiminished and influenced one and all.

Nagendra's intellectual output reflected his two main strengths. First, his knowledge of Hindu religious texts and his command over the languages, English, Hindi and Sanskrit, formed basics of his academic and intellectual pursuits which is evident in most of his writings. Second, his training and the theoretical tradition of Lucknow University was also conspicuous in his writings. Further, he had an abundant concern for social issues and the growth and development of the people and the society of which he was an integral part. A cursory glance at the various articles and writings which have been included in this volume and also of the others in different volumes and journals would point out the trends outlined earlier. Primarily, he was concerned with culture and development. He believed that socio-cultural development and economic growth were the desiderata for the elevation of the personality of the individual in the society. He used to stress that any developmental activity or growth paradigm should centre around the human being and he should be the measure of all efforts to bring about a change and improvement in the functioning of the society. He strived to find out the moral and ritual foundation of ancient Indian society. He probed the historiography of culture and called for a cultural policy for the society. He raised the questions regarding the evolution or planning of culture. He critically analysed concepts such as homo hierarchicus, nature's metropolis and nature's necropolis. Development studies and a sociological appraisal of the theory of development is his significant contribution to the debate on development in the contemporary Indian society. Women and Scheduled Castes and their changing profiles were of special concern for him. Poverty and its continued prevalence in the Indian society troubled his conscience and bemoaned the swing between rhetoric and reality. Regional disparities in development, especially the neglect of Eastern Uttar Pradesh, made him critically look into the sociological perspectives. His assessment of D.P. Mukerji, his mentor, as a sociologist, is a brilliant appraisal of the significant contribution made by him to the sociological literature. Nagendra's book, *The Concept of Ritual in Modern Sociological Theory* is a milestone and it had been adapted in the curriculum of several universities.

Having said so, I personally feel, so do many of his students, that Professor Nagendra did not do full justice to his vast intellectual potential. He could have enriched the intellectual field with his incisive and razor-sharp analytical mind. He devoted more time than necessary, perhaps, to his students, friends and immediate family. He was always ready to look to the comforts of the people around him. His early involvement with politics in general and student politics in particular had a toll on his subsequent intellectual pursuits, which account, in all probability, for the dent in his intellectual output. Is there not a spot in the cool and captivating face of the moon?

It is a rare privilege to have known, and known very closely, a humanistic intellectual like Nagendra. His humanism was unbounded. His memory will be immortal in his generations of students and friends. He was, and is, a Universal Man.

1

Moral and Ritual Foundations of Ancient Indian Society in the Age of Sutras and Early Smiritis

The ancient Indian society was the nearest approximation to what Rene Guenon calls a normal civilization, one that rests, as he says, on principles in the true sense of this word, and one in which all is ordered and in a hierarchy consistent with these principles, so that every thing is seen to be the application and extension of a purely and essentially metaphysical doctrine, that is what we mean when we speak of a traditional civilization.[1] Another essential feature of a traditional civilization, Guenon further remarks, in a different context though is "the correspondence between the man's most intimate nature with his particular vocation".[2]

In saying that a normal civilization rests on principles, what Guenon seems to suggest is that unlike a system arbitrarily designed to be its own raison d'être, a normal society presupposes the existence of a model, more inclusive and more authentic than itself, a social order in principia, which it imitates; the mimetic process consisting in a reproduction of the model through a strict, almost spontaneous conformity of its way of life with the paradigms inherent in the model. It is through such conformity that a moral society seems to enforce its order, which should not be misconstrued to mean that the order of a normal society is imposed from without, in fact the type of regimentation with which we are familiar in the context of modern societies, is wholly unknown to the traditional societies. It would be equally incorrect to describe the order of a traditional society as "mechanical" as the French sociologists Emile Durkheim has attempted to do, while distinguishing between the states of solidarity in primitive and modern societies.[3]

In fact, the self-imposing nature of the traditional norms is only an aspect of what Coomaraswamy calls the "unanimity"[4] of the traditional society[5] where agreement on willingness to believe is more prominent than agreement on unwillingness to conform. Similarly, ideas and beliefs in a traditional society are held by the community in which the individual participates, rather than by the individual himself, as is the case with modern societies where consensus on willingness to behave is arrived at by issue of whips. What is of importance to the traditional society is not what one feels about how something is to be done, but that what is done is to be done correctly; everything must be "in order" or "in form," only that being "in form" which conforms to a recognized pattern, or which, repeats an archetype. That which is unarchetypal is informal, hence ugly and profane, immoral and meaningless.

To imitate or to reproduce an archetypal model is then the ultimate purpose for which a normal society exists. We will soon take up the question of the origin and form of the model of which the traditional societies are typical reproductions. But in the meanwhile, a word about hierarchy, the central principle of their organization.

The theory of hierarchy is a natural corollary of the traditional doctrine of inherence of the many in the one which may be stated in Miester Eckhart's words as "single form that is the form of very different things".[6] It is this doctrine of inclusion or inherence on which the idea of hierarchy in Christian theology rests. In Christian theology, the universe is seen as a series of hierarchies, one class stretching upto another in a "rational arrangement of the less inclusive surmounted by the more inclusive, unless all the inclusive is attained in God".[7] The ninth century Christian theologist John Scotus Erigina divided all nature into four categories of being, viz., "that which creates and is not created; that which is created and creates; that which is created but does not create; that which is neither created nor creates".[8] The first class Erigina identifies with God which is the origin and goal of all things and "the fountain of being that floods the universe." In the second and third classes are included all beings other than God – the second comprising ideas and archetypes, revelations of the divine will, the principles according to which things are formed; and the third being made up of all created things patterned after these archetypes. Such things have no independent existence of their own as they all exist in God and manifest his will. Because each thing is a theophany, a divina apparitio the universal man, for instance, is a certain "intellectual idea formed eventually in the divine mind" and the individual man derives his reality from the universal humanita. The fourth class is non-entity that reflects nothing of the divine essence.[9]

Angelic beings according to scripture are of nine kinds divided into three groups ranging upwards from angels, archanges and principalities to seraphim, cherubim and thrones those nearest to God – with dominions, virtues and powers, in the descending order occupying the middle ranks.

As God is the all-inclusive principle of creation in Christian theology, so is Mahadeva – Narayan – Vishnu – Shiva – Mahadevi conceived as self-determined Self, the overlord of the universe in Hindu cosmology. Other angels (devahs) are principles and powers conceived in hierarchies (sthan vibhag) or collectively as Visve devah, "Angelic Host." The higher angels are powers (vibhutis) or limbs (anga) of Mahadeva, which manifest eternally without reference to any particular creation. They are supra-individual intelligences like the second and third hierarchies of angels in Christianity, ideas and archetypes, which inhere in all created beings constituting the basis of their intelligence.

The next hierarchy of the angels (devah) is that of work angels (karma devah) which comprises lesser Gods such as guardian angels (digpals), progenitive deities, patriarchies (pitras), etc.

The above somewhat elaborate reference to Christian and Hindu angelic hierarchies was meant to highlight the point that hierarchy is not an arbitrary system of classification and ranking of men based on accidents of birth, privilege or power, but an extension, as we have tried to show, of the traditional doctrine of inclusion and inherence to the human societies, an application in other words, of the metaphysical principle of the one becoming many (tad ekam) or of the impartite becoming partite.

Hierarchy on the human plane will mean a natural division of human societies into rank orders ranging from the least inclusive upwards from the bottom, to the most inclusive at the top, and in as much as the human societies are vocational organizations (karma vibhag), their hierarchies will normally consist of professional classes specializing in particular vocations, of varnas or castes as they are known in India. There are references galore in the Vedic literature which point to the principle of Brahma (the Sacerdotium) of which the Brahman caste is a living embodiment being the most inclusive and first in the order of precedence as compared to the Kshatra, Vis and Shaudra of which the other three castes, exemplified by Kshatriyas, Vaisyas and Shudras which range from less to least inclusive in the descending order and rank next in the same order in precedence.

For instance, there is a reference in the Brihadaranyaka Upanishad[10] to the divine procession which says that the Deity simple in principia as Brahma (the Sacerdotium) emanates into Kshatra, Vis and Shaudra, in the due course becoming divided into four castes of deities, viz., Brahman, Kshatriya, Vaisya and Shudra.[11] The four castes in the Hindu society constitute a true hierarchy in the sense that their rank orders are reflections of a paradigmatic model rather than an individual opinion or a group ideology. Dumont's theory of hierarchy suffers from its own pitfalls. For instance, it fails to identify the true principle of a hierarchical organization which can not be socio-historical; it runs into rough weather again while explaining the relationship between the king and the priest. In Dumont's opinion, the king by virtue of his monopoly of temporal power should not rank next to the latter in order of precedence as is the case in the caste hierarchy of India.[12]

Change in a traditional society is from order to order, which is to say that changes through which it passes, are, like those in the life of the organism, manifestations of its "becoming"; the society always maintaining the permanency of its form, retaining, in other words, its identity. Deviations from the norms can not, of course, be ruled out in view of the basic imperfectability of human nature, but they are taken care of by traditional methods of socialization and social control: the rites of passage (samskaras) and the rites of penitence (prayaschitta) including punishment for the social rehabilitation of the criminal (aparadhi) as in the ancient Indian society. The general deterioration of the order, again a natural manifestation of the organic life of the society, is sought to be controlled likewise through a strict adherence to virtuous deeds and recourse to sacrificial operations (yajna) no less through institutional reform, reform signifying restoration of the normal form and not the imposition of a new form. Revolutionary change is untouchable in the context of a traditional society, except in the form of a charismatic or divine interference when the order has declined to the point where it can not be restored through human efforts.

It is time we returned to the question of the model which, as we said at the outset, the normal societies presuppose or of which they are reproductions. The question is almost an exact version of the one posed by the sacrificers about the model of the first sacrifice performed by the Gods in the primordial beginnings. "What was the model" they asked "and what the starting point (cause) of the primeval sacrifice (performed by the Gods)"[13] (kasit prama, pratima, kim nidanam)? And the answer, as Coomaraswamy puts it, is that the model "is the sacrificial victim, for this image and this likeness by which he further proceeds, is of himself, the sacrifice, yielding, himself upto the Angels, he expressed a likeness of Himself, to wit, the sacrifice hence, one says Prajapati is the sacrifice (Atmanah pratimanam asrijat, yad yajnam, tasmad ahuh Prajapatir yajnah) (SB XI. 1.8.30)".[14]

The archetype model of all creation (the corresponding form of all forms, immortal and mortal) is then the sacrifice performed by the Gods in illo tempore, identical with Prajapati Himself. For, Prajapati is the causa exemplaris of both the immortal as well as the mortal worlds (yasya chhaya amritam yâsya mirtyuh).[15] The immortal world is a super creation (atisbristi) as compared to the latter, i.e., his own, as He Himself is a part of the mortal world.[16] The atisbristi, the higher creation consisting of the Gods such as Indra and Agni, then becomes the model for the lower creation to imitate (a devanamapi patham aganma). We will follow in the footsteps of the Gods (yat saknvam tad anupravodhaṃm) and as far as we can, we will walk on the way of the Gods. Let no impediments stand in our way[17] and as the Satpatha Brahman says "we must do what the Gods did".[18]

To imitate or to relive the sacrifice is then to go the way the Gods have proceeded, to become immortal (to become what they have in them to become) that is to say. For it has been said that the sacrifice awakens the consciousness of immortality (aran krinvantu vedim samagnim indhataam surah, tatramritasya chetan yajnam to tanvavahai). Let the priests prepare the alter and kindle the fire on it, we too then (the sacrificer and the Indra) may spread the sacrifice that awakens the consciousness of immortality.[19]

But the point must be made clear that immortality in the sense of the greatest fullness of life here with the promise of a life of hundred autumns[20] together with an unhindered flow of the "stream of wealth" (vasor dhara) and divine life hereafter is not the real mystery of the sacrifice in which the sacrificer wants to participate; its real mystery lies in what the Upanishad call everlasting immortality, the ultimate perfection of man (dhruva amritatva), the transcendence of both time and aeveternity (the relative immortality of the Gods). As the Kathopanishad says, "the wise men who comprehend the everlasting (undetermined) nature of immortality never bother about ephemeral things"[21] or as the Mundak says, "immortality is nothing but Brahman the state of absolute freedom (mukhti, from all contingent possibility,"[22] or what, we shall see later, the Dharmashastras call Paramarth, Param Purushartha or Moksha the final deliverance from individuality).[23]

Nor was it ever believed that immortality could be achieved here and now, even the Yogin who could become Javanmukta, i.e., attain self-realization or Atmaprabodh in this very life had to quit his bodily form to become finally one with Himself or ascend to the supreme light (Brahman). For the ordinary mortals, immortality was always a matter pertaining to the other world (videhmukti)[24] which he could achieve by a gradual process of passing from one state of being (loka) to another till he crossed over to the penultimate state of being (Brahmalok) which extends beyond the creation and which is the abode of "unbegotten Angels." However, not all mortals are entitled to this state of immortality which, as we said, is short only of the state of final deliverance from individuality (the jivatma has been freed in this state from both nama and roop, but it is still not in an absolutely undetermined unconditional state).

However, the privilege of attaining kramamukti is due only to the comprehensor who has lived life in full awareness of its sacrificial nature and an equally perfect awareness of the significance of the sacrifice.

This is not the place to discuss the metaphysics of videhmukti. But a brief reference to it will be necessary in any case. The posthumous journey (symbolic) of the spirit (jivatma) according to the Hindu tradition is supposed to take two routes, viz., the Uttarayan via the Moon and the Sun, and the Dakshinayan, terminating in the Moon, the northern and the southern routes, respectively. The first route is called Devayana, the path of Gods and the second, Pitriyan, the path of ancestors. The first leads over the "Sea of Life" (Samsar) Brahmalok, the abode of Brahma as Prajapati as also of the exalted souls (Siddhas and Munis) who are not touched by the pralaya, the cosmic dissolution in which the entire creation except the Prajapati of the next cycle of creation and the Siddhas who have conquered both death and the desire to beget (aprajakama)[25] but who have yet not attained "deliverance," reside till the end of the Kalpa.[26] There is no question of their return to the states of being (lokas) already crossed over by them. This method of attaining deliverance from one's individuality is known as karma mukti and is open only to the wise and faithful who by the virtue of their good deeds ascend stage by stage (from all lower state of being) to a higher state, till they reach the shore, the penultimate state of deliverance. This gradual ascent to immortality is a process of dying over and over again (punar mrityu) which involves only ascent but not descent. It is this kind of immortality that the Gods enjoy, not the absolute immortality of the true comprehensor, the Jivanmukta. The Devayana is chartered by the route via both the Moon and the Sun, but extends beyond both, to super individual states and final deliverance. The "path of ancestors," Prtriyan leads to the Moon and only upto it and then back to this world, and is the requital (istapurti) for rites performed for definite ends (sankalpita). The beings who repair from the Pitriloka to the Moon, enjoy the temporary fellowship of the Gods in the Moon but only as long as the remnant of their good work exists (yavat sampatam),[27] whereafter they are reborn, i.e., return to this earth. Among the beings returning to this earth, a distinction is drawn between those with "pleasing conduct" and those with "abominable habits." The former return as high-born men: as Brahmanas, Kshatriyas or Vaisyas and the latter as dogs, pigs and low-born human beings.

The idea is that while Devayan leads the (jivatma) to the light of lights (jyotisham jyotirekam) via the penultimate formless state (Hiranyagarbha or self-determined Self) from where there is no return, the Pitriyan leads it back to bodily form. The "Moon", as Guenon says, "represents cosmic memory" or in Coomaraswamy's words,[28] it is "tendentious," the store house of tendencies, forms or causes (purvakarmas) where, as Guenon puts it "the forms which have completed the full course of their development are dissolved" and where are "preserved the germs or forms as yet undeveloped since as in the case of forms, as of anything else, the starting point and the finishing point are necessarily to be found in the same order of existence".[29] Rebirth is the manifestation of the undeveloped tendencies in bodily forms. This is the germ of the theory of transmigration to which we will come later. But it may be made clear that there is no actual return of any ancestor individually. Heredity is only an illustration of the perpetual recurrence of forms just alluded to. Pitriyan is essentially the psyclic journey of the soul (jivatma) from gross formal to subtle formal states and from subtle formal states back to gross formal states, while Devayan is the ascent of the soul (jivatma) from formal to formless states of manifestation.

To conclude the discussion so far, the "model" (pratirupa) of which the existing societies are exemplifications (rupa) is "the sacrifice" identical with Prajapati himself, which proceeds to proximity by projection or reflection assuming many forms (rupam); and it is in this sense that the world is "in the likeness of (anurupta)" of that world (the macrocosm) and in the Sun. But it must be understood that the sacrifice by which Prajapati – the All Worker, Vishwakarma creates the worlds (vishwa bhuvanari) and gives the Gods their names and assigns them their places in the cosmic hierarchy (devanam namdha ekah eva)[30] requires the cooperation of all arts – those of "music, architecture, carpentary, husbandry, and that of warfare to protect the operation".[31] "In this man in whom sacramental life is complete, there is a hierarchy of sacerdotal, royal and administrative functions and a fourth class consisting of organs of sense and action that handle the raw material" or "food" to be prepared for all.[32]

Attainment of earthly happiness and heavenly bliss was no doubt the avowed purpose of the sacrifice and as Edgerton rightly remarks the Vedic sacrifice is most certainly the "magic key to omnipotence, absolute power, by which one becomes autonomous,"[33] by which, one could attain "siddhis" and "mahasiddhis" (charismatic power). But these power are nothing as compared to the eternal felicity, "moksha" or "dhruva amritatva" as the Upanishads call it, the true end of life which Gnosis (vidya) alone can bring forth. This explains why the sacrifice is declared as a form of "ignorance" (avidya) which can utmost enable one to crossover the sea of life and reach the shore of eternity; but nothing more. Dhruva amritatva can be attained only, as we said, through perfect self-awareness (vidya) identical with self-naughting (atma yajna) (avidyaya mrityum tirtva vidyaya armritam ashnute).[34]

Atmayajna is sacrifice of the self, renunciation of desires, that is doing what is enjoined upon one to do without self-reference motives or doing what the Bhagvad Gita calls "nishkam karma." All this is to suggest that social life is essentially a competition in giving or sacrificing; nothing more and nothing less. Man is social to the extent to which he excels others in the art of self-naughting, to the extent, in other words, to which he can transform every action into a rite.

But the sacrifice whether the literal offering of oblations to the Gods or the renunciation of desires must be executed correctly if its efficacy is to be ensured.

What then are the standards of the correctness or artfulness of the sacrificial operation? The standards (the pratimanam) of the rightness of the sacrifice are known to none other than the first sacrificers, the Gods or the ruler of the sacrifice, Agni himself.[35] The first sacrificers who knew the law and acted accordingly are fittingly described as right-willed (rita vrata). Which is to say that we have to look at the paradigms to be able to act correctly. Rita, the Law Eternal as collectively reflected in Dharma is then the ultimate standard of rightness. All human laws of right conduct collectively known as Dharma are reflections of the Law Eternal (Rita).

However, it is not an accident of history that the sacrifice (the rite) is the central principle of social organization in the traditional (normal) societies. Nor is the rite a mere foreshadowing as Jane Harrison, Ernst Cassirer and a whole lot of anthropologists and sociologists have tend to show of reason.[36] If modern societies have lost the art of ritual procedure, it is not that they are in no need of this art; the more important reason is their autotelic abnormal nature.

This brings to the last question of this part of our discussion, viz., the one concerning the source or knowledge of the archetype (pratirupa) which we have located as the causa explaris of all forms (rupa). This knowledge we do not and can not owe to human invention, which also means that it can not be a gift of history. But a gift certainly it is and a suprahuman gift at that to the chosen few who are entitled to receive it. It is in Guenon's words "inspirational knowledge," Shruti or revelation (as it is called in Hindu and Christian traditions). It is of essence to revealed wisdom that its truth is never questioned and that it is embodied in to the beneficiaries through a spiritually qualified hierarchy of teachers and deserving pupils in an uninterrupted continuity. Myth is verily the traditional vehicle of transmission of this wisdom, the source through which all archetypes are revealed to mankind.[37] In this process of transmission, the Shruti (what is heard) becomes Smriti (what has been remembered and handed down as tradition). But it must be borne in mind that this process of traditionalization does not involve any distortion or modification of the revealed truth. What may happen is that it is subjected to interpretation and counterpretation in different times, which again does not mean that it can be historicized in the sense that its truth can be retivized. Tradition is firmly rooted in Shruti and can never contradict it.

II

The Dharmasutras form part of the Kalpasutra literature recognized as one of the six limbs of Vedas, the other limbs being Shiksha (education), Vyakaran (grammar), Nirukta (hermeneutics), Chhanda (poetics) and Jyotish (astrology). The Kalpasutras have generally been classified into four types, viz., Shrauta, Grihya, Dharma and Shulaba. All these Sutras as their name suggests are aphorism collected into manuals for the procedural guidance of public and domestic rituals, or as text books of moral rules to be followed by men in the conduct of their routine business. The Dharmasutras deal mainly with acharah (folkways), samskar (rites of passage), asauch (impurities), prayaschitta (repentance), varnadharma (vocational duties), ashramadharma (duties relating to stages of life), etc

Since, as we have observed, the Smritis (tradition) can never be at variance with the Shruti (revelation,) the ideals of life as adumbrated in the Dharmasutras and Dharmashastras are only an explicitation of the revealed wisdom. The Dharmashastras are the traditional sciences of prudence, which lay down the principles of right conduct of dharma. "The whole Veda" as the Manusmriti and Dharmasutras unanimously declare "is the first source of sacred law, next the tradition and the virtuous conduct of those who know the Veda further; also the customs of the holy men and finally self-satisfaction." And whatever law has been ordained for any person by Manu that has been fully declared in the Veda, for that sage was omniscient.[38]

Dharma (the moral law of Hindus) as the etymology of the term suggests is the generic term for everything that is suggestive of norm, order, law and justice, folkways and mores, manners and morals, or that has the sense of supporting or sustaining (dhri). The Veda equates it with Indra, the sustainer (dhatri) of every sacrificial operation and with Agni, the deity whom both the Gods and men have made their chief support.[39] It would be clear from what we have said earlier that Dharma is Rita Law Eternal viewed in its transcendent and immanent forms.[40] (Dharma as the law of life and Dharma as svadharma.)

So it is that the Dharmasutras are unanimous against the violation of dharma, lest violated dharma destroy us; for the dharma being violated destroys and being preserved preserves.[41] Dharma, that is to say, like the law of nature will avenge its violation. On the other hand, those who consistently follow dharma (prescribed duties) in the right manner will reach the deathless state and even in this (life) obtain all the desires that they may have conceived.[42]

The promise of fulfillment of this two-fold aim would thus appear to be the practical standard by which the rightness of conduct was to be judged. A normal social organization knit together and sustained by Dharma like the one conceived by the Hindus, then, stood both for general prosperity as well as the individual's own happiness here and in life hereafter. It was for this end that the institutions prescribed in the Dharmasutras and

Dharmashastras were designed. These sacred texts – the manuals of conduct and ritual procedure – spell out in the minutest detail, the appropriate methods of dealing with every life situation simple or complicated, right from the cradle to ones' grave.

Social life was essentially conceived as Karma Marg by the Hindus, the way of works to realize the fullness of one's being, which consisted of both rites (yajna) and conduct (svadharma) – duties specific to one's status in life and those specific to ones own nature. But the way of works was also meant to be transcended because as it has been shown in the foregoing discussion, it can only culminate in an endless chain of births and deaths providing no relief from the bondage of pleasure and pain.[43]

The traditional Hindu sociologists had therefore contemplated a pattern of society whose institutions will lead to their own transcendence, which, that is to say, will gradually prepare the individual to give up his social mask through an increasing depersonalization of himself – not only in the sense of getting fully integrated with the society but in the sense of becoming fully self-integrated. And this, they had sought to do through the twin institutions of "varna" and "ashrama" together with an elaborate system of rites including the samskaras (the rites of passages) as they are known.

The four ashramas – brahmacharya, grihastha, vanprashtha and sanyas – as they are described in the Sutras and Smritis, are the stations of "mortification" (shrama) as Deussen beautifully puts it, "gradually intensifying ascetic stages through which a man more and more purified from all earthly attachment should become fitted for his home (astam) as the other world is designated in the Rg. Veda (X. 14.8)".[44]

In a life conceived as stages of increasing depersonalization or asceticism, "everyone is a pilgrim (shraman) whose only motto is 'keep on going',"[45] and who as it were, was determined to cross the Sea of Life and to get to its other shore. The pilgrims journey begins with his second birth in which Savitri (the sacrament) is his mother and the teacher (who administers the sacrament) his father, his first birth being from the natural mother.[46] The Upanayan (taking near the preceptor) as it is called, is the rite of initiation into esoteric wisdom. But as its procedure indicates, the whole rite is an imitation of what was done by the Gods in illo tempore. Look at the way the priest addresses the initiate, "O neophyte the garment which Brihaspati had put on Indra at the time of his initiation and the manner in which he had done so; in the same manner and with the same immortal and indestructible garment, I invest you, to make you long lived, strong and resplendent with the effulgence of Brahman".[47] The sacred strings are the spiritual umbilical cord which links the initiate to his preceptor who is Agni, the deity of the sacrifice in a likeness.[48] The Dharmasutras and Smritis prescribe an elaborate disciplinary code which the student had to observe.[49] The twice-born according to the Manusmriti who completes his studentship in strict accordance with tradition, reaches the highest abode (after death) and is not born again.[50]

But the Brahmacharin must become a Grihastha (householder) after returning (samavartan) from his preceptors' guardianship as a snatak (one who has taken the bath at the end of his studentship) to continue the line of procreation as ordained by Shruti (revelation).[51] The Dharmasutras and Smritis are unanimous about one marrying a girl of equal caste and endowed with auspicious bodily marks, and of good character, but not of one's own gotra, "pravar" or "prohibited degree of pinda."

Of the eight forms of marriage rites, viz., brahma, daiva, arsha, prajapatiya, asura, gandharva, rakshas and pishach,[52] the first six are lawful for the Brahmans, the last four for the Kshatriyas and the same four, except the rakshas rite, for Vaisyas and shudras. In the brahma and prajapatiya rites as prescribed in the Grihyasutras for the twice-born, human marriage is viewed as a repetition of hierogamy (marriage of the Gods) like the Upanayan rites. Take, for instance, the mantra recited at the time when the bridegroom offers garments to the bride "O longlived the goddesses who have spun and spread this garment have given it to you to wear it for your unblemished and long life," or the "Soma was the first to get you, it was Gandharva next and

Agni was your third husband, and I born as a man on this earth, am your fourth husband".[53]

Marriage rites like those of Upanayan were meant for this spiritual transformation of the individual and for the perpetuation at the same time for the social order in its normal form. The life of the householder or the Grihastha Ashram was considered as the yoni, the place of birth of the other stages according to the Gautam Dharmasutra as the other orders are barren.[54] Vashishtha and Vishnu Dharmasutra consider this order as the most distinguished among the four in as much as it is the grihastha who has the privilege to perform sacrifices and it is from the grihastha that the other three orders derive their sustenance.[55] The housekeeper as the Manusmriti says is declared by the Veda also to be superior to all the three.[56]

Among the most important duties of the grihastha are: offering daily oblations into the domestic fire (agnihotra) and the execution of the five great sacrifices: the panchamahayajnas (for the sake of expiating sins committed inadvertently by the householder). There are five places in the house where animals are liable to be destroyed, viz., the hearth, the grounding stone, the broom, the pestle and mortar, and the water vessel, the use of which always binds him with the fetters of sin. These five great sacrifices are called brahmayajna (teaching and studying Veda), pitriyajna (offering of water and food to mans), devayajna (offering of burnt oblations to the Gods), bhutayajna (offering of bali to presiding deities of the directions, etc.) and manusyayajna (hospitality to guests).[57]

The Grihasthashrama centres mainly around the family – husband, wife, children, manes and the rishis – the miniature society presided over by the householder as the *pater familias*. More than a human individual, the husband or the father is the image of lord Vishnu and his wife that of the universal Goddess Lakshmi, the two thus representing the union of the archetypal male and female principles.[58] The householder has to discharge three obligations (rins) as part of his dharma: towards the Gods, towards the manes and towards the sages, by performing sacrifices, studying the Vedas with a teacher and by propagation of his progeny, that is by procreating children, especially a male child. A Brahmin on being born owes a son to his ancestors.[59]

When, however the householder has discharged these obligations and sees his skin wrinkled, his hair white and has seen the sons of his sons, then he may resort to the forest, that is, become a hermit. He may retire into the forest alone or with his wife and therefore, must take the sacred fire as also the implements required for the performance of the Agnihotra, and the five great sacrifices. However, Vanprashtha is life of rigorous austerities, which one enters turning away even from his Dharma. Man now intensifies his search of himself – his Atma which transcends all the social masks he had been wearing from birth to birth.[60]

The fourth, the Sanyas Ashrama is the life of a "bhikshu," of the holy beggar or the "parivrajak" (the homeless wanderer) and begins after one has lived through the third part of his life in the woods.[61] The sanyasin renounces the works taught in the Veda, cuts himself off from both the worlds and concentrates himself to the centre of his consciousness, the Brahman.[62] But the vashishtha Dharmasutra is in favour of his continuing with the study of the Vedas least he runs the risk of becoming a Shura.[63] The sanyasin has to wander about alone without the fire, absolutely silent, accepting nothing for enjoyment that he may receive through begging. He will not desire to die, he will not desire to live, let him wait for his appointed time.[64] Sanyas constitutes the renunciation of the entire Brahmanical or traditional way of dharmic life – the sacrificial fire the sanyasin takes into his belly, and the Gayatri (the Veda) into the fire of his speech. Baudhayan Dharmasutra lays down the elaborate procedure by which a Brahman on the eve of entering the ascetic order has to perform the last sacrifice in which he burns his sacrificial vessels and offers – the pranagnihotra.[65]

The second major institution through which the order of the traditional Hindu society was sought to be maintained was its vocational organization known as the Varna Vyavastha. The Dharmasutras and the Smritis alike contain elaborate references to the four Varnas, viz., Brahmans, Kshatriyas, Vaisyas and

Shudras; the first three of which are designated as Dvijas (twice-born) and the fourth as Shudras (who have only one – biological birth).[66]

We have already seen why the Dvijas (the twice-born) are so called; they are supposed to have two births, one from the womb of their (biological) mother and the other from Savitri (the Veda) through their teacher. The twice-born (Brahmanas, Kshatriyas and Vaisyas) are naturally superior in rank to the Shudras, and among the twice-born, the Brahmans are superior to the other two as they are a higher order progenitors who give a second birth to their pupils for the sake of the Veda (esoteric wisdom). Manu therefore considers a Brahman howsoever young as Father even to an aged man.[67] Young Kavi, the son of Angiras addressed his relatives (whom he taught as he excelled them in esoteric knowledge) as "little sons" though they were much older than him in age. When they protested and complained to the Gods they were told that the child (Kavi) had addressed them properly. According to the Manusmriti, the Brahman, ignorant or learned is a divinity, just as the fire whether it carried forth a burnt oblation or art, is a great divinity, and warns the king not to incur his displeasure.[68] The earthly king has in fact no jurisdiction over the Brahmans; their king is Soma.[69]

While the Brahman is declared to be the lord of the Varnas (by virtue of his pre-eminence and special sanctification),[70] the Kshatriya holds the next rank from which Varna hails the king, who has been created to protect the Varnas.[71] The Vaisya comes next and the Shudra the last. Rank among the Brahmanas is to be determined by sacred knowledge, among the Kshatriyas by valour, among the Vaisyas by wealth and among the Shudras by age.[72]

The duties prescribed for each of these varnas in the Dharmasutras and Smritis are: for the Brahmans, studying, teaching, sacrificing, accepting gifts; for the Kshatriyas, studying, sacrificing, bestowing gifts and protecting the people with his weapons and gaining his livelihood thereby; for the Vaisyas, studying, sacrificing bestowing gifts, trading, rearing cattle and lending money besides agriculture; for the Shudras, serving the other Varnas.

The above list of the duties of the Varnas is from the Vashistha Dharmasutra.[73] The classification of duties available in the other Sutras and Smritis is more or less the same except for some minor differences here and there. However, over and above these duties, specific to their moral status, the Varnas were expected to follow certain general principles of morality (samanya dharmas) which as presented by Manu and other Sutrakaras are: abstention from causing violence (both physical and moral) to others (ahimsa), practising truthfulness (satya), abstention from acquisition of useless wealth (asteya), remaining pure (shauch) and practising control of senses (indriya nigraha).

A faithful observance of these general rules of moral conduct was necessary for leading a self-disciplined life which in turn was the necessary pre-condition for living upto the principles of one's own morality (of one's svadharma or vocation).

The Sutras and Smritis do not rule out the possibility of confusion of castes leading to the formation of mixed (unpure) castes as a result of mismatched marriages (based on transgression of marriage rules). Jati utkarsha and jati apkarsha (rise or fall of castes in the social scale) though recognized to an extent[74], need not to be considered as a normal feature of the Indian society even in that age. For it is no where mentioned that the caste duties are interchangeable or that their rank order is subject to change. In fact, the determination of caste duties as well the rank order of castes was regulated by what may be called the principle of "spiritual age" reflected in the degree of moral maturity attained by each individual through the cycle of his birth and rebirth.[75] What appears as a provision for intercaste mobility was only a concession to the deviants to attain a higher status through a consistent adherence to the norms of virtuous conduct for seven generations or loose their high status through an equally consistent deviation from the norms for seven generations. The provision made in the Manusmriti was actually a method of self-repentance.

Vocational (caste) duties, in so far as they correspond to the specific nature of the castes, could not be interchanged and hence the Manusmriti's stress on one discharging his own appointed duties incompletely than performing others' duties completely, for one who lives according to the law of another (caste), is excluded from his own caste.[76] The moral order is best sustained by every one steadfastly sticking to his own morality, for after all one's own morality (svadharma) is only an individual manifestations of the sovereign principle of morality (Dharma) rather than by trying to imitate or encroach upon other's morality.

It is not difficult to understand how a natural division of karmas (works) can assume the form a vocational order linked with birth and heredity. For what is called nature (swabhava) consists, as Guenon puts it, of two sets of qualities, viz., "gotrika": those that one inherits from his gotra (family line) and "namika": those that are unique to the individual himself, which his name should ordinarily express.[77]

It is then one's nature – his "gotrika" and "namika" qualities – which shows what we call his "spiritual age" – at the time of his birth, the high-born having a higher spiritual age and the low-born, a relatively lower spiritual age. Natural inequalities exist in every society, but only traditional (normal) societies try seriously to explain them, modern societies only wishing them away or explaining them as freaks of nature. In the Varna hierarchy so to say, it is one's spiritual age as indicated by his birth which determines his status, and not his heredity (gotrika qualities alone). But it must be made clear that the theory of transmigration of soul is just not a theodicy idea – a rationalization of the incongruity between destiny and merit in the traditional Indian society.[78] The theory on the other hand, must be viewed as an aspect of the doctrine of "exemplarism," the theory of the relationship, as Coomaraswamy describes it, between the exemplar and its imitation or between the "eternal cause" and the things.[79] For as Shankaracharya has said, "apart from the lord (Isvara) there is no other transmigrant (samsari)".[80]

We had the occasion to refer earlier to this doctrine in connection with our discussion of the principle of hierarchy when we had said that Prajapati (the Lord) himself was the exemplar of all figures and forms being the sacrifice in actual.

The point which however remained suppressed in our exposition was the one about the intelligible reason of the one becoming many or the Lord (Isvara) becoming samsari (jivatma) as the enjoyer and sufferer of happiness and misery. The answer to this conundrum as available in the Vedas can be found in the following hymn "Indra (the Lord Parmeshwar) mons multiform by his magic powers." Indra mayabhih puru rupa iyate.[81] The Lord proceeding to eternal activity (manifestation, samsar), subjecting himself to the law of karma and then receding to eternal rest by transcending this law (of karma) is part of His self-dalliance Lila, which is a mystery to be lived rather than a problem to be solved.

One more point before we conclude, the doctrines on which we have drawn to build our main argument in this discussion can lay no claim to validity, if empirical verifiability and objectivity be the touchstone of validity. But if verifiability means correspondence to truth and objectivity unanimous agreement on what is actually the case, then the tables are turned on the modern theories (scientific) which, as Barfield beautifully puts it, are at best attempts "to save the appearances".[82] The so-called objective and verifiable theories are thus only representations of representation, for all phenomenon are just appearances rather than the reality on this view. To believe the self-evident truth of the doctrines or to accept the relative truth of science is a dilemma which, and those "who know" and those "who know wisely," will resolve according to their own light.

III

The substantive point we have tried to make in this essay is that the ancient Indian society, especially in the age of the Sutra and the Smritis (600 BC to 200 AC), was the nearest example of a normal society which like modern was not a self-designed system existing for its own sake, but a principled order imitative of an archetypal model – a body of principles and values supposed to be revealed and believed to be true. This archetypal model as we tried to show, was the sacrifice co-extensive with the sacramental life of the All worker Vishwakarma, the First Principle in actual. The order of the traditional Indian society was thus conceived in perfect imitation of the division of works at the primordial sacrifice, or conversely, it was the primordial vocational order reflected in time. To imitate this order was to become divine, to become perfect or to enjoy the fullness of being on the true sense of the term. The social institutions of the traditional Hindu society as the Dharmasutras and the Smritis had designed them were all meant to lead the individual to the realization of this end. Every form of activity and every form of ritual was an exercise in man's trans-substantiation of his assimilation to his primordial essence. Man in the ancient Indian society was the "normal sacrificial man," not the "marginal homo religious of modern society."

We have not made any distinction between caste and varna, nor do the sources on which we rely make any such distinctions. We have also proceeded on the assumption that the laws that the Dharmashastras as sciences of prudence lay down are not empirical generalization, of course, they do need empirical examples to illustrate them.

Notes

1. Orient and Occident 1924, p. 234, quoted by Coomaraswamy, A.K. in his essay on Primitive Mentality, reprinted in the collection of his select articles and papers *Figures of Speech or Figures of Thought* (New Delhi: Munshiram Manoharlal, 1981).
2. "Imitation and Craft" in *Journal of Indian Society of Oriental Art*, Vol. VI, 1938, quoted by Coomaraswamy, A.K., op. cit., pp. 232–233.
3. Durkheim distinguishes between what he calls "mechanical solidarity" and "organic solidarity" as reflecting the respective states of consciousness and organicity in the primitive and modern societies. The latter, of which the index is "restitutive or civil law," he considers as representing a more evolved state of consciousness than the former, whose index is "repressive or criminal law," just the opposite of the stand we take. Durkheim's argument rests on the fallacy inherent in the theory of linear evolution. See his *The Division of Labour in Society* (London: Routledge & Kegan Paul, 1933).

4. Coomaraswamy, A.K., op. cit., pp. 218, 221.
5. Ibid.
6. See Coomaraswamy, A.K., op. cit., p. 79.
7. See Baker, Hershel: *The Image of Man – A Study of the Idea of Human Dignity in Classical Antiquity, The Middle Ages and Renaissance* (New York: Harper Torch Books, Boolingen Library, 1975, p. 190).
8. Ibid., p. 190.
9. Ibid., p. 190.
10. I-4–11–14.
11. There is a similar statement in the Aitareya Brahman according to which Prajapati first created the sacrifice and thereafter the Brahamans and Kshatriyas, Vaisyas and Sudras. The sacrifice then ran away leaving them behind. The Kshatriyas chased it but returned disappointed, but the Brahmanas overtook it. Since then, the sacrifice has stayed with (inheres in) the Brahamans. And again, one who starts the sacrifice also starts the Brahaman, for the Brahaman is verily the sacrifice (brahma vai yajna). Brahma thus is the all inclusive principle being, the sacrifice itself. See *The Aitareya Brahaman of Rg. Veda*, edited and translated by Malviya, Sudhakar (Varanasi: Tara Printing Works, 1983, Vol. II, Chapter IV).
12. Dumont Louis: *Homo Hierarchicus: The Caste system and its Implications*, translated by Sanisbury Mark (New Delhi: Vikas Publications, 1970).

    Dumont defines hierarchy in terms of the structural principle of complementarity and opposition, and accordingly explains the caste system as a rank order based on the opposition of the pure and impure, and as the pure is empirically superior to the impure, the opposition of the two constitutes a hierarchy. The Brahaman is pure and hence superior to the untouchable who is impure. But why is the Brahman pure? Dumont's answer is: because the untouchable is impure. This is only an example of circular reasoning on which the whole edifice of Dumont's theory is built. But the most fatal flaw of his approach lies in his attempt to reduce the paradigmatic to the empirical.
13. Rg. Veda, X. 130.3.
14. See Vedic Exemplarism in Coomaraswamy – 2. Selected Papers: *Metaphysics*, edited by Lipsy, Roger (Bollingen Series, New Jersy: USA, Princeton University Press, 1977, p. 184).
15. Rg. Veda, X. 121.3.

16. Brihadaranyak Upanishad (Shankar Bhasya), I. 4.5.6.
17. Rg. Veda, X. 2.3.
18. VII, 2.1.4.
19. Rg. Veda, I.170.4
20. "A hundred autumns may be before us, O Gods during which we complete the life term of a body or bodies." Rg. Veda, 1.89.9.
21. Kathopnishad, 2.21.2. The wise men who comprehend the everlasting non-modal nature of immortality never bother about worldly or ephemeral things (atha dhirah amritatvam viditva dhruvam dhruvesvih na prathayante).
22. Mundak, 2.2.11 (Brahma Vedamritam purstad Brahma daksinaschottaren, adhaschoradhascha prasutam Brahmaidam visvamidam varistam).
23. See Kane, P.V.: *History of Dharmashastra: Ancient and Medieval Religions and Civil Law* (Vol. V, Part II, Poona: Bhankarkar Oriental Research Institute, Second Ed., 1977, pp. 1510–1511).
24. For a fuller understanding of the posthumous journey of the soul (jivatma), see Chhandogya Upanishad, IV 15–5,6 and IV 10.3.7 and Brihadaranyak Upanishad, V. 10.1 and VI 2.15–16. Also, Vishnu Puran, Chapter VIII, 85–91.
25. See the Vishnu Puran,

    A system of Hindu Mythology and Tradition translated by Wilson H.H. (Vol. I, Book II, Chapter VIII-85–91, New Delhi: N.M. Publishers, pp. 328–329).
26. Kelpa is one day of Brahma, the creator, equal to a thousand Mahayugas, one Mahayuga being an aggregate of the durations of the four yugas, viz., Krita, Treta, Dvapar and Kali which together constitute one cycle of human time. Of these according to the extent of dharma (righteousness) prevailing in them, Kali has the shortest duration of 4,32,000 years, Dvapar, of twice as many years, Treta of thrice as many years and Krita of four times as many years as that of Kali. At the end of each Kalpa begins the night of Brahma (Kalpantar) when there is cosmic dissolution (pralaya) in which everything (all the three worlds: the Earth, Sky and the Heaven) is destroyed except Brahma, the creator himself and the unborn Gods the Siddhas, who have reached the Brahmaloka (a state of formlessness though not of final deliverance from individually by krammukti: This is what is called incidental (Naimittik Pralaya) dissolution.

Brahma has a life span of a hundred Angelic years which is one day of Supernal Time (of Potent Vishnu) at the end of which (His night) takes place elemental dissolution (Mahapralaya or Atyantikapralaya) in which even Brahma is destroyed. During the day of Vishnu (day of Supernal Time), there is birth within the waters of a cosmos designated as Hiranyagarbha and the following night of Vishnu (Supernal Night) is again a period of latency. See, Wilson H.H.: *The Vishnu Puran* (Book, I, Chapter III and Book VI, Chapter I). Also, Coomaraswamy: *Yakshas, Essays in Water Cosmology*, edited by Shroeder Paul (Delhi: Oxford University Press, pp. 186–187. Also, Pandey G.C.: *An approach to Indian Culture and Civilization*, (Varanasi: Banaras Hindu University, 1985, pp. 125–126).

27. Chhandogya Upanishad, II. 10.5.
28. *Yakshas, Essays in Water Cosmology*, edited by Paul Schroeder (Indira Gandhi National Centre for the Arts, Delhi: Oxford University Press, 1993, p. 184).
29. See *Man and His Becoming according to the Vedant*, translated by R.C. Nicholson (New York: The Noonday Press, 1958).
30. Rg. Veda, X.81.1, X. 82.3
31. Coomaraswamy, A.K.: *Hinduism and Buddhism* (New York: Philosophical Library, 1943, pp. 26–27).
32. Ibid., 26–27. All the four varnas according to the Rg. Veda proceed from the body of the Purusha (X. 90.11.12.), the primordial man with whom as the victim the Góds performed the First sacrifice coextensive with the creation. We are told in no uncertain terms in the Vishnu Puran that the varna vyavastha was a sacrificial organization, all the four varnas having been created by Brahma for the performance of the sacrifice, Chapter VI, pp. 6–7.
33. The Upanishads. What Do They Seek and Why? p. 118.
34. Isha Upanishad, 3.11.
35. Rg. Veda I-1.8, also X-190–1; The Law Eternal is Rita, also Dharma self-revelation of the Deity – Brihadaranyaka Upanishad.
36. See Harisson, Jane: *Ancient Art and Ritual* (London: H. Holt Publishers, 1913), Cassirer, Ernst: *Philosophy of Symbolic Forms* (London: Yale University Press, 1965), and Frazer; James George: *The Golden Bough* (Forgotten Books, 1922), *Malinowski, Branislaw, Magic and Religion*, Chapter I-VII, abridged edition of the *Golden Bough*, Watts, Los Angles, 1944.

37. It is not an allegory of nature or a fumbling primitive effort to explain the world of nature as generally understood. See for a detailed discussion: "The Concept of Ritual in Modern Sociological Theory." *Academic Journals*, New Delhi, 1968. S.P. Nagendra.
38. Laws of Manu, English translation of Manusmriti by G. Buhler in the *Sacred Books of the East* Series, Edited by Max Muller (Delhi: Motilal Banarasidas, 1964, II-6.7, II.10.14). See also, *Sacred Laws of the Aryas as Taught in the Schools of Apastamba, Gautam, Vashistha and Baudhayan*, translated by G. Buhler in the SBE series, Vol. 14, Part II.
39. Apastamba, I.1.1.3; Gautam, I.1.4; Baudhayan, I.1.6. and Vashistha, I.4.6. (in Sacred Laws of the Aryas).
40. Rg. Veda, I.2.4. and X.92.2.
41. Laws of Manu, VIII. 15–18. Also, Vashishtha Dharmasutra VI. 1–3, 6–8.
42. Laws of Manu, II-5.
43. Pravritti and Nivritti marg as the Manusmriti calls them Laws of Manu XII-88.
44. Deussen, Paul: *The Philosophy of Upanishads*, English translation by A.S. Geden Rev. (Orient Books Reprints Corporation) 54, Rani Jhansi Road, New Delhi: Munshiram Manoharlal, 1908, p. 307).
45. See Coomaraswamy, A.K.: *Hinduism and Buddhism*.
46. For a definition of the term "Dvija" see Apastamba Dharmasutra, 1.1.16 and Manusmriti, I.1.70 (SLA).
47. Paraskar Grihyasutra, Harihar-bhashya, II. 2–1.
48. Vashistha Dharmasutra, VII. 5–6.
49. Ibid., VII. 7.17., also Laws of Manu, II. 226.
50. The Manusmriti devotes practically the whole of its Chapter II to the enumeration of the duties of the Brahmacharin.
51. Prajatantum ma vyavatsechchiha – Tattiriya Upanishad, 1.11. The Vashishtha Dharmasutra leaves it to the Brahmacharin to enter any of the remaining three orders of life after completing his studentship, but the Manusmriti makes it compulsory for him to marry. Vashishtha: Chapter VII, 3rd and VIII-1, (SLA) Laws of Manu, III-4.
52. Laws of Manu, III. 21–23.
53. Parashar Grihyasutra, I-4–2–5.
54. See, Bannerji, S.C.: *Dharmasutras: A Study in Their Origin and Development* (Calcutta: Punthi Pustak, 1962, p. 136).

55. Vashishtha VIII. 14 (Sacred Laws of the Aryas Part, translated by G. Buhler, Delhi: Motilal Banarasidas) and The Institutes of Vishnu LIX-27, translated by J. Jolly (SBE series 7).
56. Laws of Manu, VI. 78.
57. The Institutes of Vishnu LIX 1.2 and 19.25, and Laws of Manu, III 67–90.
58. The marriage formula: "I am Vishnu thou art Lakshmi: thou art the Goddess, I am the God, I am Sam, thou art Rik, I am the Sky, thou art the Earth; let us marry let us produce children... let us live a hundred autumns." Parashar Grihyasutra, I-7–5–6.7.
59. The Institute of Vishnu, XXXVII-29, Vashistha Dharmasutra, XI-48; Baudhayan Dharmasutra, II-9.16. (4–8) (Sacred Laws of the Aryas).
60. See Laws of Manu, VI, 1–32.

    Vashistha, IX, 1–12, Baudhayana, II-13. (SLA).
61. Laws of Manu VI, Vashistha and Baudhayana, II-13. (SLA).
62. Baudhayana Dharmasutra, II, 6.11.26 (SLA).
63. Vashistha Dharmasutra, X. 4. (SLA).
64. Laws of Manu, VI-34–97.
65. II. 10. 17–1.45.
66. Apastamba Dharmasutra, I, 1, 1,3–1,2, Gautam Dharmasutra, X-2, 7, 49, 56–15; Vashistha Dharmasutra, II-1, 36, Baudhayan Dharmasutra, 1, 8,16, 1–16. The Institute of Vishnu, II, 1–17, Laws of Manu, Chapter X.
67. Laws of Manu, II. 150.
68. Laws of Manu, IX-317.
69. Vashistha Dharmasutra, I-46.
70. Sacred learning approached the Brahman and said to him "Preserve me, I am thy treasure, reveal me not to a scorner, nor to a wicked man, nor to one, of uncontrolled passions, so preserved I shall become strong." (Vashistha Dharmasutra, II-8).
71. Laws of Manu, VII. 35.
72. Ibid., II-153.
73. II-21. (in SLA).
74. Laws of Manu, X-64. This insight we owe to G.C. Pandey.
75. An Approach to Indian Culture and Civilization, Banaras Hindu University Publication, p. 127.
76. X-97.

77. Quoted in my: "Traditional Theory of Caste," in *Towards a Sociology of Culture in India* edited by T.K.N. Unnithan and others (New Delhi: Prentice Hall of India, 1965, p. 265).
78. See, Weber, Max: *The Social Psychology of the World Religious: From Max Weber – Essays in Sociology* edited by Gerth, Havs and C. Wright Mills (London: Routledge and Kegan Paul, 1952, p. 275).
79. See his Vedic Exemplarism in Coomaraswamy-2. Selected Essays, p. 177.
80. See, Vedant Sutras with Commentary by Shankaracharya edited by G. Thibant, SBE series, pp. 34–38, 1.1.5.
81. *The Hymns of Rg. Veda* (translation of the Rg. Veda) by Ralph T.H. Griffith (Vol. I, Chowkhambha Sanskrit Series, Varanasi, 1971, VI 47–18), Griffiths' rendering of mayabhih is "by his illusions" which we have replaced by "his magic power."
82. Barfield Owen: *Saving the Appearance* (London: Faber and Faber, 1988).

2

Historiography of Culture*

'Interpretive understanding' is a phrase we borrow from Wilhelm Dilthey[1] to describe the method which we consider most appropriate for the study of culture. Dilthey along with Windleband and Rickert had played a leading role in the development of the historical school in post-Kantian Germany. Kant's critical philosophy, especially his distinction between pure and practical reason, had become the basis for a clear-cut demarcation of the boundaries of Wissenschaften and Geistwissenschaften. Science was concerned with the study of nature, which was the realm of necessity and which could be subsumed under general laws. History, on the other hand, was concerned with the study of mind and its manifestations like art and culture which could not be dealt with by the scientific method.

But, in spite of the fact that history could not depend upon the scientific method for the study of its subject matter, a difference of opinion arose among German philosophers as regards the proper scope of history. Hegal and Marx took the view that history had to study the life of mind as a process with its general laws of evolution. History in the hands of these two masters in other words, was as much a study of the laws as was science. Against this view of history, the trio led by Dilthey took

* Lecture delivered at the National Seminar on Historiography of Indian Culture at Varanasi, March 12, 1995.

the stand that the life of mind was to be studied more in its uniqueness and specificity than its generality which was a doubtful proposition in itself. For, the generality of the cultural phenomena had yet not been conclusively demonstrated. Windleband was so sure of the nature of the subject matter of history that he proposed two different names for the two kinds of science, viz., nomothetic and idiographic; the former being the designation of the sciences of nature, the studies of the universal; and latter of the sciences of mind the studies of the unique and the particular.

Rickert had slightly modified Windleband's classification by rearranging the two basic divisions of generalizing and individualizing sciences into non-valuing and generalizing sciences such as physics and chemistry, the non-valuing and individualizing sciences such as zoology, evolutionary biology, etc., the valuing and generalizing quasi-science such as sociology, economics, jurisprudence, etc., and valuing and individualizing science such as history proper. Rickert should not detain us further as the most valuable insight into the nature of history was provided by Dilthey.

Dilthey, though tending to agree on many points with Windleband, differs from both in respect of his basic approach to the study of history. He did not accept the thesis that history was to be viewed as a continuous process; on the other hand, he favoured restricting its scope to the study of world outlooks or weltanschauungen which were all unique in their own way and the metaphysical consciousness of man, which according to Dilthey consists in man's awareness of himself and his relations, and which imparts unity to his mental life and manifests itself in his perpetual quest of the meaning of life, gives rise to three types of mental outlooks each of which becomes the basis of the outlook of the individual and also of the world outlook or weltanschauung. These three world outlooks are divided into three types, viz., philosophical (a correlate of the cognitive or knowing aspect of man's self-awareness), artistic (a correlate of the co-native or feeling aspect of man's self-awareness) and religious (a correlate of effective or willing aspect of man's self-awareness).

The study of these world outlooks, which are distinctive of particular epochs of history, is essentially a decipherment of their meanings; and since they are non-contemporaneous, the historian has to transport himself into the past to decipher their meaning. However, the interpretation of the different historical epochs is to be done by the method appropriate to their native. Dilthey called this method *verstehn* (understanding) which literally means 'standing under' and which Dilthey defines as 'the reliving of an already lived experience', the stabberment of a complete identity, in other words, with the age which the historian had to interpret.

Dilthey, while recommending the understanding method for history or the cultural sciences, was none too oblivious of the difficulties the application of this method involved. Given the plurality of the worldoutlooks characterize the historical epochs, the search must be made for a supreme science of interpretation, which could translate them into each other's language and show their interconnection and unity. This supreme science of interpretation could be no other than hermeneutics, the science which had earlier been used in the interpretation of the sacred texts of different religions.

Being the manifestation of the life of mind, culture is an essentially historical reality. Historiography of culture is therefore an oxymoran, the history of a historical form being a contradiction in terms. Not that history is not aware of this problem in fact, it has flourished along with the other sciences in its family such as sociology, psychology, political science, ethics, etc., in full awareness of the challenge that the problem poses. But they had only two ways out of the dilemma: to give up their existing scientific method and substitute it for another one suited to the nature of their subject matter; or to make their subject matter lie in the procrustean bed of their method. Since the other alternative was more acceptable to them, they found it easier to historicize the nature of man and his culture; which explains why even historians like R.G. Collingood[2] who avowedly reject positivism, eventually fall into its trap. The four characteristics of history in his view are: (i) that it is scientific, i.e., it begins by asking questions rather than telling something which he says he knows as does the author of quasi-history like legend or myth, (ii) that it is humanistic, i.e., it asks questions about the doings of man at determined times in the past, (iii) that it is rational in the sense that its answers are based on evidence, and (iv) it is self-revelatory, i.e., exists in order to tell man what he is, by telling him what man does. To these four characteristics we may add a fifth without which the philosophy implicit in Collingwood's definition of the scope of history would not be complete. We study history Collingwood says, for attaining self-knowledge.[3] If self-knowledge be the aim of history and science and rationality be its method of enquiry, then the nature of the self is also foreknown; it is what the scientific method would determine and define it to be.

II

Space would not permit us to examine at length Collingwood's scientific view of history. But we do wish to make some observations about the status of science as knowledge and its relevance to history. It is true that science is no longer a simple method of knowledge and has become a virtual replacement for epistemology.[4] But, we must bear in mind that its status as knowledge is no better than that of a working hypothesis or paradigm even till date. 'Physical science', writes Owen Barfield, 'has for a long time stressed the enormous difference between what it investigates as the actual structure of the universe, including the earth, and the phenomena or appearances, which are presented by that structure to normal human consciousness. In tune with this, most philosophy at all events since Kant has heavily emphasized the participation of man's own mind in the creation or evocation of these phenomena'.[5] Scientific theories, be they of physics or biology, are all assumptions – call them theories if you please – to save the appearances. Through the intuitive activity of the mind, reality is made to appear as 'phenomena' the first order of representation – which are further interpreted or expressed in terms of scientific concepts and theories. Scientific theories thus do not perform the same role in the knowledge of reality that the Greek 'theoria' (contemplation) played. The term as used in Aristotles' psychology referred to 'the moment of fully conscious participation in which the souls' potential knowledge (its ordinary state) becomes actual, so that man can at last claim to be awake'.[6] An echo of Barfield's view is to be found also in Kuhn's study of science.[7] The revolutions in science, as Kuhn points out, have actually been changes in paradigms rather than any real breakthrough in the understanding of reality. As all hypotheses work so all paradigms do, none rendering an earlier hypothesis or paradigm wholly irrelevant or obsolete.[8] The scientific view of history by which Collingwood sets so much in store introduces the same element of fictionality in the interpretation of history as science has introduced in the interpretation of nature, with one difference that the impact of the scientific revolution in history is likely to be more severely felt than that in nature. Manipulation and control of history and society will be the worst thing to happen to humanity after the control and exploitation of nature made possible by science.

Now, if the aim of history is self-understanding and if self-understanding is 'awakening of the self' as in the classical Greek tradition and 'probodh' or self-realization as in the Indian tradition, history must be approached through hermeneutics as suggested by Dilthey. For, much of the material which the historian has to deal with may be of dateless antiquity, and the determination of the veracity of even historical accounts is sometime so difficult that the historian has to take recourse to speculation and guess work to check upon it. In some of the prophetic religions, a science of human psychology is an indispensable part of the science of interpretation of religious texts. For instance, in Islamic theology, interpreters of the holy Prophet's sayings take the help of what they call 'Ilmul-Rijal' which enables them to determine the veracity of the statements made by persons who are supposed to know them.

We said above that cultures are historical realities, not only because we do not know their origins, but also and more especially as their traditions, more than what history has been able to know or understand of them, consist of a large body of literary material handed down by word of mouth in the form of myths, legends, art forms, fairy tales, songs, customs, etc., which are of timeless origin and which history in its present form can never adequately render into its own language, but whose content it can ill afford to disregard.

The content of the folklores, which according to Coomaraswamy is a 'consistent body of culture', is metaphysical and the difference between traditional cultures such as the primitive, the oriental or medieval and our own is one of 'sickness from health'.[9]

Though Collingwood or others of his persuasion may reject myth and folklore as quasi-history, they need to provide the clue to the understanding of traditional cultures like India. Civilizations which have arisen in the wake of the scientific and industrial revolutions are actually built upon a systematic destruction of their folklore, which invariably involves in one sense or another, as Coomaraswamy observes, the premature death of the folk, or in any case, the impoverishment of their lives. The life of 'civilized peoples has already been impoverished, its influence can only tend to impoverish those whom it reaches. The white man's burden of death'.[10] The mythology of the tribal people, writes D.F. Thompson, 'supports the belief in a ritual or supernatural visitation that comes upon those who disregard or disobey the law of the old men. When this belief in the old mend and their power ... dies or declines, as it does with civilization chaos and racial death follow immediately'.[11]

We must then look at the myth for getting to the meanings hidden in the secret recesses of racial memory of the peoples and cultures, if the culture is one where the normal form of life has yet not died out, or the one which Rene Guenon would consider as resting on 'principles, in the true sense of the word, and one in which all is ordered and in a hierarchy consistent with the principles, so that everything is seen to be the application and extension of a purely and essentially intellectual and metaphysical doctrine: that is what we mean when we speak of a traditional civilization'.[12]

III

The conventional historical method cannot therefore be a sure guide to an appropriate understanding of a normal or traditional civilization in fact it is not suited for a study of societies steeped in myth and ritual. New scholars, who have used these sources in their interpretation of the Indian culture, be they indologists, historians or sociologists have mainly looked upon them as allegories of reason rather than transrational dimensions of the human psyche.

Ronald Indane has taken up the bulk of indological research on India produced since Enlightenment by Europeans scholars for a critical assessment in his highly informative brilliant work titled 'Imagining India'.[13] His aim in this work is to 'open up', as he says, 'the closed unitary world that academic discourses have helped to manufacture with their Eurocentric world history'. The curious metaphors that he claims to have discovered in these discourses as he calls them are India as a 'female'. Indian thought as dream (Louis Renon), caste society as centrifuge and of Hinduism as jungle or even a sponge. That Indians' work is more of a genealogy of knowledge of Hinduism than a noological critique of it, is clear from the metaphors he himself has used to describe India of his own imagination. Taking the main clue from Michel Foucault, Antonio Gramsci and others he rejects Hegel (James Mill), Vincent Smith et al., as hegemonic. Likewise, he dismisses Todd, Basham, Baden Powell, Zimmer, Campbell, etc., as imperial and Eurocentric in their outlook, who all consider India either as a semi-tribal polity or as a culture lacking orderly rationality. This is not the place to attempt anything like an elaborate examination of Indane's assessment of the works of European and Indian scholars on India. The crux of his argument is that the metaphors they have used to describe India are a part of a 'discursive formation' of a language of power or a reflection in other words of their hegemonic interests. It is this mental disposition which prevents Indane from finding anything of positive value even in the works of scholars such as Hienerich Zimmer, Joseph Campbell and Ananda Coomaraswamy whose interest in the Indian tradition and culture cannot be anything but genuine and academic. Much can be said against the metaphor of 'scale of forms' Indane himself has used to describe the ancient Indian system of governance drawing upon Collingwood whose concept of history we have briefly commented upon. Indane and scholars like him fail to see the pitfalls of an archaeology and genealogy of knowledge in terms of which they try to evaluate ideas. It is a self-stultifying logic to trace every thought system to relations of power except ones' own. Even the most faithful critics of Foucault, the author of the phrases archaeology and genealogy of knowledge, have not spared him for the essential nihilistic strain in his thought.

IV

We propose to present a brief review of certain works on India which in our view are the best representatives of what may be considered as the interpretive or hermeneutic school of Indology and Indian history. Among these, we include Ananda K. Coomaraswamy, Rene Guenon, Hienerich Zimmer, Joseph Campbell and Gobind Chandra Pande. But before we do so, we would like to throw a little more light on what we consider to be a mythical clue to history. Let us begin with dispelling the prevailing notion that myth is an allegory of reason or nature used by the prelogical primitive or archaic man to understand himself and the world around him in the manner, i.e., in terms of causes and laws – of the modern man. In other words, myth is not a lower or embryonic form of reason, nor is it fiction used as a recreative sap to keep reason in good shape. It is, on the other hand, the elaboration of 'mythos' the ultimate 'word', into the narrative composed of many words, the process of this elaboration being like 'the step whereby the title of the play Hamlet becomes expanded into all the words and stimulated actions, characters, and situations of which that play is composed'.[14] The myth is only an expansion of the Essence, and when the Essence is thus expanded it assumes a quasi-temporal form and appears as a story of gods and goddess, and is concerned with things that did not happen in the same way as things happen in history. Coomaraswamy therefore calls it (itihas) the penultimate truth of which all experience is a temporal reflection. 'The mythical narrative is of timeless and placeless validity true now ever and everywhere'.[15] It is this Essence which the Greeks called the archaetype primordial images, and following which tradition Jung[16] and Eliade describe the myth as a repository of archaetypes.

Every one of the transient historical forms of life is a reflection of an archetypal possibility. For instance, there is an archetypal Sun, Sun of the Sun which is other than the physical Sun, but not an allegory of the latter. There are likewise primordial patterns of virtuous conduct, goodness, beauty, husband-wife, mother-son and ruler-ruled relationships, coming down to us from time immemorial through legends, myths and fairy tales. The archetypal First cause and then the immediate causes through which life in all forms has been explained or sought to be understood are to be looked for in the myth.

In fact, from what we said above about the opposition between the modern civilization created by the scientific and industrial revolutions, and culture organized around tradition should not be construed to mean that we posit a fundamental opposition between the truth of science and truth of religion or metaphysics. The opposition actually is between the scientific world view which has glorified appearances and their scientific representations into truth and traditional thought wherein even the truth or the solid world of science is considered as an epiphenomenon of the real or the ultimate truth. It is the vacuous nature of the reified world of modern civilization which is at loggerheads with the world of tradition. So long as scientific laws are continued to be validated with reference to the ultimate or the First principle, there can be no opposition between science and metaphysics. History will be obscuring the nature of reality rather than illuminating it, if it tries to see it through the mirror or impoverished science. The other precaution that the historian has to take is to make sure that he reads the appropriate meanings both in the text and the context, in the symbols and archetypes, and their cultural setting. There is no method of objective interpretation of history except where every bit of the historical material is interpreted as it ought to be interpreted. This is what Nirukta or hermeneutics tries to do.

We would like to refer to two main works of Ananda Coomaraswamy in this context, viz., his *'Hinduism and Buddhism'* and *'Spiritual Authority and Temporal Power in the Indian Theory of Government'*. Coomaraswamy's basic thesis in his first book is that Hinduism and Buddhism are contingent forms of the Philosophia Perennis whose universal truths no age or culture can claim as its own. Coomaraswamy begins with the myth between whose boundaries the Hindu social organization and culture are ensconced. It is the myth of eternal beginning when there was (tad ekam) the supreme identity of the one and the many. When all was deposited in the Oner, the First Principle spoken of as Purush. Prajapati, Shesh Nag, Ashvattha and all, the One which is a biunity of conjoint principles, Heaven and Earth, Sun and Moon, Sacerdotium and Regnum.

Prajapati reflects 'let me enter into my children, the sleeping and inanimate stones' 'to awaken them' and so He divides Himself into many, rupam, rupam pratirupo babhuva. Since Prajapati after coming to inhabit his children can not come together again from them, He proclaims that they shall flourish who will build me again hence: the Gods built him again and they flourish. Sacrifice is the primordial act enacted by Gods to biget or perpetuate it (yajen yajyam yajayant deva). It is, in other words, the exempler of all acts, the touchstone of all skillful and correct doing, in the language of theology, the sacred act. It is not given to man, the temporal being to initiate; they must therefore imitate what the Gods did in averternity timeless time. Human life is an imitation or reproduction of sacrifice and all prudence is an application of the principles of sacrifice on the historical plain. Actions are perfect or imperfect, in order or inordinate in the measure in which they reproduce or do not reproduce the rite. Virtue is skill in works (kaushayla).

Sacrifice in divines or on the human plain is the sacrifice of the sacrificer himself which means self-sacrifice or a perfect command of desires, the motivating force of action which means both pleasure and pains, and whose conquest means liberation from both. It is this liberation which is the ultimate end of life called amritatva.

Coomaraswamy writes, 'where there is an agreement as to the nature of man's last end, and that the Way by which the present and the paramount ends of life can be realized is that of sacrificial operation, it is evident that the forms of life will be determined by the requirements of the sacrifice and that order (yatharthata) and impartiality (samadristi) will mean that every man shall be enabled to become and by no means prevented from becoming what he has in him to become'.[17] In the archetypal man, the Purush who is the embodiment of sacrificial life, there is a hierarchy of sacerdotal, royal and administrative functions followed by a fourth function to handle the raw material or food to be prepared for the various organs of the Purusha. The vocational order in the Hindu society is thus only a reproduction of the division of functions in the life of the Primordial man. Castes are literally born of the sacrifice.

In *Spiritual Authority and Temporal Power*, Coomaraswamy addresses himself to the problem of the relationship of the sacredotium and regnum (brahmakshatra) what in the language of modern social science is called status and power. The relationship between the two is the same he observes as that between the Sky and Earth constituting as they do the syzygy of the male and female principles. The king has power which if allowed to be autonomous will degenerate into licence. It must be, as such be subjected to the discipline of a higher principle, what Coomaraswamy calls spiritual authority as represented by the priest, the embodiment of Brahma, spiritual power. The king who is the supreme sacrificer and a royal reproduction of the Prajapati and wears the ushnis, the crown, must subject himself to the discipline of dharma through the advice of the priest.

To the students of modern theory of government, the supremacy of power over status seems as obvious as of the ruler over the ruled. It is under this impression that scholars like Evola had mistaken the rank of the king as having the highest rank in the caste hierarchy. The mistake is present also in Hocart's otherwise brilliant exposition of the theory of caste. It is there in Louis Dumont also to which for want of space we may not be able to refer.

Coomaraswamy, in our opinion, is not an ordinary art historian and critic, his is, together with Rene Guenon, the most authentic interpretation of the Indian tradition. What has been sketched above is neither a fair sample of what he has said about the Indian social organization of culture, nor even a very dependable resume of his views.

The French indologist Rene Guenon who died as a Sufi in Cairo under the pseudonym Abdal Wahid Yahia has three outstanding works to his credit which must attract the attention of all students of the Indian tradition, viz., *Introduction to the Study of Hindu Doctrines*: *East and West*, and *Man and His Becoming According to Vedanta*. Guenon like Coomaraswamy considers Indian tradition as a variant of the Primordial Wisdom, regards both Shankar and Ramanuj as the best exponents of Vedanta sharing the general view that Shankar is more acceptable to the esoteric circles of India than Ramanuj. Guenon again shares Coomaraswamy's view that the Hindu social organization is an example of a natural hierarchy of the human society.

Defining caste as a function determined by the natural abilities of each individual, Rene Guenon makes no distinction between Varna and caste. He speaks of what he calls the namik and gotric qualities of the individual, which both enter into; the constitution of his nature the gotric qualities, being those which the individual shares with his consanguineous kins, while the namik are those which are his own and which his name is supposed to express. It is the latter by which he is better known and it is this which explains the variations in the dispositions of the members of the same ancestral stock. In a family of five brothers who have inherited the same set of hereditary qualities, one becomes a musician, another grows into a thief and the third may be a poet and so on. The distinctness of the individual over the rest of the members of his family is determined by his extra-hereditary qualities and both these qualities enter into the determination of his caste.

Rene Guenon also examines the Indian theory of ages, and considers the modern age as Kaliyuga and modern education as an elaborately organized form of ignorance, avidya like a typical traditional Indian scholar.

Hienrich Zimmer in his *Myths and Symbols in Indian Art and Civilization*[18] besides other symbols, has selected the Markandeya myth from the Matsya Purana to explain the secret of life according to the traditional wisdom of India. A brief account of Zimmers' commentary on the myth will be order in this context.

It can be easily seen that the myth is an account of how Vishnu, the Primeval Being manifests himself in a series of archetypes the cosmic ocean, the serpent Ananta' the divine child which are all manifestations of Vishnu and he himself is the anthropomorphic form of the archetypes of wholeness. Vishnu teaches Markandeya the identity of opposites firstly manifesting himself as a child and then by calling the ageless saint by his first name as an old friend and relative, though the two had never met. The identity of opposites, Zimmer, is the secret of Maya, a simultaneous and successive manifestation of energies that are at variance with each other, processes contradicting and annihilating each other, creation and destruction, evolution and destruction, the dream idyll of the inward vision of God and the desolate naught, the terror of the void, the dread infinite. This 'and' uniting the inempatibles expresses the fundamental character of the highest being who is the Lord and wielder of Maya, whose energy is Maya. Opposites are fundamentally of one essence, two aspects of one Vishnu. That is the wisdom, the myth undertakes to disclose to the Hindu devotee Zimmer's other similar work in which he offers a critique of the Indian titled Philosophies of India edited posthumely by his student Joseph Campbell which also we wbuld have liked to discuss but for the pressure of space.

G.C. Pande, the only Indian thinker after Coomaraswamy whose thought we propose to discuss next is basically a historian and virologist but with a deep metaphysical insight. Of his numerous works on Indian culture and philosophy we have selected only two, viz., his Pant Memorial Lectures entitled *Bhartiya Samaj Tattvik Aur Aitihasik Vivechan* and Hiranand Shastri Memorial Lectures titled *Bhartiya Prampara Ke Mool Swar* brought out by National Publishing House, Delhi. Professor Pande's interpretation of the Indian culture is also hermeneutic not in the limited sense of the word in current western usage in the hands of scholars like House Gadmar, but in its traditional meaning of Nirukta as used by Yask Sayan, Coomaraswamy, Rene Guenon and others, what we in our own way call appropriate (sameechin) understanding. G.C. Pandey bases his exposition of the Indian society and culture on the interpretation of the Purush Sukta of the Rig veda. The Purush Sukta as the myth of creation, of externity becoming time – what Coomaraswamy would call the divine procession and of the impounding of time into eternity when everything is absorbed into One (tad ekam). Everything in this world is Purusha that which is manifest and that which is to manifest, whose one part is the whole cosmos, three parts Amrita. It is this Purusha, Pandey remarks after the Gita, who becomes manifest in the universe and in the human intelligence as the cosmic germ. Man, in other words, is the abode of divinity and culture is the union of the human with the divine essence of man. It is his inner transformation or sacramental lifting up as in Christianity to the Heaven, to identify of becoming and Being. Culture therefore is a symbolic and normative order in Professor Pande's view, but not like the disjointed culture system in modern sociology. The knowledge of this invisible transcendental Purusha is obtained through revelation (Shruti or amnyai) which is ahistorical. Pandey like Coomaraswamy and Rene Guenon considers the science of social organization – call it traditional sociology in modern language – a part of autology or self-knowledge (Brahmavidya) and regards the Purush, Dharma and Atma as the revealed archetypes of Tad Ekam. Again, exactly in the manner of Coomaraswamy, Pande considers the sacrifice as the primordial act – the naval of the cosmos – to which every human action has to conform or which men have to accomplish analogically (Pratikatmak) what gods do in the usual course.

The division of gunas and karmas, the varna vyavastha in Pande's interpretation much like that in Coomaraswamy's is a reproduction of the life of the cosmic man, the Purusha.

The agreement in the views of the three scholars is so pronounced that reading Ananda Kentish Coomaraswamy, Rene Guenon and Govind Chandra Pande is almost like dipping into the same texts thrice – two in English and one in an Indian language and that is another remarkable feature Professor Pande has been able to achieve. He has ably demonstrated how the profounder metaphysical insight can be expressed through a modern Indian language. The difference among them is not one of understanding, but of the same Infinite Possibility appearing in different modalities to different viewers. Pande's professional background, however, lands him into several difficulties when he tries to save Varna from its degenerate historical form miscalled the caste system. Rene Guenon does not consider the distinction between the two worth making. The degenerate caste system is no variant of the national hierarchy of the human society. It would be an interesting piece of historical enquiry to locate the point at which the traditional vocational order became degenerate. Another point which Rene Guenon raises and which remains suppressed in G.C. Pande's work is the distinction between namik and gotrik qualities which enter into the composition of the individual's nature, which determine according to Pande his Karma which in turn constitutes the basis of the vocational organization known as the Varna Vyavastha. It is again his undue concession to history he exposes when he thinks that the misconceived conflict of tradition and mode modernity can be reconciled in terms of a new synthesis in which modernity simply be a new phase of the seeking of grapple with the problem of securing utilities for the mass of mankind.[19] The reconciliation of the two is possible only if modernity could be willing to test its principles against the primordial norm and correct them accordingly, and this modernity which has excelled tradition by sheer absolutization as Professor Pande apply remarks of the values of science and technology can never do.

Notes

1. See Hodges, William, Wilhelm Dilthey: *An Introduction*, Routledge and Kegan Paul and also (S.P. Nagendra) 'The Concept of Ritual in Modern Sociological Theory', *Academic Journals*, Delhi, 1968, p. 51.
2. R.G. Collingwood: *The Idea of History*, UK: Oxford University Press, 1973, pp. 303–305.
3. Op. cit., p. 315.
4. See Habermas Jurgen: *Knowledge and Interest Introduction*, p.5.
5. See *Saving the Appearances*, Barfield, Owen, 24, Russell Square London: Faber and Faber, United Kingdom, 1957, Introduction, p. 12.
6. Barfield, Owen, op. cit., p.49. Compare this sense of 'theoria' with that of 'Prabodh' (Hans upanishad)/Atmaprabodh (Mandukya Karita)/Pratibodh (Kena upanishad). See Dessenn Paul: *The Philosophy of the Upanishads*, London: Faber and Faber, 1957, p. 165.
7. Thomas Kuhn: *The Structure of Scientific Revolutions*, Chicago: University of Chicago Press, 1970.
8. The real scientific revolution in Barfield's view took place when the working hypotheses of science were finally declared and accepted as truth in the academic circles.
9. Barfield, Owen, *Saving the Appearances*, London: Faber and Faber, 1957.
10. Op. cit., p. 217 and f., p. 232.
11. Quoted in Coomaraswamy, op. cit., p.217.
12. Rene Guenon: *East and West*, 1924, p. 235 quoted by Coomaraswamy op. cit., p. 233.
13. Basil Blackwell: Cambridge Mass, Introduction, 1990, p. 1.
14. Burke Kenneth, quoted in S.P. Nagendra's 'Concept of Ritual in Modern Sociological Theory', *Academic Journals*, 1968, p. 172.
15. *Hinduism and Buddhism*, New York: Philosophical Literary, p. 6.
16. For a discussion of C.G. Jung's concept of myth see his *Introduction to a Science of Mythology* (with the collaboration of Kerenyi), London: Routledge and Kegan Paul, 1954.
17. Ibid., p. 26.
18. Heinrich Zimmer, 'Myths and Symbols in Indian Arts and Civilization', *Bollingen Series VI*, New York: Pantheon Books, 1957.
19. G.C. Pande, Meaning and Process of Culture. Shivalal Agarwala, Agra, 1972.

3

Homo Hierarchicus

Some Comments[1]

There are studies galore of the Indian caste system, but *Homo Hierarchicus* is a study of a different genre. For, Louis Dumont's interest is not in the substantive whole that is the caste system, but in the formal properties of the whole, not in one or another order of the whole, but to use a Levi-Straussian phrase, in the order of orders. So, *Homo Hierarchicus* is just not one or another perspective on the caste system; it is a prolegomena to the critique of "universal forms" of which the existing societies, archaic, traditional and modern, are specific modalities in space and time. It is another thing that situated as it is, structural anthropology may not be in a position to grow into any such critique. But even as a comparative study of the unique and the discontinuous, it can afford immense help to the societies to discover and understand each other, be it only by way of exposing what they mutually conceal from each other. *Homo Hierarchicus* has, thus, as much relevance to the traditional man, whose world it seeks to explore and epitomize, as it has to the modern, whom it can help to understand what he covertly desires but overtly suppresses.

Then to locate the order of orders, the structural principle of the caste system, Dumont begins peeling off the whole, layer by layer and ultimately discovers the same structural principle underlying every layer. The rank order, the division of labour, marriage regulations, commensal relations, in fact all the lived-in in orders are shown to reflect the same structural principle. The only "lived-in" order which does not resonate fully with the rest and seems to deviate from the master principle is the distribution of power and authority. But Dumont has no difficulty in bringing this alike under the same umbrella. We will see how he does it, but let us first identify the principle.

Dumont takes Bougle's definition of caste as his starting point. According to Bougle, the caste system is composed of hereditary groups which are both distinguished from the one another and connected together in three ways: (1) by gradation of status or hierarchy, (2) by detailed rules aimed at ensuring their separation, and (3) by division of labour and, the interdependence which results from it.[2] Now, all the three principles or which Bougle thinks the system is founded, can be reduced, Dumont argues, to just one principle, viz., the opposition of the pure and impure. Empirically, the pure is superior to the impure and, therefore, the opposition of the two is hierarchical, which means that hierarchy is also based on the same principle. And, since the pure castes cannot be allowed to come in contact with the impure ones, and as there can be no intermingling of pure and impure occupations either, the same principle can be seen to underly separation and division of labour also. The whole world thus seems to be based "on the necessary and hierarchical coexistence of the two opposites".[3]

The whole, no doubt, consists of numerous castes going from the highest to the lowest in an irreversible non-cyclic order, but the order remains firmly ensconced between the opposition of the pure and impure "on the one extreme being", the Brahmans who are pure and superior and on the other, being the untouchables who are impure and inferiors.

It must be borne in mind that the separation of purity and impurity on which the social reality of caste is built is not of the same nature as the separation of the pure and impure on the physical or organic plane, which results in occasional pollution of persons or groups. Pollutions associated with occasions such as birth, death, menstruation of women, accidental contact with impure persons, etc., are temporary pollutions and there are well-known methods of washing them out and restoring the affected persons to their original status. But, the separation of Brahmans and untouchables on the social plane is final and irrevocable. In this case, purity is the complement of impurity and impurity the complement of purity. The Brahman is pure because the untouchable is impure and the untouchable is permanently impure because the Brahman is permanently pure. The system is, so to say, "a totality made up of two unequal but complementary parts".[4]

Looking again at the system as a linear order of descending statuses, we can locate the same principle at work. The division of the system into castes and of castes into subcastes is actually a segmentation of the hierarchical status between a large number of groups. And since the basis of the hierarchical status is the opposition of the pure and impure, the entire transitive order of castes may be viewed as a reproduction of the same pair of opposites.

We said at the outset that Dumont's main interest is not in the substantive whole, but in the formal principle underlying it. Now, when we identify the principle as the separation and complementarity of the pure and impure, are we not mixing up the formal and the substantive? For, purity and impurity are religious notions; the Brahman is pure and the untouchable impure because purity and impurity have been attributed to them for social considerations. Likewise, when we define hierarchy in terms of the superiority of the pure and inferiority of the impure, we are making it an essentially religious notion. Dumont is quite conscious of this and even though admitting that hierarchy may be a religious notion, he would like to define it in purely formal terms. Hierarchy, he points out, should be understood "as the principle by which the elements of a whole are ranked in relation to the whole".[5]

Having thus defined hierarchy as a formal principle of ranking, he opposes it to "social stratification" the expression used by the modern societies to describe their own gradation of power and authority. Conversely, social stratification is also hierarchy, but an inverted hierarchy, "non-conscious, shame faced and suppressed".[6]

And now, a word about the concept of the whole. Dumont distinguishes between two approaches to the idea of the whole. According to one, "a system (a whole) is conceived as made up of objects each with its own essence and it is in virtue this essence together with a definite law of interaction that they act on one another; for instance, physical bodies each have their own mass and act on each other to an extent determined by this mass and their relative position. This way of thinking which separate the individual being from the relation is essentially modern. ... According to the other approach, the elements of which the system seems to be composed are disregarded and only considered as product of the network of relations, this network would then constitute a system". In sum, the whole, according to Dumont, is a system of relations rather than a system of elements.

If we transpose these formal notions to the ontic plane, we get two concepts of the social whole: one, the concept of the whole as a network or configuration of ends or values sui generic in which the individual becomes a structural reproduction of the configuration. In this whole as in Platos' Republic, Dumont remarks "the stress is placed on society as a whole, as collective men[7]; the ideal derives from the organization of society with respect to its ends (and not with respect to individual happiness); it is above all a matter of order, of hierarchy; each particular man in his place must contribute to the global order ..."[8]

The other concept of the whole that we get to is the one in which the emphasis is on the individual, the society according to it is a mere aggregate of individuals and the "kingdom of ends coincides with each man's legitimate ends and so the values are turned upside down. What is still called society is the means, the life of each men is the end".[9] Ontologically, the society does not exist.

We have no difficulty in understanding Dumont's concept of the whole except on one score: if the whole is a configuration of values, then how can it be held to sustain itself without the value of values or the transcendental value? Then, there is another question which is just a corollary of the first: if the whole is a hierarchy of opposites, and the opposites presuppose each other then, what sustains them in their co-existence? Dumont does not directly raise these questions, but the answers that he would seem to give to them are like this: the basis of hierarchy is the opposition of the pure and impure, and the pure and impure are notions of separation created by ideology, i.e., ideas and values held by the society. In other words, it is the society or the whole which is the source of the opposition and it is the opposition which constitutes the whole, the society. Is Dumont not arguing in a circle and is he not resuscitating the sociophony implicit in Durkheim's sociologism? He claims that Plato's concept of society is the nearest analogy to his own concept of the hierarchical whole. But it must not be forgotten that in Plato's Republic society is as much collective man, as man is the individual society, i.e., the individual is consubstantial with society, a relationship which can be maintained only on the metaphysical plane. In Dumont's concept of the whole, hierarchy as a principle of ranking will hardly get beyond the meaning of "social stratification", a position which Dumont disowns. At one point Dumont calls the oppositions of the pure and impure a synthetic *a priori* opposition[10], which would mean that it is a universal and necessary opposition and that its universality and necessity are not grounded in experience. What then is the ground from which this synthetic *a priori* flows? Dumont is speaking here the Kantian language and one would therefore expect him to give a Kantian answer[11] to the question. But no, his answer is different; it is not pure reason which according to kept contains the principles of cognizing anything absolutely *a priori;* for Dumont, it is the society. As we have pointed out above, in Dumont's view, the hierarchy of the pure and impure is grounded in the ideology of the Hindu society.

The principle of opposition giving the structural form to the society and the society validating and sustaining this principle is a fallacious argument having its roots in our refusal or failure to recognize that dialectical opposition as a formal principle of a space and time-bound order can be understood only in terms of a non-dual transcendental principle. "The world of pairs of opposites, affirmations and negations, good and evil", remarks Ananda Coomaraswamy, "is theophony"[12] social phenomenology and structuralism stop at the point of binary opposition and treat it as the final principle of being, or else, reduce it to sociophany.

This then accounts for the confusions which abound in *Homo Hierarchicus*: between hierarchy of caste and hierarchy of varna, between status and power, between jajmani and division of labour, between religious inferiority and secular dependence, and so on. We will have occasion to refer to these confusions in our treatment of Dumont's structural analysis of varna, marriage, jajmani system and above all, the distribution of power.

Endogamy and hypergamy are the basic features of marriage within the caste system, but as Dumont would argue, they are just applications of the principle of hierarchy. For instance, marrying within the caste is a mechanism by which the castes reproduce themselves and in so reproducing themselves, what they tend to retain and perpetuate is their respective status in the transitive order. Dumont distinguishes between the primary and secondary marriage in the case of women and between the principal and subsidiary marriage in the case of men. For women, the first marriage is the primary marriage which either gives them a superior status or circulates them within the same status group. The principal marriage in the case of men is again isegamous; there must be equality of status between the spouses. But, the secondary marriages in the case of women and the subsidiary marriages in the case of men, both lead to a status discrepancy between the spouses, although the status of the off-springs is not affected nor is the hierarchy of the wives disturbed. The prescriptions of ideology[13] as reflected in the classical Hindu theory of marriage also accord well with the principle underlying the actual marriages, viz., the maintenance of status or hierarchy.

As regards the restrictions on physical contact and eating and drinking, it is not difficult to see how they constitute one of the basic criteria by which the castes separate and distinguish themselves hierarchically from one another. The preoccupation with status can be seen to be present even among the untouchables, some of whom close themselves to others whom they consider as more untouchable.[14] It is a significant coincidence that the relative religious or status inferiority of the untouchables is in place with their economic dependence on higher or dominant castes; or conversely that the hierarchical superiority of the higher or dominant castes is reflected in their dominance.[15] Those who are powerful and economically dominant are also the purest and those who are materially oppressed are also the supremely impure.

The caste system has its own division of labour which contrasted with its counterpart in the modern industrial system is oriented as Dumont points out, to the needs of the whole. And, this structural relationship to the whole, he further argues, links the division of labour with hierarchy.[16] As things are in present-day India, there is no definite relationship between caste and profession. While there are castes which are not only professional but also bear the name of the profession[17], there are those which are differentiated internally into numerous occupational groups. For instance, the Kahars of UP or the fishermen, water bearers and servants of women or again the Khatiks as masons, rope-makers, fruit gathering and sellers of their professional label becomes a mark of separation; there is no intermarriage between the khatiks who have became pork butchers and others. In the other case, also the basis of segmentation may be something other than specialization. Among the potters for instance, some are tile makers and some pot-makers, but some use oxen and others, donkeys for transport. Would it be against the natural grain to think that these features are an insignia of their internal separation?[18]

Coming new to the jajmani system which is the basic form of division of labour in the caste system, we notice the following features: in the first place, each family has at its service, a family of specialists for each specialized service, ceremonial or customary system of presentations and counter-presentations for the services. Repayment is in kind and is not made for each presentation but is spread, instead, over the whole year – a fixed quantity of grain at the time of harvest and obligatory presents on major ceremonial occasions. The families which receive the benefit of specialized services are known as Jajmans and those who offer the services are called praja.

The system which has often been described as a religious institution is in Dumont's view, one of politico-economic dominance and dependence between those who own land and those who do not. But, this relationship of interdependence unites the villagers into a hierarchical collectivity whose orientation is towards the whole. The spirit behind what is received in the form of service and what is returned in the form of payment in kind, is totally different from the one that we come across in an industrial system where the individual is in the centre and the system on the periphery.

We may now take up Dumont's discussion of status and power. Is the distribution of power and authority the manifestation of the same structural law of separation and complementarity which, as we have discovered, is behind the caste system as a whole? Dumont's answer is no. He proceeds on the assumption that hierarchy does not presuppose power, nor does power presuppose hierarchy. But how then one may ask, does power coexist with the other "lived-in" orders within the hierarchical society? Dumont's answer to the question is very interesting: it is the Indian Lady of Mercy, the hierarchical opposition of the pure and impure, which accommodates it under its umbrella and harmonizes it with it: religious temper.

Power enters hierarchy in India through the classical theory of varnas, which Dumont thinks, contains another principle of hierarchy, viz., the hierarchy of "varnas, colours or estates whereby four categories are distinguished the highest is that of the Brahmans or priests, below them the Kshatriyas, then the Vaishyas, in modern usage mainly merchants and finally the shudras, the servants and have-nots".[19] The order of varnas is not linear, but is one of "successive dichotomies and inclusions". The four are divided into two: the twice-born and the Shudras; then the twice-born are again divided into two: the Vaishyas forming one block opposed to Kshatriyas and Brahmans who form another. The varnas have each their well-designed duties, the Brahman being the priest; the Kshatriya, the ruler or the king; the Vaishya, the farmer and the Shudra, the servant. As contrasted with the caste system, the emphasis in the varna hierarchy is on function rather than birth.

But, the most distinctive feature of the varna hierarchy is the relationship between the Brahman and the Kshatriya: the Brahman being the spiritual authority and the Kshatriya, the temporal. Status and power are clearly distinguished here. At no stage in India was there a merger of status and power, the spiritual authority never wielded power as in the Catholic west. For the emergence of pure hierarchy, it was necessary that status must be separated from power; but it was equally necessary that pure hierarchy must have justification for power; for after all power cannot be deleted from order. Indeed in the theory of purity, a vegetarian merchant ought logically to have precedence over a king who eats meat.[20] But this is just not the case on the plane of social reality. The theory of varna subordinates the king to the priest, but includes them both in one solid block, as it were to oppose them to other varnas. It is, then, with reference to varnas that the caste system validates its subordination of the vegetarian merchant to the meat-eating king. Hierarchy thus gives place to power without saying so, and it is obliged to close its eyes to this point on pain of destroying itself.[21] Having subordinated the king to the priest, hierarchy has no doubt established the precedence of status over power. But then it must not ignore the majesty of the king and must give him precedence over others, for after all, it is the king who upholds dharma.

Another important fact about the caste system though extraneous to ideology but well-covered under the cloak of hierarchy, is the territorial division of castes, with which are connected the rights over land and the relationship of dominance and dependence in the territorial unit, viz., the village. The territorial division of castes, Dumont would like to tell us, has a close resemblance to the segmentation of the system into castes, and of castes into subcastes, as if territory was an essential ingredient of this segmentation.[22] So territory also looks like being a presupposition of hierarchy. And who owns land in the hierarchical India? The question, Dumont would argue, is ill-formulated. Rights over land are nothing more or less than the rights over the grain distributed on the threshing floor under the jajmani system. The grain here is an object of communal right differentiated into individual rights which are all interdependent. The rights over land, starting from the farmer, culminate in the king, as if the whole chain was a differentiation of the king's right. "Only if the king were to give up his own right and to take care that all rights were united in the same hands as was the case with certain religious donations would something like ownership be created".[23] In conclusion, all rights over land are marked by interdependence and complementarity oriented as though, to the needs of the collectivity.

Power in the territorial base of the caste system, i.e., in the village is wielded by the dominant castes as they have been so-called by the contemporary social anthropologists. The dominant caste, Dumont would say, is a reproduction of the royal function at the village level; a sort of territorial segmentation of the royal function of exercise of authority and dispensation of justice. In fact, the system of governance and dispensation of justice starts from the king and comes down to the caste panchayat. Here, then, is a chain looking more or less like the segmentation of justice and authority. And the fact that caste from panchayats generally deepens justice by arbitration and conciliation, one may conclude that their main function is to "re-establish harmony within the group and to maintain the authority of the panchayat"[24], a replication of the function of the king.

Before closing this part of our discussion, we would like to refer to two more aspects of the caste system, viz., the place of the renouncer or the sanyasi in the system and contemporary developments in the traditional system. The renouncer in the hierarchical society as understood so far, introduces another element of contradiction to its internal order of interdependence, as he is oriented to individual rather than social ends. However, what looks here like a contradiction is essentially a manifestation of complementarity. The renouncer, no doubt, gives up his social role, the role assigned to him by his caste, subcaste or family, but he assumes a universal role which though not in the society may be considered as a specially "thought of" social role. The traditional society while apparently ignoring the individual, does not ignore him essentially; it gives him a contrived role and integrates him back into its fold. The renouncers often separate themselves from the main trunk of the society to become a sect, but the sect again gradually becomes a caste like organization.

Contemporary changes in the caste system commonly described as sanskritization and westernization may also be viewed as a diachronic reproduction of the same structural principle of separation and complementarity. There has been a long process of formation of new castes, either by a process of fission, or by the complementary process of aggregation in India. Fission accounts for the continuing subdivision of castes into subcastes as a response to the internal urge of the castes to preserve and protect their purity or status against "till-advised contacts or marriages". Aggregation, on the other hand, explains the continuing process of social climbing through "extrinsic borrowings" of the insignia of status called sanskritization or Brahmanization. Westernization is again a result of the some urge for social climbing, but the model here is the king and not the priest, and the king in this case is the west. So, a change in the Hindu society, Dumont thinks, has also been towards a permanency of form and this, thanks to the "thought of" order of the myth of the eternal return – the Indian philosophy of history which envisages a recurrent return to the same form through the abolition of time.

We began by remarking that Dumont's work is of a different kind. It is different because here is an attempt to understand the system in the true spirit of understanding; at no stage does it appear that the experience from which Dumont speaks, he has not relived with the hierarchical man in India and it is this reliving of an already lived experience which must inform every comparative sociological enquiry. There is no attempt at all either to belittle the system or to denigrate it. There is yet another merit of this work; Dumont has neatly reassembled all fragments of understanding bearing on the caste system which had been lying scattered in the works of scholars such as Blunt, Ghurye, Stevenson, Karve, Gough, Srinivas, Bailey, Meyor, etc., and woven them back into the texture of his own structural understanding.

But after we have said this, we must not forget to mention that Dumont has his own limitations, limitations imposed by the sociological apperception which he shares with the modern man. It is this apperception which is at the back of his sociocentric view of hierarchy. There is no contradiction in the hierarchical man's mind, between caste and varna, between birth and function, and between status and power. If the principle of hierarchy is separation and complementarity as manifested in the opposition of purity and impurity, then the king must take precedence over the merchant and after the priest, irrespective of whether he is a vegetarian or non-vegetarian and independently of the power which he commands over both. But separation and complementarity, then, must be understood on their own plane, i.e., as manifestations not of ideology but of metaphysics.

Dumont does not deny that even the untouchables have their statuses which they jealously guard against impurer encroachments. There can be, in other words, only relative purity and relative impurity. What is pure is only less impure and what is impure is only less pure. The king is less pure than the Brahman, but less impure than the merchant and so on. The transitive order of castes viewed from one end is a descending order of purity or an ascending order of impurity and viewed from the other end, an ascending order of purity or a descending order of impurity. There is nothing like an absolutely bipartite division of castes into pure and impure.

Nor does the hierarchical man think that the order of purity and impurity is irreversible. For, the only hurdle in its reversibility is time which he constantly tries to overcome by imitating an archetype, i.e., by transforming every action into rite. Action thus transformed into rite is action well-done and is synonymous with yoga and yajna in the Hindu tradition. In trying thus to abolish time, the hierarchical man tries to transcend the opposition of the pure and impure, for both are progenitive of each other and hence both must be overcome. The renouncer, as Dumont correctly noted, is an element of contradiction in the hierarchical order, for he is the man who has become ahierarchical; has, in other words, transcended the opposition of the pure and impure. His so-called involvement in the world is only an appearance.

So, no action is pure and impure in its own right; it is pure or impure in the measure in which it reproduces or does not reproduce an exemplary model. A well-doing Shudra is better than an ill-doing Brahman in spite of the relative purity of the Brahman's domain of work and the complementary impurity of the Shudra's domain. The relative purity or impurity of the different domains of work is again a reflection of the same principle of separation and complementarity. The domain of the Brahman's work is purer than that of the king and the king's domain of work, purer than that of the merchant and so on because in this descending order, the least pure is the remotes approximation to the exemplary model, i.e., sacrifice.

There can be no question of the Brahman trying to become a king, or the Shudra trying to become either because all of them in that case will be ill-doers. The king, the merchant and the unfree servant, as Dumont prefers to call the Shudra, will be ill-doers again if they ignore the priest, for without his counsel they cannot distinguish between well-doing and ill-doing. As Coomaraswamy points out "the Purohita literally one put in front", "One who takes precedence" like Agni or Brahaspati in divinis is the king's Brahman adviser and minister. The Purodhatr is the king himself who appoints the Purohita or more literally "puts him in front". The Devasvah are the deities – Savitri, Agni, Soma, Brahaspati, Indra Rudra, Mitra and Varuna by whom the king is "quickened" through the priest who invokes them as "king quickeners" (rajasvah), so that "It is these gods that now quicken (suvate) him, and having been quickened (sutah) by them, he is henceforth quickened" (Svah suyate, S.B.V. 3.3.11.13).[25] "In the Greek tradition", Coomaraswamy again remarks, "the heroic kind of caste alike in the soul and the community", "that part of our soul which is endowed with bravery ... and courage ..., and which is the lover of victory (Plato, Timaeus 70A), is the best part of the mortal or animal soul, superior to the affective and inferior to the spiritual and immortal part that lays down the law. As such its seat is in the heart, between the bowels and the head, it is the defender of the whole community, its function is to listen to the voice from the Akropolis, to server and cooperate in battle with the sacred principle, against the mob of appetites (within us) or of moneyed men (in the city)".[26]

The confusion in Dumont's mind between what he calls the sacrifier and the sacrificer is of a piece with other confusions we have referred to above. The Yajaman according to him is the sacrifier, "he who has the sacrifice performed" and therefore the patron in relation to the praja whom he employs for carrying out the ritual duties on ceremonial occasions. The Brahman priest is still the kingpin of the jajmani system in the villages and the towns, but no a Yajaman calls him praja; only the lower caste Yajaman assistants in the family rituals are so called. So, praja is not the complement of Yajaman in any case. The Yajaman is the sacrificer, one who performs the sacrifice or has it performed. Now, it must be remembered that in a social organization where rite or sacrifice gives form to every activity, there can be no clear-cut division of life into religious and secular. In fact, the hierarchical man knows nothing of this distinction. True that now the jajmani system looks like a system of division of labour with a religious façade. But this is true also of the social organization as a whole, which though essentially religious, looks like a secular organization with a distinct religious sphere.

The structural principle of separation and complementarity can not be given meaning in secular terms. To say that man is hierarchical is nothing more or less than to say that he is religious. Dumont and for that matter all modern thinkers refuse to see the logic of their own argument. The jajmani system is only a segmentation of the social whole which is oriented to sacrifice (yajya) wherein the king is the principal Yajaman and every other householder is either a Yajaman or a priest. That the social organization is a hierarchy of priests and Yajamans is a thought absolutely repulsive to the consciousness of modern man. But in apparently non-religious terms, this only means that the social organization is a hierarchy of vita contemplativa[27] and vita active; contemplation and action, the Sacerdotium and Regnum being the first temporal manifestations of the primordial principal of dialectical opposition. It may be remarked in passing that the separation of the Sacerdotium and the Regnum, of spiritual authority and temporal power in India to which Dumont refers, was not a separation of polities from religion. This never happened at any stage in the Indian tradition, the king was never allowed to become a despot; he always ruled according to dharma, as counseled and directed by the wise, the Sacerdotium. The king giving precedence to the priest and the priest submitting to the temporal power of the king was a mutual choice dictated by the inner dialectics of their respective functions; any other kind of choice would make them both ill-doers.

What image of himself does the modern egalitarian man, who avowedly disparages every kind of inequality, see in the mirror that *Homo Hierarchicus* holds to him? That inequality is as much a part of the values that he has chosen for himself, as it is of the values of the hierarchical man, is the plain and simple answer. For, what else are phenomena like racism, if not a recrudescence of man's traditional urge for inequality? The fact that the urge remains suppressed and concealed under the cloak of rationality, can not delete it from the life of the modern man.

Notes

1. Dumont, Louis, translation by Mark Sainsbury, New Delhi (Vikas Publications, 1970).
2. Dumont, Louis, op. cit., p. 43.
3. Ibid., p. 43.

4. Ibid., p. 55.
5. Ibid., p. 66.
6. Ibid., p. 66.
7. Ibid., p. 40.
8. Ibid., p. 9.
9. Ibid., p. 9.
10. Ibid., p. 43.
11. Even the Kantian answer is inadequate.
12. Ananda K. Coomaraswamy: *Spiritual Authority and Temporal Power in the Indian Theory of Government*, New Delhi (Munshiram Manoharlal, 1970), p. 73.
13. Ibid., p. 128.
14. Ibid., p. 136.
15. Ibid., p. 137.
16. Ibid., p. 92.
17. Ibid., p. 95.
18. Ibid., p. 95.
19. Ibid., p. 67.
20. Ibid., p. 65.
21. Ibid., p. 77.
22. Ibid., pp. 154–155.
23. Ibid., p. 157.
24. Ibid., p. 180.
25. Op. cit., pp. 8–9.
26. Ibid., p. 2.
27. Hannah Arendt: *The Human Condition*, New York (Doubleday: Anchor Books, New York, 1959).

4

The Theory of Development

A Sociological Critique

Even the most serious questions sometime get bogged down in tendentious debates because they are vitiated by the very manner of their formulation. The question of development or the wider question of social change is one such question, which was formulated with presupposed answers with the result that the concepts and theories which have grown about it over the years have not only tended to deflect it from the central issues involved in it, but imparted to it an ideological slant.

The misformulation of the question in sociology is bound up with the misformulation of the sociological problem itself. The problem before the founding fathers of sociology, as they could see it, was not what the social reality was, but how it was to be brought under the coverage of the scientific method. Their preoccupation, in other words, was not with the nature of the social reality, but with the scientific whose infallibility as a source of valid knowledge had to be established with reference to the social reality also, a preoccupation which eventually led to the reduction of the ontic to the epistemic. The method had already yielded a concept of nature as determined by the laws of space, time and causality, laws about whose universality all doubts had been set at rest by Kant. But, the social reality consisted of minded and free beings, an intuition whose validity the sociologists never questioned. The feat, then, of bringing it under the paramountcy of the scientific laws could not be achieved unless the realm of freedom was equated with the realm of unfreedom. The equation was crucial as the very possibility of sociology as a science rested on it. The sociologist then had no option but to demonstrate by hook or by crook that the social reality was nothing but a variety of the natural reality or in other words, it was what the scientific method would make of it. They did this; and by a tricky misformulation of the basic question before them. Instead of asking what kind of reality is the social reality? they asked: what kind of natural reality is the social reality? And, the obvious answer was: it is a para-natural reality. It is this 'category mistake'[1] on which sociology started building its theories; and the science has matured in the same proportion as it has succeeded in reducing the social to the natural. It is neither necessary nor possible to show how the aim of the entire range of sociological thinking from Comte to Parsons via Marx, has been to highlight the nature-image of the human society. In other words, to view it as a self-regulating, self-perpetuating and self-transforming reality which commands, constrains and socializes the individual and which is no less at peace and harmony with itself than nature. The gap between what it is and what it tends to be is no doubt always there in the society. But it is constantly at pains to fill this gap; it has its own in-built mechanisms which perpetually resolve its internal tensions and tend to keep it in a state of equilibrium.

We may now see how the theory of development derives from this official theory of the society. But, in the meanwhile, we must consider an objection which may be pertinently raised against our thesis. Is it possible, it may be asked, for sociology to escape this reductionist predicament? To say that the nature of reality should determine the method of its study is to say nothing, as there is no way to ascertain the nature of reality without reference to the method of its study. In fact, there is no escape from the position that the ontic is relative to the epistemic unless the two are viewed as parts of a hierarchy participating in a non-dual metaphysics which transcends them both. Social science methodology then must be firmly grounded in metaphysics if it is to be saved from its inherent solipsism and if it is to ensure an adequate understanding of the social reality. Even the methodologies of structural anthropology and phenomenological sociology fall short of this requirement, despite their unquestionable superiority over other methodologies.

It should be clear from what has been said about the nature of sociological theory that it must consider development as a change from a lower state of social order to a higher state, it being assumed that the model of the higher state is the harmony present in nature. Whether it is conceived as increasing 'positive mentality' as in Comte, or as increasing 'differentiation and coherence' as in Spencer or as increasing 'rationality' as in Pareto, Weber and Durkheim[2] or as 'enhancement of adaptive capacity' as in Parsons or as increasing 'communicative rationality' as in Habermas, it is in any case a change from a lower non-human state to a higher non-human state. Nor is there much to distinguish on this score between these theories and that of Karl Marx either. Development for Karl Marx also means increasing social equality and increasing self-regulativeness of the human society. Even the state as an institution of regulation and control par excellence has no place in Marx's utopia.

It is interesting to note that the sociological concept of rationality means nothing but adaptability to nature when it comes to man-nature opposition and social conformity when it comes to individual-society opposition. 'Freedom', said Hegel, is 'the recognition of necessity', words which were echoed by Marx also. But what eventually becomes of freedom, thanks to the line of development sociology which has been taken, is the ability to act in conformity with the social necessity. To be free is to act rationally, and to act rationally is to act in conformity with the social necessity. The protest against what has come to be known as the concept of 'oversocialized' man in the contemporary sociology, is a protest against this concept of socially overconstrained man. It is again against this concept of man that comes the voice of protest from philosophers such as Sartre and Hiedeggar. We will return to the problem of human freedom at a later stage in our discussion.

Thus understood, the development becomes synonymous with linear change implying a point of beginning and a point of end, of which the former is the lower point and the latter the higher. But a theory of linear change can be maintained only at the cost of rejecting the logic of change. For, how can we talk of change without reference to that which changes? If change, as Kant put it, were to consist in a possibility of 'a conjunction of contradictorily opposed predicates in one and the same object[3] then change cannot be intuited without its dialectical opposite, viz., permanence. But permanence in the like manner cannot be thought of without change; for how can we talk of that which changes without reference to the possibility of its becoming otherwise.

There has been much debate in philosophy on whether permanence is real and change an illusion, or change a reality and permanence an appearance, the first position being attributed to philosophers such as Zeno and Samkara and the second to those such as Heraclitus and Nagarjun.[4] But this again is a false attribution to both the groups of philosophers none of whom makes any mistake about the complementarity of permanence and change, of being and becoming, of the primordial and the temporal.[5] As part of a dialectical pair of opposites, change has the potentiality of becoming permanence and permanence the possibility of becoming contingent. From permanence to change and from change to permanence is a cyclic movement. 'Everything that is, everything substantive and living has its normal mode of growth declared Heraclitus and so ex hypothesis does it have its cycle. For all living things manifestly undergo cycles of genesis and decay, of life and death'.[6] As did Heraclitus, so also Plato and Aristotle, recognize the essential cyclicality of change. For Plato, 'eternity is but an endless succession' of cycles. 'Invariably one of these cycles is held to terminate in some great catastrophe, usually a flood ... with but a handful of individuals left alive to commence the next cycle of civilisation'.[7] And for Aristotle also 'the coming to be of anything, if it is absolutely necessary, that is, moving in the way it is so constituted to move "must be cyclical"'.[8] The central point in the whole classical

Greek philosophy of change as Nisbet[9] points out is the concept of 'physis'. Everything whether it was a tree, dog, man himself or the cosmos, was supposed to have its physis, its disposition to grow. Aristotle's words, in the statement cited above – 'moving in the way it is so constituted to move' – mean nothing more or less than that the idea of physis implies. Heraclitus compared physis to a 'moral police' meaning thereby that if things do not grow the way they should grow, that is, according to their 'physis', retribution will be swift.

There is a remarkable similarity between the Greek idea of 'physis' and the Indian idea of 'swabhava', the nature, the intrinsic attribute of a thing which makes it what it is and prevents it from being anything else. Swabhava is a manifestation of the primordial Being in the contingent 'becoming' and so is 'physis'.

Thus, in traditional thought, both Greek and Indian, development means becoming according to the law of one's nature, 'a determinable sequence of changes proceeding from the very structure of a thing' as Aristotle put it. The dialectical opposite of development is decay, that is, change whose sequence can not be determined, which is, that is to say, unnatural or accidental. The possibility of decay is contained in development as the possibility of development is contained in decay. However, decay is not the same thing as cosmic catastrophe of Plato's conception. The latter signifies the end of time itself when becoming is reabsorbed into Being, the end of one day of the cosmic creator, Brahma in the Indian tradition.[10] Significantly, the end of time is equated with the reduction of everything to the waters, in the Indian tradition also. The residues in Plato's case are 'a few shepherds high in the hills' and in the Indian case the cosmic Serpent called the residue or the Shesha, and the archetypal Man reclining on it in the cosmic waters.

Decay and development are processes within time and hence the interregnum between the two can be filled only by an atemporal agency which may stop the drift and initiate development afresh. One may call it a charismatic personality in the language of sociology or a divine incarnation in the terminology of the living religions.

If we keep this plain logic of social change in mind, we can not entertain the linear theory of self-realizing and self-fulfilling change with the primitive society as it's starting point and the contemporary Western society as it's end. Not that the protagonists of the theory are unaware of its loopholes; they do realize that change can not be thought of without persistence. Nor do they rule out the possibility of deviant or anomic tendencies developing within the social organization. But they consider them all sub specie tempori. Persistence is as much an attribute of time for them, as is change, and so are also order and anomie. In fact, the social reality for them is both Being and becoming.

Even the structural theory of social change in the existentialist phenomenological formulation is not free from this mistake. Edward A Tiryakian, for instance, talks both of structuration and destructuration of social reality, equivalents roughly of development and decay. He even admits that the 'ground of any genuine social revolution is an attempted overturning and radical rotation of the normative axis which frames and orders institutional life'. Again, the societal change in his view 'stems from those who are religious radicals alien to or alienated from the normative order of the ongoing society'. Tiryakian is equally clear in his mind that the genesis of social change can not be located in the political or even the economic order. But social reality for him, too, is a temporal reality containing in itself both Being and becoming: the existential ground of possibilities – the social structure as well as the actualization of this ground into social institutions.[11]

This is a ridiculous situation in which modern theory of social change places itself. But be it as it may, the theory received a big boost from intellectuals in the West because it not only established, once for all, the superiority of the Western society over all others, but also justified its paternalistic – imperialistic attitude towards them. The comparative method had shown the contrast between development as exemplified in the European society and stagnation as exemplified in what now came to be called 'primitive' and intermediate societies.[12]

II

It was in the context of these societies that the question of development was raised and particularly after the Second World War when many of them emerged into history after a long spell of colonial rule. Within the official development there was only one answer to the question, and it was that if these societies wanted to transform their sub-human existence, they must follow the example of their European counterparts. In other words, they must imitate the European model of development, which meant adopting all that Europe, including its alter ego America, stood for, in one word, modernity; and rejecting all that these societies themselves represented, in one word, tradition. Since the Western world itself had, in the due course of time, become split into two worlds, modernity also got bifurcated into two models, which for convenience sake we may describe as right-wing modernity and left-wing modernity. Thus, within the basic dichotomy of the metropolitan and dependent worlds, the global society gets further differentiated into right-wing metropolis, left-wing metropolis and the dependencies.[13] The dependencies could adopt either the modernity of the right-wing or the modernity of the left-wing or partly both the two, if they so chose, in which case, they would enjoy the patronage of both the worlds.

The distinction that we have made between the three subdivisions of the global society is of a piece with the distinction made between the First World, the Second World and the Third World, in the language of international relations.[14] The relationship between the First and Second Worlds is one of opposition, but in their unity they constitute a solid block of opposition to the Third World. It is this kind of opposition, this kind of relationship of dominance and dependence, which characterizes the drama of international relations within the contemporary global society. The drama gets going through massive economic aid from the metropolis to the Third World in the name of sympathy and help, and through an unbroken indoctrination of the intellectuals in the Third World by their mentors in the metropolis. Within the global society, it is the intellectuals who constitute the link between the metropolis and the dependencies and within the dependencies, between the ruling elites and the people. The intellectuals in the Third World silently receive the message from the First and Second Worlds, and propagate it to their people who can neither understand nor reciprocate it.

Thanks to the setting of the global drama, the developing world also gets artificially split into two worlds: one that of the dominant elites and the other that of the dependent people. The elites are obviously the agents of modernization or development and the people, virtually its patients. They are patients because their lot is only to suffer; for what they are preached to do has hardly anything to do with their development; its sole purpose being to keep the show of development going may be to lull them into silence. Incidentally, both in relation to the people and the dominant elites, the intellectuals, right-wingers and left-wingers alike, find themselves sailing in the same boat. Both are equally alienated from the people and equally aligned with the ruling elites. Nor is it by sheer accident that there is such a big gap between the intellectuals and the people, and little or no gap between the intellectuals and the ruling elites. What Julien Benda[15] calls the betrayal of intellectuals is only a logical outcome of the value premises implicit in modernity.

But even if we grant that adoption of modernity is the essence of development, the question would still arise whether or not this adoption necessarily implies a rejection of tradition. No, it does not; is one answer to the question, but the official answer and hence worthy of serious consideration. If caste is influencing politics in modern India, if that is to say, it has become a parapolitical community, the only reason could be that it had the potentiality to become so, for how else could a traditional institution like caste become a modern political institution like a pressure group? Where then is the incompatibility between tradition and modernity? Tradition is simply underdeveloped modernity and modernity, developed tradition. This is how Rudolphs argue.[16] Again, if an Indian could continue becoming more modern every day without ceasing to be Indian any bit, how could there be an opposition between tradition and modernity? 'In India', writes Milton Singer[17], 'modernization takes the form of traditionalization'. There is no substantial difference between the stands taken by Rudolphs and Milton Singer on this score: both arrive at the same conclusion and by the same method of fallacious reasoning. Their conclusion is that tradition is no bar to India's modernization; and their argument is that even though apparently different from modernity, tradition is basically convertible into modernity. As though there was nothing new in change (modernity), continuation on and the future was a sheer enfoldment of the past (tradition).

Almost the same is the upshot of M.N. Srinivas[18] well-known theory of sanskritization and westernization. The theory explains the ongoing change in the Indian society as an upward mobility of the lower, non-elite castes through adoption of the cultural values of the Brahman elites and a similar vertical mobility of the Brahman elites through adoption of the cultural values of their Western rulers, almost a case of the little tradition transforming itself into the great tradition and the great tradition changing itself into modernity.

Almost all the Western and Indian social scientists who have participated in the debate on social change, by and large, voice the same opinion, each of course, in their own way.[19] In fact, there is little to distinguish even between the right-wingers and left-wingers as regards their commitment to the official theory. Both have their affiliation with the metropolis and both orchestrate the opinion relayed to them from their respective camps.

The specious piece of theorizing which gives rise to the theory of modernity of tradition, also gives a new slant to the theory of development. For once it is admitted that tradition can take modernity in its stride, the difference between the underdeveloped traditional and the developed modern societies becomes just a matter of time lag and by the same logic development becomes a matter of speeding up the ongoing change. The theory of development in the context of these societies, then, takes the form of a theory of guided change, and the theory of guided change in turn becomes a theory of techno-economic change. Because when it comes to the question of closing the time lag, technology is the best answer. Thus, on the sociologist own showing, the theory of development in underdeveloped societies is nothing but a theory of planned techno-economic change.

Now, if it is the economist who holds the key to the development of the Third World, then an Adam Smith of poverty such as Gunnar Myrdal is the only hope for the underdogs of this World. But even Gunnar Myrdal[20] or the economists whose theories he rejects to establish the vanguard status of his own theory, have their own difficulties in making the social reality responsive to their formula. Tradition which in the economists' manner of theorizing, now becomes a symbol for the whole array of non-economic values and managed like economic values. What then happens is that when an institutional theory of development like the one proposed by Myrdal also fails to click with reality, the failure of the theory is blamed upon the 'softness' of the underdeveloped people themselves. Economists[21] like Myrdal are theoretically determined to believe that lethargy, indiscipline, corruption and social injustice are part and parcel of the very lifestyle of the underdeveloped world. Likewise, when measures of land reform fall to deliver the goods in India, the Planning Commission's Task Force on Agrarian Relations must blame the ruling elites for their failure to implement these measures with a strong political will and the political wing of the ruling elites must blame its bureaucratic counterpart or else the opposition parties or the people themselves, for their lack of cooperation with the government.

The prevailing anomie in India's public life is not a result of her slow pace of adaptation to the modernizing ideals. It is, on the other hand, an outcome of her stubborn resistance to these ideals, her refusal to accept and legitimize them. For, the adoption of these ideals would mean a complete overturning of her normative axis for which India does not yet seem ready. But that does not mean that she can not overcome her artificial crisis of poverty and backwardness which she has inherited from history. In their overzealous concern for India's poverty, let economists and social scientists not forget that long before her encounter with the modernizing ideals, India had achieved a measure of economic prosperity which was the envy of the West. Aurobindo[22] writes 'the splendour of Asiatic and not least of Indian prosperity, the wealth of Ormuz and of Ind, the barbaric doors rough with gold ... were once stigmatized by the less opulent West as a sign of barbarism. Circumstances are now strangely reversed; the opulent barbarism and much less artistic ostentation of wealth are to be found in London, New York and Paris, and it is the nakedness of India and the squalor of her poverty which are flung in her face as evidence of the worthlessness of her culture'.

A traditional society's resistance to the modernizing ideals is as natural as the resistance of the sacred to the profane. In a traditional society where man is viewed sub specie aeternitatis – as a becoming of Being, the social institutions are regarded as exemplifications of the primordial law. But just the reverse is the case with the modern society where man is considered sub specie tempori – as a creature of history – and the social institutions as sedimentations of group habits sanctified by reason. Where reason is the supreme principle of validation of values and norms, science and technology must become the governing principles of life, as they are the foremost instruments of reason. Again, when science and technology become the governing principles of life, the norms and values created by them become the norms and values of life itself. Myths, mysteries and the ultimate values, in terms of which all problematic situations in life are traditionally explained, are expelled from life and their place is taken by science and technology.

This is the stage which the society in the West has reached in the course of its development, a stage at which life stands completely demythologized, and technology glorified into a new but superior myth of life. The net result is a dehumanization of life, a substitution of life by a system of fake human values and artificial institutional means of realizing them. It is therefore not without reason that there is a loud and articulate cry[23] in the

West itself against the fake and pretentious Messiah[24], the enemy of intellect[25] that is science and the one-dimensional society[26] that is the modern industrial civilization. The predicament of the Western intellectual, however, is that when he feels oppressed by the institutions he has himself created he turns into a critical humanist or becomes an existentialist or postmodernist and cries for freedom; only that he can not step out of the unfreedom in which he finds himself strait-jacketed. But the man in Asia, howsoever unfortunate otherwise, is fortunate at least in one respect that he still has a chance to retrieve his freedom and to save himself from the unfreedom of the fortunate man in the West.

How he can do so, is a question into which for obvious reasons we can not enter here. But let us make no mistake about the fact that it is futile to think of freedom and development within the framework of the official theory, following which India has already done enough damage to her economy, polity and society.

Having been brainwashed for over a century and a half to believe that we had so far belonged to a bad society which we must now discard, we started destroying one by one all our traditional institutions, almost with a vengeance, soon after becoming independent. And alongside of this process of detraditionalization, went also modernization: legitimization of the colonial institutions and autocolonization of our own institutions. In the result what we have been able to achieve so far, in lieu of a good society, is a set of elitist social institutions not only alien to our tradition but wholly out of tune with the urges and aspirations of the people. Take any sublayer or the overlayer of modernity now covering the traditional base of the Indian society and you will see the gap between the common man – the real man – and the artificial social institutions he has to contend with. Place him in the context of any of these institutions and you will see that he is more a victim thereof than a beneficiary.

Take our system of centralist planning in which the needs of the common man are determined by an elitist agency. The only role that the common man is expected to play in this system of planning is to follow the directions of the experts. There are numerous studies showing that the benefits of planning are not reaching the common man. There is a growing realization among the experts themselves that development has failed to ensure social justice. Is not then the common man a mere object, a victim, of planning? Those who harboured the hope that contradictions in our theory of planning could be corrected by giving it a socialist twist are as much disillusioned as the protagonists of the conventional theory. In a theory where development means an artificial expansion of needs and a continued search for provisions to meet these needs, it is impossible to ensure social justice except in an arbitrary manner.

Let me illustrate. If development means a rising standard of living, it implies an ever improving consumption basket, which in turn would mean rising wages, rising costs of production and rising prices. Therefore, even if birth rate could be controlled and full employment ensured, wages cannot be equalized and a gap must always remain between the poor whose wages can not permit them to go for better consumption baskets and the affluent, who will press the economic system to produce newer and better consumption baskets for them. Even the developed societies are finding it difficult to control prices and to contain the poverty inherent in the logic of affluent development.

In an elitist theory of planning, industry is bound to get priority over agriculture and the city over the village. From the way we talk of rural development, is not the impression created that the rural society is an unnecessary appendage to the urban society? We may or not admit this fact, but our whole attitude to the villages is one of commiseration mixed with contempt, almost the same kind of attitude that the metropolitan World has towards the Third World. If the villages want to develop, they must adopt the urban way of life and since they can not do so on their own, the cities must help them. But it is not without reservation that the urban elites talk of the development of the villages. There is a push-pull theory of urbanization which tells us in so many words that the villages are congenitally poor and overbreeding, and a constant source of overcrowding in the cities. Therefore, while planning for rural development, we must also plan for the defense of the cities against the invasion of the villages.

To say that modernization is a false goal of development is one thing, but to say that it is a luxury, India in her present circumstances can not afford, is another. The cities must get priority over the villages in all matters pertaining to development because if the cities are the models which the villages must imitate, they must be made truly worthy of imitation.

In the circumstances, all that we can think of doing for the villages, in the name of development, is symbolic modernization which is already under way. It is another thing that the reaction of the villages even to a limited dose of modernization should be so wild. If village life is chaotic today as never before, and there is now greater exploitation of the villagers by political-vested interests than heretofore, the reason is not that the theory is defective, but as the ruling elite would have us believe, the people are backward and superstitious!

Space would not permit us to enter into a detailed discussion of the relationship between villages and cities in a traditional society. Suffice it to say that they are structural segments of one and the same cultural whole and are bound by a relationship of complementarity rather than fundamental opposition. The development of one at the cost of the other would therefore, mean a violation of the very structural law of the development of the whole. As parts of the whole, they have to develop complementing each other's development and promoting in turn the life of the whole. Contemporary urban sociology starts with rural-urban dichotomy and ends with rural-urban continuum, a euphemism for the concept of the village as a subsidiary of the city. Urbanization which is basically the same thing as growth of class inequalities[27], a characteristic of the industrial urban societies is shown to be the natural tendency of rural change. It is such theories of ongoing rural change that provide feed to the official theory of development, in which the village practically becomes a casualty.

III

We can thus see how the modern theory of development which begins as an answer to a false question ultimately degenerates into an ideology and becomes a vested interest in the hands of its protagonists. And it is this sinister implication of the theory, its inherent tendency to become an ideology of manipulation and control which the so called underdeveloped societies have to guard against. In fact, if they want to survive and develop as free nations, they have to free their freedom from the octopus-hold of the institutions which have stemmed from the theory, institutions which both in their design and action are meant to control them.

An alternative[28] theory of development for India and for the Third World must then begin with what Paulo Freire[29] calls 'cultural action for freedom'. This will mean in the first place, a new education of the people to break the culture of silence, in which they have been brought up so far. Once this culture is broken and the people begin to speak, they will themselves realize the threat the elitist institutions pose to their existence and freedom. In the second place, cultural action for freedom will mean the creation of an institutional set-up suited to the people's own genius, which is the sine que non of free development. What the task presupposes is not a paper revolution in values, but a radical change in outlook which can be brought about only by a cultural renaissance. Let us not labour under the illusion that the foundations of a healthy national life can be laid on the modernizing ideals. We have to rediscover our identity in the traditions of our indigenous culture and then refashion our national institutions in accordance with its own living ideals. The search of this identity had begun during our national struggle for independence with the Swadeshi movement launched by Gandhi, when a cultural renaissance seemed to be in the offing. The Shanti Niketan, Kashi Vidyapith, Bihar Vidyapith, the Banaras Hindu University, the Jamia Milia to mention only the institutions of higher learning, were the flowers of a resurgent national culture, whose principal aim was to lay the foundation of a national pattern of higher education suited to our culture. None had a greater realization of the futility of the colonial system of education than Tagore, Malviya and Gandhi. Even these institutions have lost their identity and now form part of the same sterile system of national education that we have evolved after independence, a system whose worthlessness can not be judged only by its total rejection by the younger generations whose increasing anger and growing sense of indiscipline is in no part their cultural inheritance.

But the renaissance which began during the national movement came to a sudden halt soon after independence when the creative elites became power-elites and their creativity gave way to 'mechanical mimesis' to use a Toynbee phrase. And thus began the authentication of colonial legacies and the imitation of modernizing ideals in the name of development. And the result is there for all of us to see. India's cultural pluralism is nothing new, only the deep fissions in her body social manifesting in endemic communal and caste conflicts are the recent phenomenon. A nation opposed to its own language is at odds with its own spirit. But thanks to the elitist vested interests, this is what the situation has come to be in India.

Unity within a culturally pluralist society can not be thought of except within the framework of primordial human values which constitute the core of all cultural traditions and yet transcend them each individually. Primordial values never die except metaphorically when their meanings are forgotten or when they get reduced to superstitions. A rediscovery of their meanings is a discovery of new and fresh potentialities in the human spirit. This is what we mean by cultural renaissance – a creative change from stagnation to development, which is to be distinguished both from cultural reform and cultural revival. Revival of exhausted possibilities is impossible and reform often takes the form of imposition of group ideology on living social laws. It is the creative elites who are the agents par excellence of the renaissant change.

The distinction is necessary because an archaist ideology has also become a contender of the modernist ideology as an alternative philosophy of development in India. Indianization[30] as advocated by a section of Indian intellectuals has both a revivalist and reformist tinge. Perpetuating in its outworn form and imposing it on other cultural traditions is a wrong answer to the question of cultural pluralism; it is yet another method of manipulative control which, as we have shown, is the implicit assumption of the modernist ideology.

There is no fundamental opposition between the cultural traditions of the so called majority and minority communities of India; they are contingent modalities of the same set of primordial values. It is for the creative elites to demonstrate in communicable words and imitable images that the diverse cultural traditions of India are segments of the same whole and that there is no mutual contradiction between them. There is no conflict either between any of these traditions and the idols of freedom, justice and equality on which we avowedly want to build our national life. For, no tradition has ever despised freedom; no tradition has ever scorned justice and no tradition has ever been averse to equality before law. They are perennial human values and by no manner of means the Western society's unique gift to humanity.

They come in conflict with tradition only when they are juxtaposed to it in their modern inverted forms. The traditional man has no difficulty in understanding natural justice, but he finds it difficult to understand modern justice, mediated, costly and delayed, which often runs counter to his own sense of natural justice. He knows his dharma and also knows that it is dharma that rules and the king only reigns, but he can not understand the intricate rule of law in which men rule and the law only reigns. This explains the traditional man's aversion to modern values which he can not place anywhere in his real life.

Nor is it a case of tradition versus reason, for reason has its own place in the traditional hierarchy of values. It is subordinate to intellect[31] and can never aspire to supersede it except at the cost of its own identity. Reason that is to say presupposes a transrational principle of guidance in the absence of which it can exist only as unfettered rationality. And it is this unfettered rationality that is the name of reason constituting the central point in modernity. Therefore, there can be no question of a synthesis of tradition and modernity.[32]

But, the compatibility of development with tradition is as axiomatic as its incompatibility with modernity. Development a la modernity is a manipulation of man and the society according to a set formula devised by a historically successful group. But development a la tradition is growth of man and the society according to the law of their being, according to their 'physis' as the Greek tradition would have it or according to their 'swabhava' as the Indian tradition has it. A theory of development, therefore, presupposes an adequate understanding of tradition and culture whose source is myth and folklore now consigned to the limbo by contemporary sociology.

It would be wrong to believe that India's economic problem is more pressing than the political or that the political is more important than the cultural. It would be equally incorrect to assume that the solution of the economic problem would ensure the solution of all other problems. In fact, there can be no economic development without political stability and there can be no political stability without a real consensus on the ends of political action. In a democracy based on real consensus, there can be no gap between the ruling elites and the people; such a gap can exist only in an opinionated democracy like the one India has borrowed from the West. Traditional polities are based on real consensus – on unanimity – where there is collective ideation and where aristocracy takes the form of democracy. Modern polities, on the other hand, are based on manipulated consensus – a majority opinion – where there is only formal discussion instead of ideation and where democracy takes the form of aristocracy. The only ground from which we can expect the emergence of a unanimous polity is tradition, the store house of archetypes and primordial values. And a unanimous polity alone can sustain a cultural unity under which different cultures can grow and flourish without fear of anyone being absorbed into another.[33]

If development means man's becoming what he has in him to become, in other words, his self-realization, as is the implication of the concept in all traditions, then the ends of development can not be served by the consensual democracy where the individuals' 'communicative competence' is determined by the vested interests of his political party and where the individual himself has been shaped and socialized to serve the needs of the system, rather than the system serving his own needs. It was not without reason then that Gandhi not only despised modernity in all its forms, but rejected the entire paraphernalia of modern civilization as utterly unsuited to the normal development of humanity. Gandhi's love for swadeshi, traditional village communities, a need rather than an acquisition-oriented economy, organized around the virtues of asteya and aparigraha (non-stealing and non-acquisitiveness) can be matched only by his relentless opposition to universalized, abstract and impersonalized systems of education, health, law, etc., which could never serve the genuine ends of life.

A full-length discussion of Gandhi's social philosophy, particularly his scheme of social reconstruction will not be possible here. But let there be no doubt about the fact that there is no better answer, to date, to the challenge of globalized ordism[34] with all its sinister implications for the so-called developing societies, than Gandhi. There is, of course, no dearth of scholars and social activists who still believe that modernity could be tamed and yoked with tradition to produce a better world than the one to which we have willy-nilly come to being.[35]

If taming modernity means putting reason in place, which will be tantamount to divesting it of its autonomy and showing it the place which belongs to it in the hierarchy of life, then the two could really work in unison and bring about a saner and healthier world. But this will be an impossible task to accomplish, for the flow of time just can not be reversed except through a process of 'charismatic resurrection'.[36]

That modernity is the natural trajectory of history and by the same token the destiny of tradition, and hence, there should be no conflict between the two as such, is another familiar argument. However, the theory of social change that sustains this argument fails to explain how societies can change without losing their identity. Another flaw in the theory is that by standardizing social change, it not only reduces it to a process of mechanical mimesis but also robs man of his intelligence, creativity and freedom. If we have 'to imagine mankind pursuing a single way of life' as Levi-Strauss said 'mankind would be ossified'.[37]

It is unfortunate indeed that the successor to the traditional civilization of India, the contemporary Indian society, instead of offering a creative response to the challenge of modernity, has been virtually behaving like a hungry body, subsisting upon its own reserves of energy – trying at times to revive its old traditions without understanding what they stand for and at others, to trace the dominant values of modernity to its own traditions. It is this pathological state which is the breeding ground of disvalues such as nepotism, casteism, communalism and religious fundamentalism, which contrary to the prevailing impression are not the values of the traditional society, but disvalues synthesized by a sick society unable to face this challenge of modernity in a creative way. And hence, the urgency to hark back to Gandhi who had shown the way to renaissant change.

Notes

1. We owe this phrase to Gilbert Ryle: *The Concept of Mind* (London: Penguin Books, 1963).
2. Weber's concept of rationality in this context refers to 'substantive' and not to 'formal (purposive-instrumental) rationality' which, contrary to the expectations of Enlightenment can not lead to the realization of freedom; it can on the other hand, only create an iron cage of bureaucratic rationality from which there will be no escape. (Bernstein R. Habermas and Modernity: Oxford, 1985 quoted by Harvey, David: *The Condition of Post Modernity: An Enquiry into the Origins of Cultural Change* (Oxford: Basil Blackwell, 1989, p. 15). Durkheim's concept of rationality is again slightly different from that of Pareto. While the former like Weber's is tempered with moral considerations, the latter stands for unmixed instrumental rationality.
3. Kant Immanuel: *Critique of Pure Reason* (London: J.M. Dent and Sons, 1950), p. 49.
4. See for example, Daya Krishna: *Considerations Towards a Theory of Social Change* (Bombay: P.C. Manaktala and Sons, Private Ltd., 1965), p. 130.
5. See especially Sri Aurobindo: *Heraclitus* (Calcutta: Arya Publishing House, College Street, 1947). Also, H. Zimmer: *The Philosophies of India*, Ed. F. Joseph Campbell (New York: Meredian Books, 1956) Chapter IV and Rene Guenon: *Man and His Becoming according to Vedant* (New York: The Noonday Press, 1958).

6. Robert A. Nisbet: *Social Change and History* (New York: Oxford University Press, 1970), p. 36.
7. Ibid., p.37.
8. Ibid., p. 39.
9. Ibid., p. 23.
10. One day of Brahma is equal to one thousand cycles of development and decay in the Indian tradition. One cycle consists of four aeons representing full, three-fourths, half and one-fourth dharma or order, respectively, in the decending order. The shortest in duration is the last aeon known as Kali, of which the ascending aeons are respectively twice, thrice and four times as much in duration as Kali. The four aeons taken together make one cycle or one Mahayuga; and a thousand such cycles or Mahayugas constitute a Kalpa which is one day of Brahma, the Creator. Each Kalpa is divided into 14 Manvantaras, each ruled by a Manu (See especially, Hienerich Zimmer: *Myths and Symbols in Indian Art. Art and Civilisation* (Bollingen Series, New York: Pantheon Books, 1953), Chapter I.
11. Mc Kinney and Edward A. Twyakian (eds.) *Structural force in Theoretical force* (New York: Meredith Corporation, 1970), p. 126.
12. Talcott Parsons: *Societies* (Foundation of Modern Sociology Series, Englewood Cliffs, NJ: Prentice-Hall, 1966).
13. The so-called 'dependency theory' of development was put forward by the Latin American Intellectuals as an alternative to the prevailing 'modernization' model which as the advocates of the theory argued was skewed in favour of the affluent as against the poor nations. The theory in spite of its Marxist façade was, as we argue, also a species of the modernization model. The fact that we have also chosen to borrow the same terminology to enforce our argument need not mean any commitment on our part to the basics of the theory.
14. After the collapse of the USSR, the globe has, as it is said, become unipolar. But considering the existing gap between the rich and the poor countries, the re-emergence of a middle block in between the two which may revive the old distinction between the First, Second and Third Worlds is not totally ruled out. There is a growing volume of opinion that failed in Russia was not Marxism or Communism, but Stallinism, a system characterized not only by one persons' rule, but by 'a hierarchically organized control of all aspects of social life, political, economic and cultural by a narrow oligarchy, seated at the apex of the party apparatus' (A. Callinicos: *The Revenge of History: Marxism and East European Revolution* (Cambridge: Polity Press,

1991), p. 15, in David Held: *Liberalism, Marxism and Democracy in Theory and Society*, Volume 22, April 1993, p. 261.

15. Julien Benda: *The Betrayal of Intellectuals*, trans. Richard Aldington (Boston: The Beacon Press, 1955).
16. S.H. Rudolph and L. Rudolph: *The Modernity of Tradition: Political Development in India* (Chicago: University of Chicago Press, 1967).
17. Milton Singer: Modernisation or Traditionalisation? In *Contributions to Indian Sociology* (New Series V, 1967).
18. M.N. Srinivas: *Caste in Modern India and Other Essays* (Bombay: Asia Publishing House, 1962).
19. Illustrative examples are: T.N. Madan: 'Study of Social Change in Contemporary, India', in *Studies in Social Change*, Eds K.S. Mathur and others (Lucknow: Ethnographic and Folk Culture Society, 1973).

    S.C. Dube: 'Formulating the Goals of Change', in *Some Aspects of Social Change in India*, Eds Kuppuswamy and Mehta (Delhi: Sterling Publishers, 1968).

    Y. Singh: *Modernisation of Indian Tradition* (New Delhi: Thomson Press (India), 1973).

    David G. Mandelbaum: *Society in India* (Volume II, Bombay: Popular Prakashan, 1972).

    Some notable exceptions are: Tariq Banuri: 'Modernisation and its Discontents: A Cultural Perspective on the Theories of Development' in *Dominating Knowledge, Development, Culture and Resistance* eds. Frederique Apffel, Margin and Stephen A. Margin (Oxford: Clarendon Press, 1990) in Fred Dallmayr: Modernisation and Post-modernisation: Whither India? *Alternatives* 17 (1992): pp. 421–452. Banuri rejects what Foucault would call 'hegemonic panopticism' 'inherent in "Western liberalisms" method of binary opposition", 'that is in its hierarchical rather than dialectical correlation of modernity and tradition, of universality and contextuality'. Banuri argues 'that many of the seemingly insoluble problems of today's world stem precisely from the implicit assumption of a dichotomy and a hierarchy between the impersonal and personal spheres of culture and that in our search for solutions we need to replace this hierarchy with the notion of a tension or a dialectic between the two'. Banuri's vision of the future in the Third World can be expressed in terms of 'decentralized polity, economy and society' (Fred Dallmayr, op. cit., pp. 441–442).

Ashis Nandy, likewise, lays emphasis on the revitalization of indigenous culture or cultural traditions in the face of relentless Westernization and uniformization of the World. For Nandy, development essentially means 'expansion of the awareness of oppression in society', and awareness or resistance to oppression in the Third World countries as a component of development, would involve resistance to modernity, in particular, to such concepts as 'development, growth, history, science and technology which have become not only "new reasons" of the state, but mystifications for new forms of violence and injustice'. (A. Credo: Cultural Frames for Social Transformation. *Alternatives* 12(1987): 113–117) in Fred Dallmayr, op. cit., p. 442.

For Rajni Kothari also, it is not the expansion of 'technocratic or managerial controls but liberating transformation, which holds the key to development, liberating transformation referring to freedom and democracy in human affairs and the institutions that sustain it. Kothari favours a 'strengthening of local self government and an invigoration of indigenous cultures and grass roots movements, especially among marginalized groups'. 'Ethnicity and pride in indigenous cultures', as he points out 'are a response – including reaction – to the excesses of the modern project of shaping the whole of humanity (and its natural resource base) around three pivots of world capitalism, the state system and a "world culture" based on modern technology, a pervasive communications and information order and a "universalizing" "educational system"', *Rethinking Development in Search of Humane Alternatives* (Delhi: Ajanta, 1989) in Dallmayr op. cit. Kothari advocates an open-ended engagement among cultures and an agonal dialogue among people (lokayan), an engagement that alone area in his opinion can pave the way to equal respect among religions and cultural groups and to an alternative world.

20. Myrdal Gunnar: *Asian Drama* (Pelican Books, 1968) 3 volumes and *Challenge of World Poverty* (Vintage Books, 1971).
21. See also William K. Kapp: *Hindu Culture: Economic Development and Economic Planning in India* (Bombay: Asia Publishing House, 1963). Kapp also attributes the retarded economic development of India to her traditional culture.
22. Sri Aurobindo: *The Foundations of Indian Culture* (Pondicherry: Sri Aurobindo Ashram, 1959), p. 73.
23. The cry is heard in the form of 'post-modernity' or 'post-structuralism' as exemplified in the works of Nietsche, Hiedeggar, Foucault, not least Habermas. Habermas has full faith in

the self-correcting potentialities of reason and hence his tough resistance to the acceptance of any theory of 'post-modernity' or 'post-structuralism' as an extension of the project of Enlightenment. But neither 'communicative rationality', the new potential of Enlightenment reason discovered by him, nor his concept of 'communicative competence' grounded thereon, nor again his theory of 'generalisability of norms', whereby Habermas seeks to resolve the dichotomy of 'fact' and 'value' can emancipate modernity from it's self-stultifying logic. Likewise, the project of post-modernity or post-structuralism – the manner in which it has been conceived – is bound to end up as nihilism as has actually happened. See Jurgen Habermas: *The Philosophical Discourse of Modernity*, trans. F. Larence (Cambridge, MS: MIT Press, 1987); Jurgen Habermas, Towards a Theory of Communicative Competence, *Enquiry*, 1970 13: 360–365.

24. Mills, C. Wright: *The Sociological Imagination* (New York: Oxford University Press, 1959).
25. Jaques Barzun: *The House of Intellect* (New York: Harper and Bros., 1959).
26. Harbert Marcuse: *The One Dimensional Man* (London: Routledge and Kegan Paul, 1964).
27. See for example, Beteille, Andre: *Studies in Agrarian Social Structure* (Delhi: Oxford University Press, 1974).
28. Alternative theories of development such as those advanced by left-wing intellectuals like Gunder Frank do not move out of the duality which they consider as the Achilles heel of the received theories, the duality implicit in the assumption that development is either transformation of a poor economy and society into another, supposed to be developed or acculturation of a traditionally stagnant, immobile and underdeveloped society into a modern one through a diffusion of knowledge, skills, values, technology, etc., by its modern Western counterpart. By attributing separate social structures to the developed and developing countries, the received theories split the structural whole into two and thus ignore the role played in creating the duality of wealth and poverty. We have no quarrel with scholars like Gunder Frank as far as their rejection of the numerous versions of the official theory is concerned. For our part, we find precious little to choose between one or the other version of the theory, if development according to it means carrying out the project of modernization as a promotion of European rationality. Gunder Franks' suggestion that an alternative theory of development 'must reflect the structure and development of the

system, which has given rise to, now maintains, and still increase both structural development and structural underdevelopment as simultaneous and mutually produced manifestation of the same historical process, (see his *Latin America Underdevelopment or Revolution*, New York and London, Monthly Review Press, 19, p. 62, 1970) again does not lead us anywhere beyond the point that the official theory in its actual implementation produces both development and underdevelopment simultaneously, a point which can not be accepted within the framework of the normal theory of development to which we subscribe. The official theory according to our understanding can neither lead to development nor underdevelopment, but only to a battle of ideologies over what development is and what it is not. For once an attempt is made to quantify development, there will be as many models or theories of development as there will be objectified goals of development. For instance, minimum needs, standard of living, quality of life, etc., the principle ingredients of the hedonistic calculus in terms of which development is sought to be measured, can be defined or objectified in innumerable ways.

The world, in other words, to which a model of development will resemble, will be its own projection; anything that the model fails to represent will be eliminated from its scope. The literary archetype of modern development is to be found in the feat executed by Goethe's epic hero Faust who 'prepared to destroy religious myths, traditional values and customary ways of life in order to build a brave new world out of the ashes of the old, is in the end a tragic figure. Synthesizing thought and action, Faust forces himself and everyone else (even Mephistopheles) to extremes of organization, pain and exhaustion, in order to master nature and to create a new landscape, a sublime spiritual achievement that contains the potentiality for human liberation from want and need. Prepared to eliminate everything and everyone who stands in the way of realization of this sublime vision, Faust, to his own ultimate horror, deploys Mephistopheles to kill a much loved old couple who live in a small cottage by the sea shore for no other reason than the fact that they do not fit in with the master plan'. 'It appears' says Berman 'that the very process of development as it transforms the wasteland into a thriving physical and social space, recreates the wasteland inside the developer himself. This is how the tragedy of development works' (see David Harvey: *The Condition of Post-modernity: An Enquiry into the Origins of Cultural Change* (Oxford: Basil Blackwell, 1989), p. 16.

29. Paulo Friere: *Cultural Action for Freedom, Pedagogy of the Oppressed* (London: Penguin Education, 1973).

30. Balraj Madhok: *Indianisation* (New Delhi: Orient Paperbacks, 1970).

    Archaism is a term used by Arnold J. Toynbee to describe the mentality of the people who try to take refuge in the past to overcome the sickness resulting from the schism in the soul of a decadent civilization. Futurists are the people who similarly try to live in the future, to escape from the present. Archaists may be fundamentalists also, people who mistake the truth of their myth as historical and act accordingly. See his: *A Study of History*, Abridgement of Volumes I-VII by D.C. Somerville (London: Oxford University Press, 1984), pp. 375–376.

31. For a fuller understanding of this meaning of 'intellect', see, Frithjof Schuon: *The Transcendent Unity of Religions* (London: Faber and Faber, Ltd., 1984).

32. Contrary to the impression created by Ashis Nandy and Fred Dallmayr what they call 'critical traditionalism' is not a synthesis of tradition and modernity, but only a method of exploiting traditional material for bolstering up modern social institutions. For, tradition and modernity have their own distinct languages of discourse which cannot be rendered into each other. Tapping the liberating potential in tradition and combining it with its counterpart in modernity will not be possible unless tradition could be reduced to a mere rehearsal of modernity. In which case, it would be meaningless to speak of 'critical traditionalism'. Nor was Gandhi a 'critical traditionalist' or a 'marginalist' in this sense. See Fred Dallmayr, op. cit., 421–452 and also his *Margins of Political Discourse* (Albany, NY: University of New York Press, 1989).

33. The traditional village communities provide the nearest example of a local polity based on unanimity and participatory democracy, communities which are facing extinction all over the world today in the wake of increasing political homogenization. In the USA, there is a strong movement, for populist politries and revitalization of communities, to undo the excesses of modern spectacular politics ('which requires the prepackaging of whatever political issue is advocated to fit the media form' and 'in which mainly intellectuals and lawyers pretending to represent virtue, goodness, beauty and the American way', participate, instead of the people at large). Populist politics aims at developing institutions which will ensure the growth of truly democratic politics based on face to face interaction of the people. "This does not mean politics understood in the sense of Enlightenment ideology gone mad, ... but the establishment of an adequate mode of representation, and expression of what is irreducibly private and its public otherness which

integrates it within a social whole". Restructuring of communities likewise implies restoring to them their particularity, specificity and otherness getting erased as a result of social homogenization. See Telos, November 87, Spring 1991: *The Empire Strike out: Roundtable on Popular Politics*, Kenneth Anderson Russell A Berman, Tim Lake, Paul Piceone, and Michael Tanes), pp. 6–7.

34. FORDISM is the name of the organizational and technological innovations initiated or perfected by Henry Ford in America in the beginning of the 20th century which not only boosted production, but resulted in the creation of a new type of worker and a new type of man. 'What was special about Ford (and what ultimately separates Fordism from Taylorism), was his vision, his explicit recognition that mass production, meant mass consumption, a new system of reproduction of labour power, a new politics of labour control and management a new aesthetics and psychology, in short, a new kind rationalized, and populist democratic society'. (David Harvey, op. cit., pp. 125–126).

35. See for example E.F. Schumacher: *Small is Beautiful* (Delhi: Rupa & Co. Paperback, 1990) where in the pleads for 'a new orientation of science and technology, towards the organic, the gentle, the non-violent, the elegant and the beautiful'. What we expect from science and technology is to provide us with methods and equipment:
    - cheap enough so that they are accessible to virtually everyone,
    - suitable for small scale application, and
    - compatible with man's need for creativity. (p. 27)

    Consistently with his stand, Schumacher recommends a decentralized system of production (not mass production but production for the masses) based on an intermediate/appropriate technology. There is much in Schumacher's economic philosophy to commend itself. He wants economics to be grounded in traditional wisdom, comes very close to Gandhi in his espousal of the philosophy of non-violence, non-stealing and non-acquisitiveness. But we have our own doubts if Schumacher's formula will go any way towards cutting modern science and technology down to size and bringing about the intended revolution in values.

36. See especially Sorkin Pitirim, *The Crisis of Our Age*, E.P. Dutton & Co.inc, 1951 (USA).

37. See Kebede, Messay, On the Relationship between the Spiritual and the Material: The Lessons of Underdevelopment (Diogenes Number 162 Volume 41/2 1993), p. 122.

5

Nature's Metropolis or Nature's Necropolis?

*The City and Urbanization**

The theme that I have chosen for my lecture is "The City and Urbanization." Josiah Strong, in prophetic words, had observed in his book *The Twentieth Century City*, more than a hundred years ago, way back in 1898, that the "new civilization is certain to be urban; and the problem of the twentieth century will be the city".[1] Strong's prophecy has come true; the city has been the central problem of the century we have just left behind. But what kind of problem has it been? The main title of my theme, *Nature's Metropolis or Nature's Necropolis* which I have borrowed from William Cronan's novel on Chicago would reveal it. *Nature's Metropolis* is ironically the city from where nature has practically been banished. Hence, the poser: Is the city on the eve of the 20th century (in 1890)[2] nature's abode or nature's graveyard?

The point I argue is that urbanization is an irreversible process, but in the 21st century, both man and nature face extinction in the new urban world again ironically called the "global village". Is that then the final outcome of the prolonged battle of wits between man and nature? If the answer is yes, then whose is going to be the last laugh? Man's or nautre's?

---

* R.B. Das Memorial Lecture, 2001, delivered at the Centre for Urban and Environmental Studies, Lucknow University on June 1, 2001.

II

A wholly unexpected though extraordinary gain for the French anthropologist Claude Levi-Strauss from his field work among the tribals in a Brazilian countryside was the insight that writing is "artificial memory", which reinforced his belief that in spite of the prevailing sociological opinion to the contrary writing was not the dividing line between barbarism and civilization. How Levi-Strauss arrived at this conclusion is an interesting story. While camping in the Brazilian countryside, one night he distributed among his respondents – the tribal chief and his kinsmen – loose sheets of paper and pencils, and was intrigued to find that in imitation of the ethnographer's own note-taking exercise, the tribal chief pretended to read from a text of "preliterate scribbling". He might be apparently emulating the ethnographer's style of writing, but was he not mocking at the literate man's loss of memory – his alienation form his mythical roots – which forces him to learn writing?[3]

Some Neolithic people had built a full-fledged civil life without being familiar with the art of writing. But the collective memory, we call history was not possible without the development of writing, which means that the dividing line between people with history and those without history is mot definitely writing. Levi-Strauss, therefore, concluded and rightly that the primary function of written communication is to facilitate slavery. Apart from the fact that there is reliable evidence to show that writing has been associated with the "creation of cities and empires", it has been instrumental in the spread of European imperialism or human enslavement in general.[4] The so-called civilizing mission of the white man was nothing more than an attempt to impose literate European reason on the "mythic" innocence and orality of the traditional people.

It is not without reason therefore that in the 18th century Europe, the city was looked upon as a symbol of progress and civilization. It is another thing that to scholars like Oswald Spengler, civilization symbolized the decay of culture, of which the rise of the city was the initial stage. Spengler traced the life history of societies to the emergence of an adolescent early-culture stage, followed by a late-culture stage and finally culminating in the decadent stage of civilization comparable to senile decay. At the early-culture stage, the society has a predominantly rural organization where man is deeply rooted in his soil. Culture reaches maturity, growing from the stage of town (the polis) to the regional city (metropolis) and finally to the world city (megalopolis).

What happens in this process of organic growth of societies is that culture is sucked out of the villages, the perennial source of its life and concentrated in the regional city, the metropolis and further absorbed into the world city (the megalopolis). When the polis grows into the megalopolis, culture reaches its destiny that is the final stage of civilization which is paradoxically both the zenith and the nadir of the life cycle of culture.[5]

The Indian city as it exists today is an extension of the European city, which is just to say that all post-medieval cities were created in India to cater for the needs of the colonial administration. The medieval cities were essentially fort-cities established as capitals of kingdoms. Some of them were established for trade and commerce on river routes; but they were not part of a market or an acquisitive economy. In Europe also, as Weber has shown, the modern urban community emerged as a successor to the Roman city. "An urban community", he writes, "in the full meaning of the word appears only in the occident." To constitute a full urban community according to Weber, the settlement had to represent a relative predominance of trade–commercial relation with the settlements as a whole displaying the following features: (1) fortification; (2) a market; (3) a court of its own and at least partially autonomous law; (4) a related form of association; and (5) at least partial autonomy and autocephaly.[6] However, it is the market which gives the city the essential character that belongs to it, viz., economic versatility.

A detailed reference to Weber's concept of the urban community was necessary to trace the similarity between the post-medieval Indian city and the modern western city, of which as we have said above that the latter is an extension. But, before we proceed to do so, we must say a word about why the oriental city could not become part of a market economy as the occidental city did. We have to rely on Marx to explain why a capitalistic mode of production could not develop in India, which was a precondition for the rise of the modern city in the West. In 1853, Marx and Engels came out with an important thesis, namely, that the "dominant economic system in the orient, the only significant exception being Japan, should not be confused with either slave or feudal economy (both based on private ownership of land)." What they called the "Asiatic mode of production," was the basis of a sui genris social formation wherein the "comprehensive unity standing above all these little communities appears as the higher proprietor or as the sole proprietor; the real communities hence, only as the hereditary possessors." It was the bureaucratic and managerial despotism of the orient which actually prevented if from developing capitalism. This despotism acts like a huge bureaucratic managerial apparatus, with the power to quash everything which comes in its way.[7]

It combines both the monopoly of violence and the monopoly of production, material and spiritual. It was almost impossible therefore for the Asiatic mode of production (governed by bureaucratic despotism) to break lose from the chain of feudalism. The oriental society was thus economically and politically determined to lie stagnant. In the West, on the other hand, capitalism and the city were basically one and the same thing. Adam Smith had already located in medieval cities, especially in Italian cities, the first motor of capitalist development. In the tussle between the city and the state in which the former clamours for autonomy and the latter wants to extend its control over everything, the cities were systematically defeated in the east while in the west, they "came out on top; at least in Italy and Germany, they were able to enjoy complete autonomy".[8]

Europe's break with feudal economy was largely on account of the autonomy enjoyed by the cities, which allowed them the opportunity for economic change. Mention may also be made here of another equally important characteristic of the Asiatic mode of production, viz., the close connection of cities with landed property and agriculture. "Asiatic history," writes Marx, "is a kind of indifferent unity of town and countryside".[9] A conflict between the two can exist only in the context of private property.[10]

Cities in the orient were alongside the villages' good exit points for external trade "where the head of the state and his satraps exchange their revenue (surplus product) for labor". In short, the oriental city was simply the seat of government and its executives. In any case, it did not belong to merchants and artisans, "over whom it extended its invisible hand" of central political power. In Europe also, the cities were founded on land in classical antiquity; but their development in the middle ages moved in the direction of discontinuity between town and countryside, the modern age being the age of urbanization of the countryside rather than that of ruralization of the city, as in the antiquity.

We are not interested in the history of the city in the West. The main purpose of this elaborate reference to its development was to show how the modern Indian city is almost a replica of the western city. Whether as an over-layer of the medieval city or as an independent new location for industry, trade and commerce, it has been developed on the lines of the western city.

While the economic background of the western city has made it a cog in the vast machine of the capitalist mode of production, the Indian city however, escaped this fate, although all through its colonial history lasting over three centuries and post-colonial history lasting over half a century, it has also been moving in the direction of universalizing its politico-economic structure and integrating itself into a single-world economy, rapidly urbanizing at the same time the country side and sharpening the rural-urban divides.

If in 1901, India had only one city with more than one million population in 1991, it had 23 such cities and if the population of million plus cities was 5.8 per cent of the total urban population in 1901, it was 32.54 per cent of the total urban population in 1991. Right upto 1941, only two cities had a population of over one million each, but between 1981–1991 11 cities joined the list of metropolises. About one-third of the total urban population of India now lives in million-plus cities.[11] In 1901, 10.01 per cent of the total population of India lived in cities and urban agglomerations. But in 1991, this percentage had reached the figure of 25.73 per cent. Urban population has increased at a very fast rate since 1961; between 1901 and 1961, the total urban population increased by 53.1 million, but during the three decades between 1961 and 1991, it has increased by 138 million.[12]

This exponential growth of the urban population is mainly attributable to the rural push, that is, the pressure on land in rural areas, but the industrial development and establishment of new towns and cities have been equally responsible for it. Another distinctive feature of urbanization in India had been the increase in the number of Class I and Class II cities, which means that bigger cities have been adding to their population in every decade, they have even been attracting the population of smaller towns. The Census Report 2001 is still awaited but as per earlier projections, India's urban population by 2001 was likely to exceed 350 million, of which over a 100 million was expected to be living in the slums. Kolkata with a density of is 88,135 per square kilometre[13] is about 19 times more congested than London and nine times more congested than New York. We will however come to these problems in the next part of our discussion. At this point we only want to highlight the role the colonial city has played in distorting, even destroying the traditional pattern of relationship, social, ecological and economic – between the village and town.

Before we proceed, a word about the nature of the colonial city. Colonial cities, as we observed, were built by Europeans from about 1500 to 1925 in their colonies to serve the needs of the empire. The five major colonial powers, as is well known, were Spain, Netherlands, Portugal, France and Great Britain, of which only the latter three are directly relevant to India. Colonialism let us observe in parenthesis is generally understood as "the establishment and maintenance, for an extended time, of rule over an alien people that is separate and subordinate to the ruling people."

The colonial city, as King has rightly pointed out, has been a major instrument of incorporating the colonial state into the world economy.[14] The integration of the colonial city with its metropolis has been so complete that both in respect of its built environment as well as physical extension it looks like the counterfoil of the core city. The European bungalow (dwelling), the physical segregation of the cities into the civil lines, slums, etc., are universal features of cities in the West, which have come over to India through diffusion. The British East India Company and the French East India Company, the early colonizers who practically established Kolkata around 1696, segregated the city into "white Kolkata" and "black Kolkata", the present-day Esplanade and the rest of Kolkata. This ethnic separation is the general feature of the Indian city. Needless to say that the idea of urban planning and administration is also western.

However, developments after 1950 have been quite interesting in that after independence, India, instead of docolonizing its economy and polity, has launched upon a programme of auto-colonization (sub-conscious voluntary acceptance of values and beliefs by an individual or a group earlier imposed upon it by others) under the cover of modernization and development. It is not surprising, therefore, that debates centring around urbanization in India in which both Indian and western scholars have participated equally enthusiastically, have focused mainly on the role of cities in economic development and modernization. Cities, in other words, which were considered earlier as instruments of colonization, are being looked upon as centres of diffusion of modernity. Political imperialism has today assumed a surrogate form; it now operates as trade imperialism exercising control over the dependant market de facto rather than de jure.

The imperial powers which ruled their colonies as sovereign masters have yielded place to new hegemons who are literally presiding over the destinies of the free world without wielding any formal political power, in the name of their modernization and development. Since modernization is only a method of imposing, as we said above, literate reason over the traditional people, cities have been identified as convenient centres for the diffusion of modern values. Not surprisingly, therefore, western scholars such as Hoselitz have come forward with theories emphasizing the role of cities in economic development. Hoselitz has distinguished between "parasitic" and "generative" cities – those whose growth is conducive to the economic development of the region of their location and those whose growth is not so conducive. Urban growth which is accompanied by a diversification of the occupational structure of the city, i.e., by engagement of an increasing proportion of its workforce in secondary rather than primary industry, is considered generative and urban growth which does not result in such diversification is considered parasitic.

There is no dearth of theories of cities as growth centres, but the difficulty with these theories is that they completely overlook the fact that modern cities have been powerful engines of the growth of corporate capitalism. Which is also to say that they have been both enclaves of the wealthy and affluent, as well as *ghettos* of the poor and the underfed. The distinction between East and West which has now been replaced by the one between South and North gets distorted in Indian cities where the difference between the consumption – affluent middle classes and their counterparts in the North has been obliterated. We may call these classes the "white-enclave" in the South or the "black-enclave" in the North. As we shall show that much of the urban challenge in India including the problem of sustainable development of the cities emanates from this gap between the consumption needs of this "white south enclave" and the residents of urban slums, the Anandnagars as Lipiere calls them.[15] It is these affluent people of the Indian cities who constitute the worldwide TV-watching middle classes and who are most vocal admirers of the virtues of globalization.

The problems that urban India has to face largely emanate from the high concentration of population in her mega cities. Bombay, for instance (now Mumbai), showed a remarkable growth of population from 9.7 millions in 1981 to 12.57 million in 1991, Calcutta's (now Kolkata) population likewise increased from 9.19 million in 1981 to 10.86 million in 1991. Delhi's population rose to 8.38 million compared to 5.7 millions in 1981. Madras (now Chennai) had a population of 5.86 million in 1991 as against 4.2 million in 1981. Not unexpectedly, these metropolitan centres are under severe strains as regards water – supply, sewage disposal, environmental sanitation, housing, transport, etc. Water pollution is a major health hazard in all the cities. Air pollution is increasing in the cities due to an alarming rise in the number of automobiles. The daily pollution let out in the air in Bombay was about 2,971 tonnes in 1992 of which 52 per cent came from automobiles, 2 per cent from domestic fuel and remaining 46 per cent from industries. In areas recording higher levels of air pollution, chest-related ailments were on the increase.[16] Children below 5 years and old men above 50 years were the worst affected. Based on the quality of life, Bombay's rank was 40th out of the 40 cities of Asia. Fifty-five per cent of Bombay's population lives in slums.

New Delhi is heading for an environmental disaster with regular migration of people from the neighbouring areas. Delhi has the dubious distinction of being the world's fourth-most polluted city. The daily let out of air pollutants alone is to the extent of 2,090 tonnes in the capital. The transport system of the city is chaotic with the vehicle population growing from 5,92,585 in 1982 to 1.97 millions in 1992, choking the roads and polluting the air with their noxious emissions. More than 76 per cent people in metropolitan Kolkata suffered from respiratory ailments. The density of population in the city is 21,933 inhabitants per square kilometre, but in certain parts of north Kolkata population is about 1,75,000 per square kilometre. Things are so bad in Kolkata that quality of life index did not apply to the city. About 80 per cent of Kolkatans use coal for cooking, which is a major source of pollution by smoke. Madras (Chennai) has nearly one-third of its population living in slums.[17]

India's rate of urbanization at 27 per cent in 1991 is not as high as china's (30%) or Pakistan's (35%), yet it's three metropolitan cities – Kolkata, Mumbai and Delhi figure in the list of world's 15 largest urban agglomerations. From being at Number 5, Mumbai is expected to become the world's second largest city in 2015 – after Tokyo, Karachi and Dacca.

According to a Central Pollution Control Board survey, in 241 Class II towns in 17 states, 90 per cent of the water supplied is polluted; only 1.6 per cent of the water gets treated. There has been little expansion in the urban infrastructure during the decade ending 1991 and only half of the population in the 4,000 urban centres has partial or fully covered sewerage facilities. Even in the national capital New Delhi, only 73 per cent of the total population is served with sewerage or low-cost sanitation services. Gross housing shortage which has touched 40 million by now is another big problem urban India has to face: the growing percentage of slum dwellers in the big cities adds to the problem. As per the World Development Report 1994, only 44 per cent of the urban population had access to sanitation. We have already referred to the over-exposure of our megacities to air pollution. While East Asian cities spend $72.5 per person on amenities, government in the South Asia spend as little as $15 per urban dweller. Significantly, urban areas command 50 per cent to 80 per cent of the developing countries' GNP and are capable of solving their problems. The shift in the strategy of urban management as reflected in the draft approach paper to the Ninth Plan and in the report of Rakesh Mohan Committee on Infrastructure is indeed a welcome development, as both the documents recommend privatization and decentralization of urban services and empowerment of the urban local bodies in the wake of the 74th constitutional amendment which provides for the election of Nagarpalikas.[18]

The National Commission on Urbanization, appointed by the Ministry of Urban Development in 1987, which submitted its find report in 1988, had laid particular stress on the need for reversing the trend of deterioration of urban services and pauperization of the urban centres. The second strategy for urban development that the Commission had suggested was for making the cities truly "generative" in their functioning. Urbanization in the opinion of the Commission would make a positive contribution to the economic growth when the cities could generate economic momentum, their economic base could expand and productivity increased. To operationalize these objectives, the Commission had identified 329 urban centres out of the existing 600 and 49 urbanization regions for developmental inputs. These urban centres were called GEMS (Generation of Economic Momentum).

Mention may also made in this context of the report of the Task Force on Planning and Development of Small and Medium Scale Towns and Cities appointed by the Ministry of Works and Housing, to implement the suggestion of Prime Minister Indira Gandhi for the development of small towns and cities, at the All India Local Self Government Ministers Conference at Bhopal way back in October 1975. The Ministry in pursuance of the Task Force recommendations had prepared detailed guidelines for selection of the urban centres under the IDSMT Scheme. But of the 329 GEMS, 109 towns (about 32.5%) were covered under the IDSMT scheme during the Sixth and Seventh Plan periods. The scheme however did not work well and for understandable reasons. Among the GEMS selected, Moradabad town was from UP.

To view the urban problem in perspective, we must bear in mind the fact that rural India with its meagre resources still supports more than two-thirds of the country's population, which urban India is cracking under the weight of even less than 30 per cent of our total population. Let us also not forget that the poverty of rural India is one of the major causes of the decay and degeneration of the cities. The growing size of the urban slums is largely attributable to the migration of villagers to the towns in search of means of livelihood or better employment opportunities. Decongestion of cities by diverting the surplus population to small satellite towns or putting a check on immigration from the villagers has its own relevance to the management of the urban crisis in India. Control of population growth through family planning is an equally understandable strategy of limiting the size of the cities. But all this only amounts to saying that the best way to meet the urban challenge is to develop the cities in a manner that would transform them into engines of development. This is what the National Commission on Urbanization suggested in its recommendation for changing urban centres into

GEMS. However, recommendations like these completely overlook the fact that given the existing stratification of the city population into the affluent and the poor, gains of development are likely to be cornered in large measures by the former. In other words, growth with social justice cannot be ensured within the existing framework of the urban society.

Also, urban expansion which can not be stopped if the city dwellers' growing needs of housing and transportation are to be satisfied is bound to result in increasing diversion of forests, pastures, cultivable land and cultivable wasteland under common village use. According to the Ministry of Agriculture and Rural Development, 1.7 million hectares of land under use in the villages was diverted to other purposes between 1981–82 and 1982–83. In other words, explosive urban expansion is bound to result in pauperization of villages, matters little whether they are marginalized as hunter lands of the cities or villages are proletarianized as dwellers of urban slums. Planned urban development which requires cities to play a generative role so called, has, that is to say, its own perils. In the veiled but highly meaningful language of Levi-Strauss, development in so far as involves adoption of modernization ideals or following in the footsteps of the modern west becomes auto-imperialism, a kind of self-imposed slavery. Let us then see where walking along the western highway is likely to lead us to.

Urbanization in the West during the last 150 years has proceeded at such a galloping speed that while in 1850, 19.6 million of America's total population of 23 million lived in rural areas (defined as places below 2,500 persons), the country has now 96 per cent of its population living in cities. England at this point of time despite being the model for industrialization was not at all industrial. Less than 50 per cent of its population lived in towns in 1851. But, as of today, more than 91 per cent of England's population lives in towns. Prussia in 1852 had 72 per cent of its population classified as rural. Likewise, in France, in 1851, only 10.5 per cent of the total population lived in towns. But the corresponding figures for urbanization in West Germany and France today are over 85 per cent and 78 per cent.[19]

The rising trend of urbanization which has led to the complete disappearance of the village from the West has triggered a simultaneous process of displacement of man from his natural habitat – his soil – which has been reduced to what is now called "environment". The city itself is one such environment which as we have shown above came into existence as an artificial community in Europe in the wake of the Industrial Revolution. There are quite a few novels on American cities such as Chicago and California, which give a vivid description of these cities as man-made worlds that "seemed in defiant counterpoise to nature."

Writing about Chicago, Gerry Wills says, "The city was an act of will a defi, an imposition, a triumph over circumstances. There was nothing natural about it." Cronon's title (*Nature's Metropolis*) for his novel in Chicago is ironic.[20] The 13–story medical building in Robert Herriks *The Web of Life* (1900) is "knife-edged" as a scalpel and as heartless. The doctor hero of *The Web of Life* chooses the muddy flats of the south side where he can administer to real needs over the hygienic clinics of the skyscraper where neurotic rich people are cared for. The very technology of the medical building is resented by the hero as it is soulless.[21] *The Octopus* (1901) by Frank Norris[22] is a novel about California' gigantic rail road but in Joan Didion's words, "it remains perhaps the most complete statement to date of the California condition and a deeply ambiguous work... *The Octopus*, if there is one, turns out to be not the rail road, but indifferent nature," "a gigantic engine, a vast cyclopean power, huge, terrible, a leviathan with a heart of steel, knowing no compunction, no forgiveness, no tolerance, crushing out the human atom standing in its way with nirvanic calm, the agony of destruction sending never a jar".[23] Josiah Royce, the Harward philosopher (from 1885 to 1916), remembers California (in one of his recollections of the city) as a "community of irresponsible strangers (or in another references "a blind and stupid and homeless generation of selfish wonders") a community not of the loyals but of men who have left homes and families, who have fied from before the word of the Lord and have sought safety from their old vexatious duties in a Golden paradise".[24] Loyalty, according to Royce, is the basic value, the moral law essential to the creation of a "community".

Let us recall again that the world made by man as Homo-Faber came into existence as a second nature and also as an exhibit of man's power over first nature. The city was also a part of this world, but in course of time it gave birth to its own way of life which eventually became known as "urbanism" and also got delinked from its source of origin and acquired the status of a new value. But urbanism itself was a part of a higher order, the rational-technical order created by the Industrial Revolution which had become a substitute for the natural order. The change that the Industrial Revolution had brought about was the replacement of the zig-zag pattern of nature, by a universal homogeneous pattern defined in terms of logicality and technical efficiency. This new pattern, in course of time, ceased to be a symbol of man's power over nature and became instead a symbol of the power of technical rationality over man. Lewis Mumford,[25] a keen student of techniques and civilization had compared the emerging rational technical order to a mega-machine, which like the Octopus in Frank Norris' description of California that crushes the human atom coming in its way. The human atom or the human individual is no longer the fabricator of "second nature," he is himself a creation of it.

Thanks to the operation of this mega-machine which has now become the engine of corporate multinationalism, the world in which we live has shrunk into a "global village". There are now about 300 multinational corporations whose production of goods and services adds up to about $300 billion a year, a figure higher than the GNP of every country except the US. If one takes 100 largest economic units in the world, only 50 of them are nation-states, the other 50 are the largest of these 300 multinational companies. These multinationals, the mega-machines of post-industrial capitalism not only claim to produce for the satisfaction of the needs of men all over the world, they also create their needs and simultaneously. Such is the logic of the functioning of these mega-machines that in the process of their working, they both satisfy and create these needs, landing mankind into the vicious circle of commodity – production –consumption or need – satisfaction – need. And the needs of the individual consumer are there because the system of corporate production needs them. The needs of the individual consumer fed back into the system of corporate production are a kind of investment of capital.

Leach writes, "since 1890 on American corporate business ... began the transformation of American society into a society preoccupied with consumption with comfort and bodily well-being, with luxury spending and acquisition, with more goods this year than the last, more next year than this. American consumer capitalism produced a culture almost evidently hostile to the past and to tradition, a future culture of desire that compared the good life with goods".[26] "We bring good things to life" is the motto of General Electric. The standard of life is determined not so much by what man has to enjoy as by the rapidity with which he tires of the pleasure. To have a high standard means to enjoy a pleasure intensely and to tire of it quietly.[27]

Not that man in the 21st century must have lost his sense of awareness of what is happening around him. He is deeply conscious of his predicament; he only does not know how to get out of it. The mega-machines of trans-natural corporate capitalism which control the power-strings of the existing welfare states too can not allow any changes to take place within the system which will disrupt the status quo. Movements such as postmodern populist ecology, environmentalism, rurbanization, sustainable developmentalization are all alternative, though supposedly better methods of maintaining the same system of commodity-production consumption.

As some eminent environmentalists of the West have pointed out, "exploitation of resources at sustainable levels, i.e., using resources today in ways that do not for close future options to these resources is impossible. In their view resources are inevitably over exploited often to the point of collapse or extinction".[28] This manner of exploitation of nature or resources accords well with Bacon's philosophy that nature must be "hounded in her wanderings" bound into service and made a "slave." The aim of the scientist according to Bacon is to "torture nature's secrets from her".[29] Likewise, if the country and the city are technologically integrated and corporately managed to function as parts of the mega-machine of production, balancing the two becomes an impossible task. Rurbanization is not a practical proposition.

The deep ecology movement which seeks to revive man's traditional attitude to nature – of viewing flora, fauna, earth and man as parts of one cosmic whole and relying exclusively on self-balancing technology for the exploitation of nature is of course a healthier development than shallow environmentalism. Capra refers to a study conducted by the Stanford Research Institute in 1976, which estimated that four to five million adult Americans had voluntarily reduced their incomes and gave up their high positions in their consumer economy to embrace a simpler life style based on drastically reduced needs. What Capra and others like him have in mind as an alternative to consumerist life style favoured by the modern urban civilization is a return to a normal pattern of living, a living which rests on principles, which in other words, is imitative of an archetypal model. The life that normal man tries to live can not be rationally reinvented: it can only be lived in accordance with tradition. Modern man as such is incapable of reliving a life which he has himself destroyed.

Urban India's problems are different from those of urban America or urban Europe. Urbanism in the West now stands for a replacement, almost total of tradition and memory by history and literate reason. It began as modernity claiming to liberate man from "oppressive traditions" and remained confined to the so-called developed nations of the west. But, it gradually grew into a globalized institutional modernity and was transformed into an instrument of western domination over the rest of the world where tradition and memory still held sway. The discourse of modernity became a universal discourse significantly called the "philosophical discourse of modernity" by Jurgan Habermas. After the Industrial Revolution established man's supremacy as a fabricator, as the maker of a new world, ephemeral though, as a counterpoise to the world of nature.

Even upto this point, pristine nature had not become a plaything of the new technologies of production – the mega-machines of trans-natural corporate system. But after the second Industrial Revolution as it is called, that is, the rise of the new form of production, nature has been practically abolished, as new technologies of self help individuals to effect changes in their own bodies and souls which enable them to conform to the requirements of happiness and perfection as dictated by the consumerist economy. It is the disease of civilization with which man in the west is laid up today.

In India, tradition and orality still constitute the dominant values of life, although looked upon as obstacles to development and progress. The problem of urbanization in India stands on a different footing therefore as compared to that in America or Europe.

Since India has yet not come under full control of the mega-machine of multinational globalism, both the men and nature are still in their proper places despite what is considered explosive urbanization even at the low level of 27 per cent. The concentration of population in the megacities of India and the infrastructural problems spawned by it is not beyond management if we have the right political will to tackle the more basic problem of poverty of the villages. What is needed is a change in our attitude to development. If affluent Americans can cut down upon their needs, change their affluent style of consumption, why can not Indians do it? And, the "white enclave" in India does not constitute a sizeable percentage of the population. It is this class which has to scale down its standard of life in the interest of the teeming millions steeped in poverty. India must seriously try to decolonize her economy. What we mean is that we must try to recultivate the traditional Indian values of simplicity, frugality and non-acquisitiveness.

It is worth noting the contrast between the slums of American cities and those of the cities of India. Josiah Strong wrote in 1898, "ignorance, vice and wretchedness combined constitute the social dynamite of which the American slum is a magazine"[30] and 70 years later Dominique Lapierree wrote about

Miami, "Florida burglaries, armed robberies, muggings, rapes a whole array of violent crimes, engendered by drug addiction and dismal poverty... became such common place events in Miami that only the most outrageous amongst them inspired the city's headline writers." Go great was the psychosis of fear that many residents preferred to move to safer places in the US. But "for all the poverty of its slums," Lapierre goes on "Indian city unlike its American or European counterpart is still not nature's necropolis, and if planned properly can be converted into a normal habitat for man."

Notes

1. New York: Baker and Taylor (1898), p. 53, quoted in by Max Weber (1962): *The City* (New York: Collier Books, p. 19).
2. The novel was published in 1890.
3. See Kerwin Lee Klein (1995): In Search of Narrative Mastery: Post Modernism and People without History. *History and Theory: Studies in the Philosophy of History,* Vol. 34, No. 4, p. 278.
4. Ibid., p. 278.
5. See Oswald Spengler (1928): *The Decline of the West* (New York: Alfred A Knopf, translated by Charles Francis Atkinson, Volume II).
6. See Max Weber (1962): *The City* (New York: Colliere Books, p. 59).
7. See Karl Marx: *Grundrisse,* p. 472 (quoted in Luciano Pellicani (1987–88): The Genesis of Capitalism. Telos, *NY Quarterly of Critical thought,* No. 74, winter, pp. 52–53).
8. See Adam Smith (1937): *An Enquiry into the Nature and causes of the Wealth of Nations,* The Modern Library (quoted in Pellicani, op. cit., p. 56).
9. Pellicani, p.57.
10. Marx and Engels: *The German Ideology* (International Publishers, 1939, p. 44).
11. Census of India 1991, quoted in *The Inevitable Million Plus,* Ed. Vasant Gowarikar, Delhi: Progressive Printers by M.N. Buch.
12. See Uttar Pradesh Mein Nagrikaran, Bhumi Upyoga Parishad, Government of UP, Lucknow, p. 5.
13. UNDP 1991 Human Development Report, Quoted in *The Inevitable Billion Plus,* Ed. Vasant Gowariker and P.V. Indiresan, p. 143.

14. See Meera Kosambi (1990): "The Colonial City in its Global Niche", a review article on Anthony D. King's (1990) *Urbanism, Colonialism and The World Economy: Cultural and Spatial Foundations of the World Urban System*, London/New York: Routledge, in *Economic and Political Weekly*, December 22, p. 2776.
15. The reference is to Dominique Lapierre's book *The City of Joy* (United Kingdom: Random House, Arrow Books, 1985).
16. See *The Statesman*, New Delhi, November 11, 1992.
17. Ibid.
18. *The Times of India*, New Delhi, February. 1, 1997.
19. See Daniel Bell (1974): *The Coming of Post-Industrial Society* (Indian Edition, New York: Harper Colophon Books), pp. 49–50.
20. Chicago, Underground, in *The New York Review of Books*, 30th Anniversary Issue, Vol. XI, No. 17, October 21, 1993, p. 18.
21. Ibid., p. 18.
22. Frank Morris, *The Octopus*, London: Penguine Publication, 1901.
23. Ibid., p. 87.
24. Ibid., p. 86.
25. Lewis Mumford (1967): *The Myth of the Machine Techniques and Human Development* (New York: Harcourt, Brace and World Inc., p. 264).
26. Leach (1993): *Land of Desire, Merchants Power and the Rise of the New American Culture* (New York, p. XIII).
27. Semon Patten (1892): *The Consumption of Wealth* (New York: Lippen Company, p. 51).
28. Donald Ludwig, Ray Hilborn and Carl Walters: "Uncertainty, Resource Exploitation and Conservation Lessons from History" quoted in Telos, No. 103, Spring 1995, Special Issue on Populism by Emery M. Rose in his "Commentary on Sustainable Development and Populism," p. 151.
29. Quoted by Capra Fritzof in *The Turning Point* (London: Flemingo Edition, Fontanna Paperbacks, 1982, pp. 40–41).
30. Jusiah Strong (1898): *The Twentieth Century City* (New York: Bacon and Taylor, p. 67–68).

6

Towards a Cultural Policy in India

*Can Culture be Planned?**

In his analysis, Professor D.P. Mukerji argues as contained in his famous essay on Indian culture that the Indian middle classes were essentially the creation of the political and administrative exigencies; the British rule created them to man the liberal professions which it had thrown open to the English educated Indians. They therefore differed both from the former in being 'non-productive' and from the latter in being 'non-commercial'. How then could they be a perfect replacement for the traditional Indian literati, the Brahmins, who were not created by a government fiat, but constituted an organic class within the larger Indian society? At the same time that their English education had entitled them to the membership of the privileged professions and services, it had cut them off from their umbilical chord, the myths and living symbols of their civilization on which the traditional Indian intellectuals were nourished. It was in fact, the living contact of the latter with the people both through the vernaculars as well the language of the great tradition, which enabled them to retain their cultural distinctiveness and yet remain organically united with the whole. The

* Based on oral presentation at a symposium organized by the XXI All India Sociological Conferences held on 19–21 December 1994 at Jawahar Lal Nehru University, New Delhi, in the honour of the late Professor D.P. Mukerji in his birth centenary year.

new intellectual elites on the other hand, maintained their distinctiveness not in their organic unity with the whole, but in their fundamental separation or alienation from the whole. Also because of their obscure social origins, they are bound to be consumed by political passions, that is, they are ever ready to play the second fiddle to the power elites. They are therefore lacking in that sense of detachment and objectivity which is the indispensable condition of creativity. The middle class soul which is alleged to be the originator and the repository of culture is stricken by a malady. It is simultaneously preyed upon by a new sense of guilt and a feeling of denial. It knows that it does not belong to India and must cover its shame in the loudness of arrivestes' assertion or by a cloying complacency. The middle class has also apprehended the closing of its career and must find the enemy.[1] Professor Mukerji actually wants culture to be rescued from politics through a cultivation of scientific neutrality by the middle classes which does not necessarily mean non-commitment to any ideal or value. The scientist is after all not neutral as between superstition and scientific laws.

Professor Mukerji was deeply concerned about the cultural outcome of the national movement. But, for Gandhi, none of the leaders of the Indian National Congress, in his opinion, thought of the national struggle in terms of a cultural renaissance. Patriotism was all right, but it was emotionally carried to a point where it virtually ruined our culture. The complaint about growing corruption in public life, and more especially in the high places is only an indication of the fact that our sense of patriotism or nationalism was only skin deep; and since it was never a part of our tradition it could not be translated into a moral value. Thus nationalism which was propped up as a new religion, produced a culture without its corresponding ethics which, more than any other fact, accounted for the loss of the moral tone among the Congressmen. The national movement, besides producing an ersatz culture, did get on their disservice to Indian culture and that was by subordinating regional sentiments – a truer reflection of the ways of the living of the people – to a vague all-India feeling. What thus happened was that while the regional cultures were weakened, the Indian culture was not strengthened. The culture of the middle classes, again, being a spurious culture could not be transmitted beyond this class. The spread and extension of national consciousness was, in other words, at the cost of quality of culture which explains why the literature, music, painting, sculpture, in fact all that is generally called culture produced during this period is so poor both in corpus and quality in comparison with what was achieved before 1920 in the different regions of the country.

Now even if we could create an intelligentsia which had both the intellectual equipment and sense of detachment needed for rescuing culture from political partisanship, can such a body of men achieve this feat? With the legacy of caste still standing intact with us, there is no guarantee that our new intelligentsia will not get converted into a caste. But supposing that this does not happen and we do have a class of politically detached intelligentsia, can such a body of men plan culture? 'In my view', says Professor Mukerji, 'culture as such cannot be fully planned. If culture comprehends the whole of life, then, surely a large segment of living formed by the unconscinds would have to be recognized, respected and allowed freedom. This is true of individuals, more true of groups and still more so of strata of people whose living is one long pervasive obedience to tradition'.[2]

Professor Mukerji's 'unconscious' is neither Freudian nor Jungian. 'It is hardly necessary for me to say that the unconscious to which I am referring is nothing mystical or mysterious. Being the precipitate of history, it is not outside history'.[3] This unconscious element in culture is like the motif, form or pattern which enters a work of art as the contribution of the artists' own genius, it is the *a priori* element of a cultural creation which constitutes and gives meaning to the conscious. When it is said that the culture produced by the middle classes in India ever since their emergence, has been of a low quality, what is implied is that this culture is the creation of a sick and alienated mind whose conscious and unconscious layers have, kind of, fallen apart. Likewise, all literature and culture which we call propagandist is of this nature, wholly unconnected as it is with the subterranean regions of the mind or with the living cultural symbols stored in the myths and legends of the people. But the conscious and the unconscious are not basically inimical to each other; they are, on the other hand, complements each of the other – 'the one can be drawn into the other and brought out of it' – which is however not to say that they do not act as cross purposes; their disunion does lead to critical situations at times. If the situation is revolutionary, depending on its spontaneity the unconscious will definitely have the upper hand over the conscious and we can have absolutely no control over it. But in other situations it should not be difficult to tame the unconscious and bend it to creative purposes. But taming the unconscious does not mean controlling it directly; it only means infiltrating into it and bringing it 'out of its lair, that is, creating conditions which would facilitate its free expression'.

Planning of culture for Professor Mukerji, then, is creating the conditions of culture and conditions of culture mean freedom, and 'freedom involves choice, which relates to purpose formation, instrumentalities, which relate to the means for achieving the purpose, and full enjoyment of the ends achieved and controlled. The first demands freedom of discussion and opinion, the second freedom of association and action and the third freedom for securing distributive justice by removing fear of want and obstacles to the enjoyment of prosperity. These sectors freedom are the very conditions of a culture-system'.[4] Professor Mukerji agrees with Malinowski whom he quotes extensively to make his point that 'in a free culture people can form their purpose, undertake activities and enterprises and enjoy the gains from work thus undertaken'.

Applying this touchstone of freedom to the present-day conditions in India, Professor Mukerji is at a loss to understand how the present state of wealth and its distribution and enjoyment can assure each individual or an institution 'the enjoyment of his own differential freedom, in the measure to which he has a part in planning, a full access to means of execution and a share in the rewards', i.e., the preliminary conditions of culture. The freedom of private enterprise, in Professor Mukerji's considered opinion, is not a condition of culture, 'it is the privacy that kills freedom'. Nor is the freedom to vote, which with its mechanical conformity with other people's wishes, is all that adult franchise may confer upon an individual.

About two points Professor Mukerji is very forthright: one that the lifestyle which is called capitalist culture, far from being conducive to freedom and culture, tends to accentuate the tension between their conscious and the unconscious elements through inequitable distribution of opportunities, and denial of the right to work and to enjoy the fruits of that work, and two, whatever be the intensity of the moral crisis facing the country at the moment, it is neither desirable nor possible to let Indian culture remain where it stands, or to let it be taken back to past. In other words, no manner of revivalism is the remedy against the situation. It will be an offence against the law of change.

II

Culture in so far as it is an attribute of man cannot be controlled or planned, exactly as man qua man cannot be controlled or planned. If the planner were an agent other than man, and if he knew what man or culture, i.e., his material of planning was, one could surely think of planning culture. The great teacher of Hasidism who 'wanted to write a book on Adam which was to be about the whole man, but, who 'ultimately decided not to write it'[5] has given us the right clue to the story of man's understanding of himself. Since in the study of himself man is both the subject and object of his study, his understanding of himself can never be complete. If he could reduce himself to an object, as he has been able to do with the help of the scientific method, he would be studying only a paramechanical phenomenon and not man, which decidedly can not be his aim. On the other hand, if he concentrates on the whole man, he cannot be the object of knowledge; only a mystery to be lived and realized according to one's capacity and skill inherited from tradition. Likewise, if culture could be reduced to goods or commodities – symbolic[6] or real – it can be definitely manipulated and planned, but then it will no longer be culture. In any case, if culture can not be seen or experienced in disjunction from life, the question of its control or planning does not arise. Some such reservation seems to be lurking at the back of Professor Mukerji's mind when he asserts that culture can not be fully planned; his distinction between its conscious and unconscious layers is also significant, to which we may return later. Meanwhile, a word more about the meaning of culture.

To say that culture is an attribute of man is to say that it is a specific dimension of human action, as of course are economics and politics, with the one difference that while other dimensions are end-oriented, culture is its own end, i.e., unlike economics and politics, culture is valuable for its own sake. But we will not say as per Weber that culture is a category of value-rational action, nor as per Parsons and others that it is not a dimension of action but a thing of the normative order existing outside action, but at the same time structuring it. Nor is culture something to which we respond without thinking about it, in which sense, as C.P. Snow puts it, scientists have a culture of pragmatic optimism[7], and men of arts and letters, a different culture.

The etymology of the word links it with 'cultus', wherefore, its meaning as 'celebration of divine worship' or 'incarnation of religion'[8] or 'art of life', by which phrase Whitehead means the art of living, the art of living well and the art of living better[9]; or as the art of virtuous and prudential living, call it the pursuit of excellence or participation in truth, beauty and goodness. It is another thing that in the culture of modern science, which for Snow is the model to be imitated by the other culture that of the humanities, no virtue or prudence is required to know the truth.[10]

The best illustration of culture as art of life or as skill in works is provided by the traditional and archaic societies where life is one seamless whole without any sharp division of things into religion and economics, music and gymnastics or culture and physical training. Even the so-called division of life into the sacred and profane much talked of by Durkheim and others, is meaningful only to the outsider who is accustomed to thinking in terms of what Bourdieu calls 'monothetic logic' – the logic of science and of theoretical arguments. Life in the Kabylia in Algeria, he says, is based on 'polythetic logic' if at all we are required to describe it in logical terms. 'The Kabylia does not possess a distinct set of fine arts divorced from religious or practical use. Their poet, rather than being an oppositional figure, is the wise man whose particular efficiency is apparent in crises. Then he must restore society as ambassador or warlord, lest the meaning of the world slips away. These who dominate in Kabylia create the model of the virtuously lived life – they offer' .

'The art of living raised to an art for arts sake, founded on a refusal to acknowledge ... that 'business is business' or 'time is money' on which the unaesthetic life style of the harried leisure classes in so called advanced societies is based'.[11]

Again, as Coomaraswamy says, 'in the traditional doctrine of art "value" is never taken to mean an exclusively spiritual or exclusively physical value. It is neither advantageous nor altogether possible to separate these values, making some things sacred and others profane: the highest wisdom must be mixed with practical knowledge, the contemplative combined with the active life, the pleasures that pertain to these lives are altogether legitimate, and it is only those pleasures that are irrational, bestial and in the worst sense of the words seductive and distracting that are to be excluded. Plato's "music and gymnastics" which correspond to our "culture and physical training" are not alternative curricula, but essential parts of one and the same education; philosophy is the highest form of music (culture), but the philosopher who has escaped from the "cave" must return to it to participate in the everyday life of the world and quite literally play the game'.[12]

The tribal wise man or the traditional Kavi is the archetypal man of knowledge, the cosmic contemplative principle – the sacerdotium or the spiritual and immortal part of the soul (in the Greek Tradition, Plato, Timaeus 70A) that lays down the law; to which all other parts are subordinate and from which the active part, which is the defender of the whole community must take guidance.[13] In fact, a vocational order based on the distribution of work according to the natural abilities of each individual is present in one form or another in all these societies, this being one of the constitutional requirements of the life of the whole. Hence, sociologist, poets and artists, all alike, have recognized the indispensable role of 'clerisy', 'intellectuals' or 'elites' in the transmission and preservation of tradition and culture as also in the organization and direction of the will of the community. 'Poets', wrote Shelley, 'are the unacknowledged legislators of the world'.[14] Coleridge likewise considers some form of intellectual labour essential for the maintenance of traditions and the organic functioning of the community. This he calls 'clerisy' whose primary institutions are the Universities, the Pastorate and the parish schools, and who should each 'be working on the same end and determined in the choice of their means and the directions of their labours by one and the same object – namely, in producing and reproducing, in preserving, continuing and perfecting, the necessary sources and conditions of the national civilization'. Which will involve forming and training up the people of the country to be obedient, free, useful, organizable subjects, citizens and patriots living to the benefit of the state, in a nutshell to inculcate in them the virtue of civility which for Coleridge stands for all the qualities essential in a citizen.[15]

Eliot is of the same view. The preservation and transmission of tradition, he thinks, is the specialized task of an elite, the one that serves but does not identify with, the interests of any particular class. Which will be the community of a disciplinary elite – 'the Community of Christians', of faithful and practicing Christians, of superior intellect and spiritual attainment.[16]

Of direct relevance to the theme under discussion would be a reference to Hannah Arendt's distinction between the three dimensions of vita active or human life, viz., 'labour', 'work' and 'action'. What Arendt calls 'labour' is the activity of man which consists in combining his labour power with nature to produce things for his consumption. The exercise has no other end except its repetition as it is concerned with perpetuation of life and is man's normal response to the challenge of his biological needs.

Though apparently possessed of utility, the things produced by labour are intrinsically futile as they are consumed as soon as they are produced, leaving nothing behind them to remind them of the effort that has gone into their making.

As contrasted with labour, 'work' is not a service to biological nature, but its transformation. When archaeology reconstructs the history of peoples and civilizations, it digs up their memory not as labourers and consumers, but as makers, as men who had made durable things – tools, buildings, vessels and ornaments, which outlive their biological lives. This activity of man which gives him the identity of a civilized creature, or on account of which he is defined as Homo Faber, Arendt describes as 'work'. Work is not compliance with the dictates of nature; it is, on the other hand, an exercise involving domination and control of nature to create the conditions of a civilized existence. But even the world fashioned by Homo Faber is not truly immortal, as it is subject to destruction save its design, which though more durable than its physical body, does not entitle him to the immortality which his deeds and works confer upon man. It is this realm of immortality which man enters, with his activity, Arendt calls 'action'.

The human condition of action is plurality, the fellowship of men characterized by the living presence of each man in his individuality and uniqueness, despite his 'species' character. In action, man not only transcends the realm of necessity both biological and sociological, but initiates deeds and speaks words like Achilles[17] which reveal his true being. Action is not the 'role' man is supposed to play as a member of the social collectivity built upon an atrophied existence of his person. Under conditions of both labour and work, man is subject to the iron law of necessity. He does enjoy a little freedom under the condition of work, as he knows what he is making, but is still subordinate to the end-product, which survives him but tells nothing about him except that he was capable of making it.

The condition of action is the condition of freedom where man initiates deeds, and vies with his fellows in creating a culture of excellence which confers upon him true immortality.

Hannah Arendt constantly adverts to the Greek *polis* which provided the public space within which men could reveal themselves. The *polis* was an association of free citizens who were all equal and free and who were all engaged in a healthy competition with one another for everlasting name and fame. This public space, the *agora,* was different from the private space of the household, where the slaves laboured to cater for the biological needs of their masters, slaves who had been kept under bondage for toil in lieu of their life. There was no freedom inside the household where the master ruled like a despot. But in order to exercise his freedom, even the master had to come out of the darkness of the household to see the light of freedom in the *agora*. Politics, the public activity of the *polis,* was thus characterized by equality, persuasion and freedom.[18]

The human condition of plurality then is the sine qua non of culture. Man must enjoy a measure of freedom to reveal what he has in him to reveal or to become what he has in him to become. Should this freedom be taken away from him, i.e., should action be reduced to labour, man will cease to be man.

III

When we talk of planning today, be it economic, social or cultural, we do not have the same meaning of term in mind which Karl Jaspers had when he quoted planned activity with any arrangement with a purpose and aim.[19] Planning as a subject of academic debate has had to do with the role of institutions, more especially with that of the state, in the arrangement or rearrangement of things. The need for economic planning, for instance, arose as an alternative to laissez-faire; the need for what came to be called 'democratic planning' or planning for freedom, likewise, arose as an antidote to totalitarian planning. The state's direct involvement in affairs cultural began with the growing prestige of the theory that culture, more than a genuine expression of creativity, is an 'ideology' a 'superstructural phenomenon' reflecting the vested interest of the classes which had traditionally held its monopoly. If authentic culture, the one genuinely expressing people's tastes and feelings had to be rescued from vested interests, the state had to take an active interest in the culture of the people. Such authentic culture could also include the dying folk cultures whose art forms – songs and dances in particular – could be used to enliven the celebrations of the high culture patronized by the state. Thus, it is that the state in all people's democracies assumed the role, among other things, of the watchdog of culture.[20]

Not that the demand for an aesthetic realism or progressive art and literature was wholly propagandist; experience has shown that culture did become a disciplinary state apparatus under capitalism and the cultural elites had legitimated the change. Walter Benjamins' remark that 'there is no document of civilization which is not at the some time a document of barbarism'[21] is a statement of hard fact. Pierre Bourdieu's works highlight the manner in which artistic knowledge has degenerated into an ideology for justifying social inequality and domination. Thanks to the lead taken by Kant in installing a permanent divide between culture and nature (declaring the sublime and the beautiful literally out of bounds for those lacking culture, i.e., for the savage who in Kant's opinion can have a feeling of fear on observing thunderbolts, but who can not recognize their sublimity) 'the capitalist society has come to recognize two natures, one nature, naturally cultivated and another nature naturally natural'.[22] And it is this confusion of natural and social which is the true source of 'meritocracy', the much-vaunted ideology of late capitalism. The meritorious according to this ideology are those who possess non-cultural capital, who, that is to say, are more resourceful than others and who do not allow the less resourceful to enter their enclave. However, a mere demystification of sociology would be no solution to the problem which Bourdieu has so ably analysed.

IV

If culture, as we have tried to show in the foregoing discussion, is not a special enclave of life, but something which encompasses the whole of it, then one can not but agree with Professor Mukerji that culture cannot be wholly planned. For, even if it were possible to manage its conscious layer – what man knows he has made or done – the behaviour of its unconscious layer can not be predicted. But, the condition of culture, viz., freedom as per Professor Mukerji's line of thinking, which is the central point in Coleridge's and Eliot's thoughts about culture as well, can definitely he planned. Incidentally, there is much in common between the condition of freedom as suggested by Professor Mukerji and that of plurality as conceived by Hannah Arendt. It is in the company of others that man initiates deeds, which according to her, bring him out in his uniqueness and unpredictability and make him immortal. Plurality, therefore, is the essential ground of culture as is freedom.

The foremost issue in the formulation of a cultural policy for a country like India with a pluralist national culture and a democratic ethos is, then, whether pluralism is to be raised on a prefabricated unity conceived as 'central or mainstream culture' as already embedded in our tradition, or as emerging out of the long interaction between tradition and history; or on the pre-existing transcendent unity of the cultures comprised in the Indian nation. The basic difference between the two concepts of unity is that while the former is a class concept constructed as a type to be imposed on the people, the latter as atypal – unanimous, spontaneous and self-imposing.

The 'mainstream culture' theory though prima facie innocuous may become the thin end of a totalitarian wedge, which is to say, that it may lead to uniformization of culture in the form of imposition of the social philosophy of the dominant – numerically preponderant or otherwise powerful – culture on other cultures. The increasing identity consciousness among the cultural communities manifesting in movements for autonomy or independence is partly a result of their apprehension of being swamped by the dominant culture.

Pluralism, therefore, should not be allowed to float on the surface of any politically contrived idea of unity. What we have in mind when we speak of the transcendent unity of cultures is the unity reflected in their values and beliefs, folkways and mores.

What Bourdieu calls 'monothetic logic', the logic of science and theoretical argument, characterizes the mentality of a very small segment of our cultural communities; their predominant mode of thinking is still 'polythetic' or 'prelogical'. This mentality which we moderns consider as one of inferior intellectuality, is more conducive to plurality than the antipodal monothetic or logical mentality, in the sense that is averse to imposing a cut and dried 'form' of life as the modern mentality is wont to. The polythetic mentality thus provides for the realization of one's individuality in an infinite number of ways, at least in more ways than possible within the limits of uniformity imposed by the latter. And it is in this sense that the unity in traditional and folk societies, unlike the one in modern democracies and dictatorships is self- or immanently imposed rather than imposed from outside by individuals or classes.

A liberal state must therefore ensure that its democratic ethos and pluralist culture complement and enforce each other. It should accordingly avoid doing anything overt or covert which may hurt the sense of districtness of any cultural group or result in the destruction of the variety and richness of its self-consciousness. Even in the name of reform and development a lot of damage is being done to the rich cultural heritage of the folk and tribal communities. In fact, besides creating conditions in which the intelligentsia could enjoy the maximum freedom – at least freedom of expression and freedom of conscience, and play its social role effectively, it should take positive steps to promote the culture of plurality – not necessarily by an activist interest but at the same time must take care of the fact that no cultural group is able to impose its way of life on another, and the purpose of education is not conceived in a manner that it should encourage the growth of a uniform personality type rather than a variety of cultural types.

It is unfortunate indeed that the programmes of development have been carried to a point where they have become a cultural liability. Development has virtually been allowed to become a vested interest in the hands world power blocks. A cultural policy instead of allowing culture to be exploited for the success of development programmes conceived by particular individuals or classes, should insist on the development policies being in consonance with the cultural urges and aspirations of the people.

Notes

1. Mukerji, Dhurjati Prasad: *Sociology of Indian Culture* (Second Edition, Revised and Enlarged, Jaipur: Rawat Publications, 1979, p. 205).
2. Mukerji, D.P.: *Diversities* (New Delhi: Peoples' Publishing House Pvt. Ltd., New Delhi, 1958, p. 191).
3. Op. cit., p. 182.
4. Op. cit., p. 192.
5. Buber, Martin: *Between Man and Man* (Translated and introduced by Professor Ronald Gragor Smith, Collins, London: The Fontana Library, 1947, p. 148).
6. Pierre Bourdieu makes a distinction between the field of large scale cultural production which submits to the laws of competition for the conquest of the largest possible market, and that of restricted production which tends to develop its own criteria for the evaluation of its products, thus achieving the cultural recognition accorded by the peer group whose members are both privileged clients and competitors. Thus while the field of large-scale cultural production is oriented to making economic profit, the restricted field is oriented primarily towards the acquisition and accumulation of 'symbolic capital', i.e., recognition, kudos and celebrity status among peer groups. *The Field of Cultural Production* (Edited and introduced by Raudal Johnson, Cambridge, USA: Cambridge Polity Press, 1993, p. 115) quoted by Paul Crowther in his review article entitled 'Sociological Imperialism and the Field of Cultural Production'. *The Case of Bourdieu in Theory, Culture and Society*, Vol. II, No.1, February 1994, p. 15.
7. Snow, C.P.: *Two Cultures: And A Second Look* (Cambridge: Cambridge University Press, 1964).
8. For 'the Christian cultus unlike any other, is at once a sacrifice and a sacrament. In so far as the Christian cultus is a sacrifice held in the

midst of creation which is affirmed by this sacrifice of the God-man, everyday is a feast day, and in fact the liturgy knows only feast days being *feria*. In so far as the cultus is a sacrament, it is celebrated in visible signs. And the full power of worship will only be felt if its sacramental character is realized in undiminished form, i.e., if the sign is fully visible. In leisure, as was said, man oversteps the frontiers of the everyday workday world, not in external effort and strain, but as though lifted above in ecstasy. That is the sense of the visibility of the sacrament, that it should be the means of lifting man, out of himself, so that he is rapt to the heavens' (See Pieper, Joseph: *Leisure the Basis of Culture* (Translated by Alexander Dru with an Introduction by T.S. Eliot', 24 Russell Square, London: Faber and Faber, 1962, p. 80). Pieper grounds culture in leisure which is not cessation of work, but transformation of work into worship 'God we are told in the first chapter of Genesis "ended his work which he had made" and "behold it was very good"... so too it is leisure which leads man to accept the reality of the creation and thus to celebrate it resting on the inner vision that accompanies it (Ibid., p. 55). 'Leisure is possible only when a man is at one with himself, when he acquiesces in his own being, whereas the essence of acedia (idleness) is the refusal to acquiesce in one's being' (Ibid., p. 51). See also Eliot, T.S.: *Notes Towards the Definition of Culture* (24 Russell Square, London: Faber and Faber, 1962, p. 28.

9. See specially, Jentz, Arther H. (Jr.): *Whitehead's Philosophy: Primary Texts in Dialogue* (Lanham, Maryland: University Press of America, 1985, pp. 49–50).

10. See for example, Foucault, M.: *On the Genealogy of Ethics: An Overview of Work in Progress: In The Foucault Reader* (Ed. Paul Rabinow, New York: Pantheon Books). Quoting Rene Descartes, Foucault says 'to accede to truth, it sufficed that I be any subject which can see what is evident ... Thus I can be immoral and know the truth. I believe that this is an idea which more or less explicitly, was rejected by all previous cultures. Before Dascartes, one could not be impure immoral and know the truth. With Descartes, direct evidence is enough' (pp. 371–72).

11. See, Fowler, Bridget: 'The Hegemonic Work of Art in the Age of Electronic Reproduction: An Assessment of Pierre Bourdieu'. *Theory Culture and Society*, Vol. 11, No. 1, February 1994, p. 136.

12. Coomaraswamy, Ananda K.: *Figures of Speech or Figures of Thought* (New Delhi: Munshiram Manoharlal Publishers Pvt. Ltd., 1981, pp. 21–22).

13. See Coomaraswamy, Ananda K.: *Spiritual Authority and Temporal Power in the Indian Theory of Government* (New Delhi: Munshiram Manoharlal Publishers Pvt. Ltd., 1978, p. 2).
14. Shelley, P.B.: *In Defence of Poetry* (Ed. Needham, London: Givri Co., 1931, p. 109).
15. Colleridge, Samuel Taylor: 'On the Constitution of the Church and the State'. In *Collected Works of Sumuel Taylor Coleridge* (Vol. 10, Ed. John Colmer, Princeton, NJ: Princeton University Press, 1976, pp. 53–54).
16. Eliot, T.S.: *The Idea of a Christian Society and Other Writings* (London: Faber and Faber, 1982, pp. 64–65).

    However, between 'elites' and other groups generally known as 'classes', Eliot has a distinction to make. While some kind of a functional differentiation is present in the society at every level of its development, this differentiation is sharper at higher than at primitive or lower levels; some functions at the higher level being more honoured than others. As a result, what is mere functional differentiation at lower levels takes the form of class differentiation at the higher honour and privilege being accorded to an individual not so much because he is a functionary, but pre-eminently because he belongs to a class. Eliot thinks that at this stage of the society, classes themselves become agencies of preservation and maintenance of culture, both of their own group as well as of the society. But in an open or classless society, the situation will be quite different. When classes disappear, their cultural role will be played by 'leaders' and 'elites', the former being men endowed with powers of government and administration, and the latter being men gifted with powers of understanding, analysis and reasoning who will constitute the creative core of the society. The elites, then, will be drawn from all classes although rather than belonging to a fixed class, they will oscillate between class and a classless elite. (*Notes Towards the Definition of Culture*: 24 Russell Square, London: Faber and Faber Ltd., 1962, pp. 36–44.

    Mannheim assigns a still more crucial role to the intellectual elites whom following Alfred Weber, he calls 'socially unattached intelligentsia' and who thinks, carry out the work of interpretation and intertranslation of perspectives to facilitate cross-contextual (intersubjective) understanding. However, not all intellectual elites are socially unattached or neutral. 'The more intellectuals became party functionaries, the more they lost the virtue of receptivity and elasticity which they had brought with them from their previous labile situation' (Mannheim, Karl: *Ideology and Utopia* (Trans. Louis Wirth and Edward Shils, London: Routledge and Kegan Paul and New York: Harcourt Brace, 1936, p. 30). This equally applies to intellectuals who have become salaried functionaries of business, government or even universities (see also Simonds, A.P. and Mannheim, K.: *Sociology of Knowledge*, Oxford: Clarendon Press, 1978, p. 129, ff.)

On the contrary, Gramsci's 'intellectuals' who articulate the philosophy and ideology of the masses and who help the ruling classes to exercise their hegemony over the people, become 'organic intellectuals' of the class to which they belong when they understand the direction in which history is moving. 'The intellectual organically linked to the revolutionary class, becomes a member of the political party, which provides the leadership for that class'. The organic intellectual is no mere orator; he is a constructor, organizer and permanent persuade (see especially Gramsci, Antonio: *Selections from the Prison Notebooks*, Ed. and Trans. by Quintin Hoare and Geoffery Nowell Smith, London: Lawrence and Wishart and New York: International Publishers, 1971, and also James Joll: *Gramsci* (New York: Fontana Modern Masters, 1977, pp. 89–94).

17. The greek hero in Homer's Head who was a doer of great deeds and speaker of great words and who was also invulnerable except in heel.
18. See for a detailed discussion of Arendt's theory of Vita Activa her: *The Human Condition* (University of Chicago Press, 1958), Passimand and also Canovan Margaret: *The Political Thought of Hannah Arendt* (London: Methuen and Co. Ltd., 1977).
19. Jaspers, Karl: *The Origin and Goal of History* (London: Routledge and Kegan Paul, 1953, p. 106).
20. Marxist aesthetic criticism according to George Steiner has taken two main forms, one, which recognizes only those works as genuine and good which display an unabashed partisanship; this line of thinking is primarily inspired by Lenin's writings in which he demanded Tendenzliteratur (partisan-literature) as an alternative to aesthetic formalism at the turn of the century and which were codified by Zhdnov at the first Soviet Writers conference in 1934. The second line of criticism which Steiner considers more faithful to Marxism is the one which, following the lead of Engels, evaluates art not so much by the intention of its author, but primarily by its social context, which may not be always commensurate with the intentions of the artists and which may express much more than his

class interests. This is the line pursued by non-Soviet bloc socialist critics who are also sometime called para-Marxists. (see Jay, Martin: *The Dialectical Imagination. A History of the Frankfurt School and the Institute of Social Research 1923–50* (Boston/Toronto: Little Brown and Company, 1973, p. 175).

21. Quoted in Jay, Martin, op. cit., p. 173.
22. Bourdieu, Pierre et al.: *The Love of Art: European Art Museums and Their Public* (USA: Cambridge Polity, p. 111, quoted in Fowler, Bridge, op. cit., 1991, p. 139.

7

D.P. Mukerji as a Sociologist

Centenary Shradhanjali

When D.P. Mukerji started his academic career in the early 20s of this century, Enlightenment Reason had already completed a life span of a more than a hundred years in Europe, a life span of earthly immortality by Indian standards. But rather than being honoured in the evening of its life, it came in for severe drubbing, as if, to be finally rejected as a false and pretentious Messiah. With the rejection of Enlightenment Reason had also begun the process of unmaking of the modern episteme through a total repudiation of its ontological premises together with the rationalization which had lent support to them. The term 'postmodern' did not become part of the vocabulary of the social sciences until the late 60s of the 20th century, although in the literary circles, at least, of the Latin American countries it had come into circulation as early as 1930. D.P. had had a full view of modernity, but the rise of postmodernity he did not live to see. These developments in the intellectual history of Europe had not an insignificant part to play in the evolution of D.P. Mukerji's thought.

He was a contemporary of Karl Mannheim (born 1893), Horkheimer (born 1895) and Herbert Marcuse (born 1898) to mention only the Frankfurters in Europe, and as we will see in what follows, there was a great deal common between him and his European contemporaries. A brief reference to Enlightenment Reason and what it stood for would therefore be in order, before we proceed with a discussion of D.P.'s own thought.

Enlightenment, as Kant defined the term, referred to the emergence of humanity from its self-imposed immaturity, where immaturity meant one's inability to see his understanding, without any guidance from another. Clarifying the meaning of the term in his essay 'An Answer to the Question what is Enlightenment', written in 1784, Kant said that man's Enlightenment or his awakened historical consciousness should reflect his increasing confidence and ability to explain the present without reference to the past – taking the present in its presentness – or future, suggesting thereby, as Habermas puts it that reason should be able to create its own normativity out of itself through self-reflection. 'Have courage to use your own understanding'[1], was the famous motto that Kant had prescribed for enlightened humanity as a maxim of conduct.

In its historical projection, Enlightenment Reason means living in a self-transcending 'now' which promises to become increasingly perfect and sublime with each passing 'now'; the modern being qualitatively less good than the contemporary. In other words, time is no longer the connecting link between one experience and another, it is the essence of all experience, and history no longer occurs in time; it rather occurs through time; nor is there a 'gap in time'; if anything, there is only a 'gap of time'. Above everything else, as both Habermas and Foucault interpret it, Kant's essay 'inaugurates a philosophical discourse of modernity' or tries to create a universal language into which all languages describing modernity – the life of Enlightenment Reason – could be unified.[2]

In July 1793[3], that is, about 10 years later than the appearance of Kant's essay on Enlightenment, Marquis de Condorcet also wrote an essay highlighting the salient features of Enlightenment Reason which he entitled as 'Sketch for a Historical Picture of the Progress of the Human Mind', which was published after his death in 1795 (Condorcet died the day after he was apprehended and dragged to prison in April 1794). Condorcet divided the history of mankind into 10 states, the 10th being 'The Future Progress of the Human Mind'. By progress he meant not much growth, development and differentiation, as movement towards indefinite perfectibility of the human species. The hero of progress, its *raison d'etre,* its telos, or the moving spirit behind it, was Reason; and since progress was conceived as a teleological movement, it was not reversible either. With each succeeding stage of progress, justice, virtue, equality, freedom and happiness became more and more perfect. A firm belief in the infallibility of reason and efficacy of the social sciences to improve the lot of humanity was another article of faith with Condorcet.

While Condorcet set such great store by Reason, Max Weber, an equally ardent supporter of Enlightenment Reason was a bitter critic of its actual role in recent history. Weber wrote, 'no one knows... whether at the end of this tremendous development, entirely new prophets will arise or there will be a great rebirth of old ideas and ideals, or if neither mechanized petrification embellished with a sort of convulsive self-importance. For, of the last stage of this cultural development, it might well be said 'specialists without spirit, sensualist without heart; this nullity imagines that it has attained a level of civilization never before'.[4] Weber like Condorcet had no illusions about the innate goodness of reason, particularly about its natural tendency to be on the side of justice, freedom and democracy. But there was absolutely no connection, he said, between capitalism and democracy or between capitalism and freedom and yet capitalism was the inevitable result of economic development. How then are freedom and democracy possible under high capitalism? Weber asked, and answered 'freedom and democracy are only possible where the resolute will of a nation not to allow itself to be ruled like sheep is permanently alive ... The historical origin of modern freedom has had certain unique preconditions which will never repeat themselves'.[5] Weber also questioned the assumption implicit in Condorcet's version of progress that sciences (natural, moral and political sciences) will determine both the 'end' and the 'means' of progress. In answer to the question what the meaning of science is, he says:

> Tolstoy has given the simplest answer with the words 'Science is meaningless because it gives no answer to our question, the

only question important for us. What shall we be and how shall we live? That science does not give an answer to this is indisputable. The only question that remains is the sense in which science gives 'no answer' and whether or not science might yet be of some use to the one who puts the question correctly'.[6]

Space would not permit us to examine Weber's concept of rationality (Zwekrationalitat) at any length. Through a minute analysis of rationality, Weber tries to show that increasing rationalization of the society and the bureaucratic organization of work to which it leads, constitute both development (in the sense of emancipation of man from the slavery of nature) as well as dehumanization or reification (in the sense of 'mechanized petrification' – reduction of man to an anonymous inanimate nullity). We mention this point in spite of the fact that it is a sore spot in Weber's theory of action because it provides the much-needed context along with other Enlightenment concepts such as time, history, freedom, progress, etc., for a proper appreciation of D.P. Mukerji's views on the modern organization of work and community life.

II

Modernity has been a major influence in the intellectual development of Professor Mukerji, which can be traced to his mental socialization through the English language. In Professor Mukerji's own opinion, the English language has played a big role in the modernization of traditional Indlan elite. But modernization in their case has meant only their Anglicization. The Indian intellectuals as Professor Mukerji says 'were not westernized; they were only anglicized';[7] all that they learnt about the modern west was through the English language which acted both like a window and an 'iron curtain' against continental ideas. However, in saying that Indian intellectuals were only anglicized, Professor Mukerji is not saying that they were not modernized; he is only suggesting that all that they learnt about the modernizing ideals was through the English language. They had no exposure to modern ideas and values through other

European languages. But, the fascination exercised by the English language on the mind of the new elite was so deep that even writers in the vernaculars such as those writing in Bengali were getting habituated to processing their thoughts in English before expressing them in their own language. As a result, the self of the writer was split and has ever remained split. It is another thing that this split personality, according to Professor Mukerji, was mot suited for creative work.[8]

These observations of Professor Mukerji's on Indian intellectuals, in particular about the Bengali writers, have an autobiographical touch about them – it is perhaps D.P. Mukerji himself speaking of his divided personality – his fascination for modernity as well as his love for the roots. This explains why in every piece that he has written, be it on economic theory, planning, Indian culture or personality, his divided loyalty to his anglicized and Indianselves stands in bold relief. However, it will not be very safe to describe D.P. either as a thorough-going modernist or a down-right traditionalist. But one can easily see the difference between the D.P. Mukerji of 'Personality and the Social Sciences' and the D.P. Mukerji of 'Modern Indian Culture'.

III

Personality and the Social Sciences is an introduction to a theory of society, of which personality as the core concept and progress, equality and freedom as subsidiary concepts, constitute the central point. The latter three concepts and the social reality they represent have been, as would be clear from what we have said above, the major preoccupation of Enlightenment thinkers. D.P. Mukerji's main thesis in this essay is that freedom, equality and progress are the sine qua non of the development of personality, which is another way of saying that they essentially derive their meaning from their relationships with personality. 'Social progress', writes Mukerji, 'in the sense of a mere movement of the milieu of folk, place and time, becomes an obstruction, a process without values, if we exclude the individual'.[9] Looked at from this angle, all social change is a means to the realization of a single objective, viz., the development of personality; neither can social progress as a determination of social change have any end other than this, that is, the development of personality.

Personality, as Professor Mukerji understands the term, is that residual element of the person – *Purusha* – which remains unexplained after every ostensible layer of man's life – biological, social and cultural – has been explained in behavioural terms. It is that element which determines how acts are to be invested with values. The person of the individual can be psychologically divided into as many 'personalities' as there are spheres of action or valuation. But since none of these personalities is autonomous and capable of existing without the other, they all presuppose a transcending principle of organization and coordination; the principle which can neither be dissociated from the individual like other dimensions, nor explained in terms of any of these. It is this principle, or the super personality which D.P. Mukerji calls personality proper, but which as he further remarks 'need not be god, need not be soul, nor any other such mystic substance'.[10] Had the term not become discipline specific, one could equate it with the Reality envisioned and described in the Upanishads as 'Shantam, Shivam and Advaitam' or as the first principle of Godhead, in the western classical and medieval traditions.

The first ingredient of this triad is the principle of harmony which sustains the universe amidst all its incessant changes, the second is the principle of coordination in the social environment and the third is the principle of Unity, 'which transcends all the diverse form of states, behaviours and conflicts, and permeates thought and action with ineffable joy'.[11] We thus arrive at a three-fold concept of the Ultimate Value, viz., of Peace, Welfare and Unity. Life becomes charged with meaning only when the individual begins seriously and consciously to realize this three-fold principle in his life, and it is in and through such realization that he attains to the height of his personality.[12] Progress then consists in the development of personality through a conscious realization of the three-fold Principle of Harmony, Welfare and Unity.

D.P. Mukerji, in another context, distinguishes between the *Purusha* and the *Vyakti*.[13] The term *Vyakti*, the individual, he says, has rarely been used in the sense of the human person in the sacred literature of the Hindus. The individual in the modern societies is nothing more than an abstract entity, conceived as part of the reified collectivity called society; it matters little whether we designate him as a free or a sovereign entity. On this point, there is a remarkable similarity between the views of Mukerji and those of Martin Bubber[14] who draws a similar distinction between the 'community' and the 'atrophied collectivity' and again between those of Mukerji's and Tonnie's[15] who also contrasts the 'living community', the Gameinschaft with the 'abstract association', the Gesselschaft, basing the former on 'natural will' and the latter on 'rational will'. The French orientalist Rene Guenon, very much like D.P. Mukerji, translates the Purush of the Vedic mythology (also of the Samkhya philosophy) as 'Personality'. The *Purush* or Personality according to Rene Guenon is the First Principle of life.[16]

Mukerji, however, avoids identifying the First Principle with anyone of its determinations like God or soul, from which one gets the impression that in Mukerji's philosophy the Purusha or Personality is not a metaphysical principle but basically the 'precipitate of history' injected into the human person like Kardiners'[17a] concept of 'the basic personality structure' or Pierre Bourdieu's concept of 'habitus'.[17b]

Again in his subsequent lectures and essays such as Philosophy of Indian History, Indian Tradition and Social Change, and Modern Indian Culture, something like a historistic vision is prominently flashed out. But as we shall have an occasion to see in what follows, D.P.'s philosophy of history is different from those of conventional historicist such as Karl Mannheim, etc. Young D.P. in his 'Personality and the Social Sciences' is a traditional Indian sociologist trying to interpret the otherwise abstract and vacuous concepts of freedom, equality, progress, etc., born of the age of Enlightenment in terms of Hindu metaphysics.

Let us take, for instance, Mukerji's view of 'time', the concept which figures so prominently in the Enlightenment philosophy of history. Time, for Mukerji is the principle which imparts dynamism to events, if at all a separation of events from 'time' could be thought of. He examines the concept of time in all its three senses of 'abstract time', 'social time' and 'timeless time'. The first two imply succession – an irreversible moment – of the past, present and the future. But, the third is a state in which unlike in the first two cases, there is no movement, no direction, no succession; it is time as conquered by Indian mystics a glimpse of which can be had from the state of *sushupti* (dreamless sleep) or what the Upanishads call prajna. But Mukerji has nothing to do with any of the two concepts of abstract time and durationless time. His own preference is for the concept of 'social time' which is constructed by each individual under the influence of the society in which he lives. In other words, time for Mukerji is a social category, basically a dimension of life; time conceived as metaphysically prior to the universe is nonsense, and the victory attained by the mystics over 'time' in their nirvikalpa *samadhi* is only a pyrrhic victory as it is gained at the tremendous cost of losing touch with the society.

D.P. Mukerji is *a la* Whitehead, does not consider time as an independent terminus of knowledge. For, duration in his opinion, can be experienced only through our senses. That is to say, time has meaning only because it is the connecting link between events, which link requires an individual or a group to perceive or contrive it. In other words, it is the individual, the human being who confers meaning upon abstract time by transforming it into action. In this process of endowing abstract time with meanings and values, the individual also attains freedom from the necessity of conforming to an external series of temporal constructs.[18]

It is clear then that Mukerji does not accept the modernist concept of time which is the defining principle of history; according to him it is history which gives meaning to time. His rejection of timeless time, however, is relative; he never tries to reduce it to social time or to view it as a reflection of social time as do Durkheim and others like him.

The question of social equality is again taken up by Mukerji in the context of his theory of personality. Social equality for him is essentially a value, an ideal superimposed upon the uneven surface of biological inequality. How to reconcile the claims of social equality with the hard fact of biological inequality is then the problem that the theories or egalitarian planning have to resolve. He cites some important studies like the one conducted by Karl Pearson to show that the gradation of the body social is not a historical anomaly; but 'the result of long continued selection, and economic differentiation in the classes'. But who will be inclined to accept such research findings in the post-Gandhi era in India, Mukerji asks. It is nevertheless true that there cannot be perfect equality in the society, nor will any such utopian state be conducive to general welfare. Modern philosophers of equality like Rawls, therefore, take the stand that inequality that can promote general welfare and ensure greater efficiency in the performance of social tasks will not be inconsistent with the idea of equality.[19] Dahrendorf's justification of social inequality is based on similar grounds.[20]

In D.P. Mukerji's view, the real test of equality is whether it can provide the right opportunity for self-expression to the individual or in other words, whether it can promote the development of personality. Thus understood, equality is the symbol of personality; it is 'the mantrum' as he says 'to exercise the group mind'. The idea is that lesser the regimentation of the individual, the greater will be his freedom for self-expression, which is an essential ingredient of personality development. If the individual has the right milieu to give proper expression to his workmanship without any interference from the group or the society, he will be truly equal to others. As he puts it, '... a proportionality of social stimulus with reference to the responsiveness of the individual is the equality which is the most important condition precedent to the development of personality'.[21]

D.P. Mukerji next turns to social control to examine its relevance to the theory of personality.[22] The two pre-suppositions of social control according to him are the necessity for order and secondly, the existence of a particular controlling authority, which has its own scheme of order believed in by itself. For an Indian sociologist, there are two types of social control imaginable, viz., the western type by class and the Hindu type by caste, both of which have been found to be out of date or inconsistent with the dignity of man. In the class type of social control, the existing order is sought to be substituted by a new order as has been done in Soviet Union. The Russian type of social control has its own merit, but it has not been able to ensure the emergence of the ideal personality as envisaged by Marx and Gorky. The other type of social control as exemplified in the Indian caste system has triggered violent reactions against itself, in the form of organized protests from the depressed classes.

However, these developments in India are not the result of a planned change; they are on the other hand outbursts, spontaneous and unconscious of pent-up feelings. Communism therefore has a natural appeal to the Indian mind as it is outwardly more rational and fairer than the Indian system. But, if communism disturbs the traditional makeup of the Indian mind, as it wants to do, it will not only be met with opposition but rejected as an impracticable and undesirable[23] alternative. India has always been ruled by what Mukerji calls *samaj-dharma* as revealed in the *srutis* and as perpetuated by the *smritis*. Caste *panchayatas, shrenis, pugas,* etc., have been the ultimate repository of power in India, the monarch being only the agent of *samaj-dharma*. Hence, the situation in India is still not favourable to the emergence of a system of social control like that in the west, which means that 'before communism is introduced, national memory will have to be smudged and new habits acquired'.[24] Out traditions do not favour the formation of such habits. Nor is the Indian society, as it is today, favourable to the development of personality. For, what is involved in personality development is the principle of Unity: a discovery and realization of harmony, i.e., oneness with the absolute and the prescription of a course of action by the master, the guru, in the initial stages of spiritual life to which social life was also meant to lead.[25] Accordingly, the Hindu scheme of life had provided a curriculum for every stage of the individual's life. A system of self-culture by direct realization, with the assistance of a guru is thus the keynote of the Hindu culture of personality, which is different from the communistic culture of collective guidance by an impersonal authority. However, *samaj-dharma* was ultimately to be subordinated to *swadharma* without which the individual could not become a real king in his own kingdom. In fact, family life or social life was only a stage in the self-realization of the individual through communion with the absolute.[26]

D.P. Mukerji blames the British administration for not offering India anything like its own institution of citizenship in place of the caste system which it has sought to destroy. He would favour the rejection of the communist system of social planning and the replacement at the same time, of a caste system by what he calls a 'creative civic sense' which alone could ensure that the controlling authority is vested in the people who instead of being interested in the controlled development of others, will be interested in their own development in accordance with the abiding principle of self-culture or *swaraj* for becoming *swarat*, kings of their own selves. Only a creative civic sense understood in this sense can foster a feeling of disinterested love and fellowship among the people.

IV

We have tried to trace the development of D.P. Mukerji's thought in chronological rather than the logical order for one good reason that the various aspects of his thinking on man and the society are a reflection of the level of his participation in the intellectual debates of his time. He was trained as an economist and a historian. He came to sociology not for pursuing the subject for its own sake, but for the development, in his own words, of his personality through the study of man. Everything that he studied, and his vision was encyclopedic, was part, in other words, of his larger quest of himself. He preferred to choose a career in history and sociology rather than in natural science as he was able to discover early in his career that social sciences could provide a surer lead to tautology than the natural sciences. This explains his repeated emphasis on the fact that sociology like all our *shastras* 'will have to show the way out of the social system', i.e., to show the path to self-knowledge, *atmavidya,* rather than remain enclosed within its own shell. This is truly the way how knowledge could be liberating; such liberation through knowledge being different from the emancipation of man as contemplated under the guidance of Enlightenment Reason. Liberation identical with self-knowledge is enfranchisement of the individual, his final release from bondage, the root cause of both worldly pain and pleasure. The different social disciplines to the Indian person, according to Mukerji, are the rings of the tree of life which for him has the roots up and above, with no Yaggadrasil to burrow from below.[27]

The nature of sociology being what it is, viz., a method of self-knowledge to be finally discarded – Professor Mukerji does not consider sociology to be the final science, which he says he may abandon some day – it is not enough that the Indian sociologist be a conventional sociologist extending the principles of European sociology to Indian culture. In fact, he must be an Indian first and a sociologist later. For, he must share the folk-ways, mores and customs of his own society for a proper understanding of what is beneath and what is beyond it; and to be able to so understand it, he must be fully conversant with Sanskrit or any such language through which Indian traditions have been transmitted. It is not for nothing therefore that he decries the Indian scholar's craze for modern scientific techniques imported from the outside for the study of his own society or culture. These techniques are too superficial to be able to render a complete account of the Indian social reality revealing itself as it does through traditional symbols which conceal more than they express.

Mukerji takes tradition both its historical and metaphysical aspects. *Shrutis, smriti* and *itihas* are all equally valid sources of tradition. But while its revelatory character is not under dispute, the historicity of traditions can also not be questioned. They are, as he says, 'quoted, recalled and esteemed', which is to say that they change. The task of dynamic sociology is to study, particularly the indigenous or immanent changes in tradition because exogenous changes may be well-known.

He laments the 'theory-shyness' of Indian social scientists, by which phrase he means narrow vision; they take one or two variables and try to deduce isolated propositions from them. Theory, for Mukerji, is a 'generalization which logically hangs together the isolated propositions of the social discipline from which statements of invariance can be derived'.[28] More than an abstraction, Mukerji's concept of theory is a live picture at that, not a disconnected set of isolated propositions but an integralist corpus of social facts.

In equating the subject matter of sociology with tradition, Mukerji brings sociology closer to history, which again in his own style he calls the study of culture. If sociology is basically the study of tradition, then it cannot be a variant of an abstractly conceived theory of society as the European fathers of the discipline had thought it to be. In this respect, he totally departs from the Enlightenment tradition of a single uniform theory of society, a single uniform government and a single uniform theory of moral and legal disciplines. If comparison need be made, D.P. would come closer to Montesquieu who, despite his Enlightenment legacy, took the stand that since the rules of life varied with the conditions of existence and also in view of the diversity of societal types, all must be considered equally normal and no attempt be made to lay down the rules valid for all people.[29]

Theoretical pluralism is modern sociological craze; all post-modern social theorists, rejecting everything resembling a grand narrative or an overarching theory of man emanating from Enlightenment Reason. We preferred instead to place D.P. in the line of Montesquieu rather than any post-modern philosopher because in Montesquieu, there was a social thinker in Europe in the 19th century who had the courage to disagree with the prevailing philosophy of the age, being in this sense a rebel. Nearer home in India, we have in D.P. another early 20th century social philosopher who unlike his Indian contemporaries like Biony Kumar Sarkar and others who were writing on the positive background of Hindu sociology, was trying to invest the concept of positive sociology with traditional Indian meaning or putting life and blood into it, another rebel of the same order.

One more point and we close, and that about D.P. Mukerji's view of history. We have already seen above how Mukerji virtually equates sociology with history in its dynamic aspect. It is another thing that Indian history has not lived up to his expectation of being a study of culture and has focused instead on the rise and fall of kings and kingdoms or else on the Indian middle class's false sense of patriotism. Yet, another drawback from which history in general has suffered is its obsession with value-neutrality, the ideal of objectivity as propagated by physical science. This obsession has created among other things an artificially though unnecessary divide between theory and practice in the sciences, a divide which has not left even history untouched. He does not accept the ideal of value-neutrality either for science or for history. His stand, on the other hand, is that neither can the physicist study physical phenomenon without getting involved in them, nor can the historian study culture without participating in the life of culture. He fully endorses Edgar Wind's view that a pure mind can never study physics nor can a pure mind ever study history. Neither is the physicist a physical apparatus, nor is the historian a historical document.[30]

D.P. Mukerji thus rejects the reductionist view of history implicit in the theories of western historians who try to reduce unique cultural events to general laws. History is not an extension of mechanistic methodology to cultural phenomena; in fact, it has its own philosophy, which of course can not be universal, instead it is culture-specific. If the Indian history looks like a lifeless record of external changes in the body social of the Indian culture, it is only because it has failed to look at the Indian culture in the way scholars like Aurobindo have looked at it, i.e., in its essential spiritual aspect. Among the western historians, Mukerji would be inclined to accept the view of Wilheim Dilthey, with reservations of course, as Dilthey despite his rejection of the natural science method for the study of history, and his preference for the hermeneutic method for Geistwissenschaften, makes the past an extension of the present, the present which has hardly any presentness about it in the Kantian or Enlightenment sense of the term. In Mukerji's view, the present is only a reliving of the past. Understanding the past in terms of the present as suggested by Dilthey cannot therefore be accepted as the proper scope of history.

D.P. Mukerji again thinks that the artificial divide between theory and practice has made the traditional Indian history a vehicle of static recurrent time. Transcendental time which describes the ascent of the soul through various stages of time to a stage when time is transcended (known as Kaltyag) and the soul becomes one with absolute reality may be most useful in the individuals' salvation; it has a philosophy of change but the change is of the individual, and not of the living collectivity. But it will not do today. What we need today is a concept of time, which will be 'open and responsive to deliberate changes of collective efforts and living. Through this change from transcendental to human time philosophy will become one with history or philosophy will be at least worthy of history'. This is how the divide between theory and practice could be removed.

It would appear that he neither accepts the traditional concept of history, nor does he accept the traditional concept of time. This impression will not be wholly incorrect but what would be misleading, is the view that Mukerji accepts the modernist concept of time or the modernist concept of history, in any one of its forms. For all his advocacy of a philosophy of change and of the making of history, D.P. never identified himself with any ideology, for it was a part of his conviction that ideologies reflect vested interests and philosophies often protect status quo. He was constantly on guard against being dubbed a vulgar Marxist. He often contributed articles to journal under the pen-name 'Marxologist', suggesting thereby that his approach even to Marxism, a philosophy of action for which he had great respect, was not one of a doctrinaire, but of a critical sociologist.

The historicist bias as we hinted above is definitely present in his thought. But unlike Mannheim, he does not absolutize it. Against the claim of Enlightenment philosophy that history could be transcended by claiming a privileged position for the 'formal categories of Reason', Mannheim had come forward with the thesis that the categories of Reason undergo a process of alteration of meaning in the course of intellectual history. But he was fully conscious of the damaging consequences of both 'an ahistorical formation and a subjectivistic historicism' and it was to undo these consequences that he proposed a new branch of sociology, viz., the sociology of knowledge, to see how an inter-translation of perspectives could be accomplished and how the objective core of non-perspectivist thought could be identified. It is another thing that Mannheim could not take care of the historicality of his own thought.[31] In emphasizing the social-historical nature of time, Mukerji not only bids goodbye to the concept of formal time, but puts time in place. He does not discard the idea of *kaltyag*, nor does he reject the notion of timeless Time; he only regrets the over intellectualization of the Indian tradition which eventually led to its bifurcation into great and little traditions. Philosophy becoming history or becoming worthy of history is just another way of saying that philosophy in India was always meant to be lived; it was no toying with ideas, no dilettantism; which explains the identity of knowledge-as and knowledge-of, in the Indian tradition. His mind has always stayed on the margins of thought, for after all he was a modern scholar and an anglicized Bengali intellectual to boot. His stress on the unity of theory and practice is again not to be mistaken as a Marxian predilection. There is much talk in Marxism about this unity in revolutionary action under socialism.

The meaning of the word 'theoria' in the Greek tradition, particularly in Aristotle's psychology is 'contemplation' which means a fully conscious participation in Being in which the soul's potential knowledge (its ordinary state) becomes actual, so that man can at last claim to be 'awake'.[32] Self-knowledge which is identical with self-realization in the Indian tradition is also a state of 'awakening' of the self, *atmaprabodh* as *Gandpad* calls it, when the distinction between knowledge and the so-called object of knowledge is dissolved. The unity of theory and practice in revolutionary activity in Marxian philosophy is notional unification of two reified concepts. Horkheimer like D.P. also had an aversion for closed philosophical systems; he not only criticized

Hegel's metaphysics of the unity of the spirit and phenomenon, but was critical of ossified Marxism too. Hegel's spirit he wrote, 'may not be a mere abstraction but it will never be identical with reality'. Horkheimer again disagreed with Lukacs' theory of identity of subject and object of history – the proletariat. There is much in D.P.'s writings to mistake him as a Lucknow Frankfurter. Horkheimer was equally fascinated by Dilthey but like D.P., he did not accept his philosophy of history in toto, for different reasons though. D.P. thought Dilthey was reducing the past to the present, while Horkheimer thought the meaning of history could not be fully grasped even by an intuitive understanding of the past because the past, after all, has been made by man consciously, behind the backs and against the wills of man as Marx said. But unlike the Frankfurters, D.P. was not trying to rescue Marxism from European Communism; neither culture from the basic structure of the society, nor man from both socialist and bourgeois alienation. But he did share with them their critical outlook and cultural suavity. The direction of his intellectual interest, to my mind, lay in his effort to discover new meanings in the traditional Indian symbols which could be conducive to the argumentation of personality even in this age of fading lights and broken cultures.

Notes

1. Kant, Immanuel: An answer to the Question what is Enlightenment, quoted in 'Modernity is a Qualitative not a Chronological Category' by Osborne Peter, *New Left Review* 192, March-April, 1992, p. 79.
2. See Habermas: *The Philosophical Discourse of Modernity*. Cambridge: Polity Press, 1990.
3. See Bernstein, Richard: *The New Constellation*. Cambridge: Polity Press,1990, pp. 333–341.
4. Weber, Max: *Protestant Ethic and the Spirit of Capitalism*. Trans. Talcott Parsons, New York: Scribner's, 1958.
5. Weber, Max: *From Max Weber: Essays in Sociology*. Trans. H.H. Gerth and C. Wright Mills, New York: Oxford University Press, 1968, p. 71.
6. Weber, Max: 'Science as a Vocation', in *From Max Weber: Essays in Sociology*. New York: Oxford University Press, 1948, p. 143.

7. Mukerji, D.P.: *The Intellectuals in India, in Diversities*. New Delhi: Peoples' Publishing House, 1958, p. 247.
8. Ibid., p. 148.
9. *Personality and the Social Sciences*. Calcutta: The Book Company, 1924, p. 15.
10. Ibid., p. 33.
11. Ibid., p. 35.
12. Ibid., p. 35.
13. *Indian Tradition and Social Change, in Diversities*, New Delhi: Peoples Publishing House, 1958, p. 235.
14. Buber, Martin: *Between Man and Man*. London: Fontana Books, 1947.
15. Tonnies, Ferdinand: *Community and Association*. London: Routledge and Kegan Paul, 1955.
16. Guenon, Rene: *Man and His Becoming According to Vedant*. Trans. Richard C. Nicholson, New York: Noonday Press, Inc., 1928.

17a. See for example, Kardiner, Abram: *The Individual and His Society*. 'The basic personality structure' is made up of the cultural imperatives reflected back in the personality, i.e., the ways of acting, feeling and thinking of the individual. It is the mould in which individual behaviour is shaped.

17b. 'Habitus' is a term used by Pierre Bourdieu, a contemporary French sociologist, who defines it as 'the strategy generating principle enabling agents to cope with unforeseen and ever changing situations a system of lasting and transposable dispositions which integrating past experiences, functions at every moment as a matrix of perceptions, appreciations and actions and makes possible the achievement of infinitely diversified tasks.... It expresses first the result of an organizing action with a meaning close to that of words such as social structural; it also designates a way of being, a habitual state (specially of the body) and in particular a disposition, tendency, propensity, or inclination'. 'Habitus' is akin to the intention in action of Searle or to the 'deep structure' of Chomsky except that instead of being an anthropological invariant, this deep structure is historically constituted, institutionally grounded and thus a socially variable generative matrix. (Pierre Bourdieu and Loic Waequant: *An Invitation to Reflexive Sociology*. Great Britain: Polity Press, 1992, p. 19, including Footnote 33.

18. Op. cit., p. 28.
19. Rawls, John: *A Theory of Justice*. Cambridge Mass: Harward Unuversity Press, 1971. Rawls is of the view that we need not spurn

inequality if it helps everyone including the worst off, and ensures everyone a chance to reach the top. The benefits earned by a few could be justified if the situation of the worst off thereby improved; if for instance because of the performance of the managing director who is more equal than others, the peon also gets bonus.

20. Dahrendorf, R.: 'The Nature and Types of Social Inequality' in *Social Inequality*. Eds Beteille, Andre, London: Penguin Books, 1969/1984.

    The system of inequality that we call social stratification is in Dahrendorf's opinion only a secondary consequence of the social structure of power. There is no society which is without power or authority. 'The very existence of social inequality' says Dahrendorf 'however is an impetus towards liberty because it guarantees a society's ongoing dynamic, historical quality', p. 42.

21. *Personality, and The Social Sciences*, Florida Book Co., 1924, p. 68.
22. Ibid., pp. 123–152.
23. Ibid., p. 127.
24. Ibid., p. 136.
25. Ibid., p. 144.
26. Ibid., p. 148.
27. *Indian Tradition and Social Change, in Diversities*. New Delhi: Peoples Publishing House, 1958, p. 240.
28. Ibid., p. 240.
29. Ambivalent Cartesians; Durkheim, Montesquieu and Method by Jones, R.A. *American Journal of Sociology*, July, 1994, p. 19.
30. *Philosophy of Indian History, in Diversities*, New Delhi: Peoples Publishing Houses, 1958, p. 144.
31. Mannheim could not effectively defend his stand as taken in the 'Sociology of Knowledge' or in his discussions on 'historicism' against the criticism that his own thought was imprisoned within the historical context of meaning. Nor could even Gadamar and other exponents of the hermeneutic method overcome the dilemma of self-reference by the idea of 'a hermeneutic circle' which after all remains a circle and a vicious one, the part being explained through the whole and the whole through the part. See for example, Simmonds, A.P., Mannheim's *Sociology of Knowledge*. Oxford: Clarendon Press, 1978, p. 86.
32. See Barfield, Owen: *Saving the Appearances*. London: Faber and Faber, 1957, p. 49.

8

The Concept of Ritual in Retrospect

A Critical Review

The important point that emerges from the foregoing review of the various theories of ritual is that ritual is a special type of action standing in direct contrast to ordinary actions and that it is a universal feature of both primitive and modern societies. A problem is thus presented before the sociologists: how to explain the significance of actions which are neither rational nor even irrational, for they form an indispensable part of social life. Implicitly or explicitly, all the thinkers agree that the study of such actions is essentially the study of symbolism and its role in the society.

Durkheim takes religion in its entirety to be the symbol of society which in his theory is the basic ontological category. He makes it quite clear that religious action is purely symbolic and it would be futile even to attempt a rational justification of it. According to Weber also, ritual is a meaningful action par excellence but an action whose meaning is not the function of its motive, for it is entirely a motiveless action. Thus, the contrast between rational and ritual actions stands in equally sharp relief in both Durkheim's and Weber's theories, and both the thinkers seem equally aware, although in their own ways, of the need for according a special treatment to religious action. Much the same awareness is reflected in the views of Malinowski and Radcliffe-Brown, in spite of the fact that they approach the problem from the still narrower angle of the social anthropologist. Malinowski explicitly recognizes the non-instrumental character of ritual and places it in the category of integrative imperatives. Radcliffe-Brown goes a step further than Malinowski, although his theory in no way involves any radical departure from the basic functionalist stand of the latter, and unequivocally admits the symbolic character of ritual as well as the need for a semantic method for its study. The crucial issue in the sociological theory of ritual would thus seem to revolve around the question: what is the precise relation between rational action and symbolic action? The question obviously involves a consideration of the nature of symbolic action and its place in the theoretical framework of sociology. The sociologists have considered the question each in their own way. And as we said, there is no basic difference in the manner of their formulation of the issue. Nor is there much difference in the solution that they each suggest for it. Ritual has invariably been shown to be a socially necessary act, as one which promotes group cohesiveness (Durkheim); or as one which sacralizes tradition and acts as a guarantee of legitimate order (Weber); or again as one that allays anxiety, protects the social organization against the forces of instability and keeps it in a state of balance (Malinowski and Radcliffe-Brown).

Ritual is a transcendentally[1] necessary act, which means that the reality that it symbolizes is neither social nor moral, but metaphysical. Since modern sociological theory begins with a repudiation of the metaphysical basis of social order, the only explanation that it can offer for symbolic forms such as myth and ritual must be conceived in rational terms. So, while every theory begins with a distinction between ritual and rational actions, it ends up by showing the former to be a specific instance of the latter. If the routine concept of rationality fails, another broader concept of rationality implying social purposiveness is posited and made to account for all other activities which do not come within the meaning of the former. On this score, there is not much to distinguish between the causal-functional and the causal-meaningful theories. Durkheim and Weber, Malinowski and Radcliffe-Brown, all alike, treat ritual as an exemplification of social rationality.

The concept of rationality does not figure at all in Durkheim's theory. But it is quite obvious from his manner of formulation of the distinction between the sacred and profane that Durkheim is thinking in terms of the distinction between ordinary rationality and social rationality. The profane activities, in his view, are all purposive activities occupying the major part of the life of the primitives; they are concerned with the fulfillment of specific rational ends. But, the sacred activities are non-purposive in this sense; they are performed on special occasions and if at all they have a purpose, it is pre-eminently a social purpose; they promote, perpetuate and revitalize the collective conscience. So in spite of all the emphasis that Durkheim lays on the discontinuity of the sacred and profane, he fails to evolve a truly distinct concept of the sacred and ultimately makes it a type case of the profane. To suggest that sacred activities serve collective ends, is just another way of saying that they serve larger rational ends, while the profane activities serve only smaller rational ends.

The main source of confusion in Durkheim's theory is to be found in his failure to distinguish correctly between collective representations and that which they represent. If social facts are collective representations, then the reality which they represent must be other than what they themselves are in other words, it can not be social. Durkheim seems quite anxious, no doubt, not to confuse between society and social facts which he only regards as indices of the former.[2] But if he had been serious about this point, he would not seek to derive the categories of understanding such as space, time, class, etc., from the physical arrangement of clans and dispersion of activities in the primitive world. Here then is a blatant contradiction in Durkheim's theory: he considers society as a transcendental reality but at the same time he equates it with such relative phenomena as clan solidarity, sacredness, division of labour, etc. Consistently with his stand, he ought to have placed society above the dichotomy of the sacred and profane, moral and immoral. But by making sacredness and morality it's defining criteria, he virtually reduces society to a relative category.

The cardinal point of Durkheim's theory is the presupposed discontinuity of the sacred and profane. But, in effect, his concept of the sacred is nothing but a continuation of the profane. Having failed to discover any rational motive behind religious actions, he proceeds to analyse them as symbolic actions. But then, instead of explaining symbolic action in its own terms, i.e., in terms of a theory of symbolism, he tries to explain it in terms of its function. Thus, he seems to accord the same treatment to religious actions in the context of society as he accords to profane actions in the context of individual. Durkheim's whole argument can be summed up in two sentences: profane actions are rational-purposive; even so are symbolic actions rational-purposive but the rationality of symbolic actions is quite different from that of profane actions; it is pre-eminently social.

It can be easily seen that Durkheim's concept of ritual is built upon the self-same mistake which has underlain sociological theory since its inception. It has been the main concern of sociologists from the very beginning to prove that sociocultural phenomena can be described in the same categories as are generally employed for the description of natural phenomena. Both the traditions of sociological thought, the positivistic and the idealistic, proceed on the assumption that social reality can be subsumed under the general law of nature. In fact, the only difference between the two traditions is that while the former tries to subsume the entire range of social facts under the law of causality, the latter allows a little margin for the residual elements (certain meanings, values and norms) which are not reducible to any aspect of nature. It is mainly for this reason that we have alternatively called the latter tradition causal-meaningful. In principle, no doubt, Durkheim is opposed to the reductionist approach. This is evident from his stress on the uniqueness, the *sui generis* character of the social reality. But his approach fails him and he slips into the same reductionist position which he is all too keen to avoid. While on the one hand, he makes nature an epiphenomenon of society, reducing space, time and causality to certain specific states of social life, on the other hand, he reduces sacred action, the truest expression of the social to a specific state of rationality (profaneness). The logical fallacy involved in the reductionist interpretation is what Ryle calls the fallacy of wrong disjunction of terms.[3] It is not only Durkheim, but as we shall see below, Weber, Malinowski and Radcliffe-Brown all alike have perpetuated this fallacy in their interpretations of ritual in one way or another.

Weber's approach upto a point is quite logical and realistic. He proceeds with a typology of action, analyses each type and then considers their mutual relationship. But in his theory of action too, religious action remains as problematic as it is in the theory of Emile Durkheim. He too, like Durkheim, admits that religious action must be looked upon as a complex of meanings, as symbolic action to put it in other words. In fact, all actions according to him are meaningful and in a way his whole approach to sociology is semantic. When we say that his approach is realistic what we mean is that Weber makes out a particular case in terms of a theory of symbolism. The distinction that he draws between *zwekrational, wertrational* and traditional actions can be properly grounded only on a theory of symbolism. But even though he formulates the problem correctly in the beginning, he fails to pick it up and tackle it properly, if he had followed the logic of his approach consistently he would have been obliged to formulate a theory of meaning which would have not only helped him to arrive at a correct understanding of the symbolism of rite, but it would have also enabled him to show the proper relationship between symbolism and social actions.

Weber clearly admits the transcendentality of ritual when he brings in the concept of charisma to explain it, for charisma in his treatment is undoubtedly a trans-social and trans-rational category. It is equally clear from his analysis of the role of religious action that he considers ritual as the primary basis of social organization. For Durkheim, it is only a part of the social tradition, but for Weber it is the very source of the latter. But Weber's commitment to the positivistic methodology was too strong perhaps to allow him to maintain this stand throughout and ultimately he also drifts into the same reductionist position into which Durkheim eventually found himself. He too reduces ritual to a specific form of rationality. As we have already pointed out, Weber fails to distinguish religious action from *wertrational* and traditional actions. Although his main aim seems to be to show that traditional actions are different from *wertrational* actions and that religious actions are only a species of the latter, yet in his actual treatment all the three types are bracketed together and rendered semantically equivalent to one another.

It can be easily seen that his confusion is rooted in the very structure of Weber's theory of action. Weber's theory of action, as we have shown, revolves around the concept of rationality, which is used by him in two senses. In the first place, he uses it to designate actions which involve adjustment of mean to ends without any commitment to ethical norms or values considered absolute by the actor. Secondly, he uses it to refer to actions which involve adjustment of means to ends within a given normative framework. The former he calls formal rationality and the latter, substantive rationality. Measured along this scale of rationality, the four types of action mentioned by Weber can be viewed as expressions of formal rationality (*zwekrational* action) or of substantive rationality (*wertrational* action) or of irrationality (traditional and affectual actions). That is to say, Weber's classification of action like Pareto's is based on the distinction between rationality and non-rationality (logical and non-logical in Pareto's terms). And like Pareto, Weber also subdivides non-rationality into trans-rationality (substantive rationality) and irrationality.

Now because of the crucial role that ritual plays in a social organization, Weber is unwilling to dismiss it as a residual type. At the same time, he is unable to find any rational basis for it. Therefore, the only way in which he could explain it was to view it as a special type of rational action. This explains why at times he seems to be equating it with *wertrational* action and to others with traditional action. Thus even though he attaches considerable importance to religious action, in effect he regards it as a mere substitute for rational action. In fact, despite all his stress on the understanding of meanings, Weber fails to ground his theory of action on a sound theory of symbolism. His initial approach was quite logical; he wanted to evolve an independent method of sociological analysis.

But he never succeeded in his aim and sociology in his hands remained tied to the apron strings of the natural sciences. What actually misled Weber into the reductionist position was, perhaps, his attempt to demonstrate the nomothetic character of interpretive sociology. He was an exponent of sociological idealism but he never seriously stuck to his stand. If sociology was concerned with the understanding of meaning relationships, then it could not rest content with the causal explanation. The way Weber has tried to handle the problem of meaning gives the impression that meaning is nothing but an arbitrary superimposition on the cause-effect relationship. It is no wonder then that he should try to reduce the significance of symbolism to its social efficacy. There is nothing surprising again in Weber's attempt to narrow down the meaning of understanding to a causal explanation of actions and their underlying motives. As we have remarked earlier, meaning relations are hardly amenable to scientific explanation. Therefore, if they are to be admitted as a component of social organization, they must be treated on their own plane. To subsume them under familiar categories just because we are unfamiliar with the categories into which they can be adequately expressed, would be a mistake.

As we said, the functional theories have developed as a part of the positivist tradition of sociological thought. Obviously, therefore, their main aim is to evolve a scientific concept of ritual or, in other words, to show that ritual or for that matter all symbolic forms are susceptible of a causal explanation. The principal concern of both Malinowski and Radcliffe-Brown is to show that magico-religious practices, for all their dissimilarity to routine activities, are rooted in the same vital needs as constitute the basis of the latter. The basic needs and problems of both primitive and modern man are almost the same. But while modern man makes increasing use of rational mechanisms for the solution of his problems, primitive man, for the most part, depends on traditional mechanisms. Thus, symbolic action according to this view serves the same practical ends in primitive social organizations as rational actions do in modern societies. The distinction between the sacred and profane or the symbolic and rational actions, on Malinowski's and Radcliffe-Brown's showing also, happens to be a distinction between two forms of rationality: one lower and the other higher. In this respect, the functional theory of the ritual is as much reductionist as the Durkheimian or the Weberian theory.

In fact, the whole structure of the functional theory is built upon the reductionist mistake. It may be noted that the functional approach in anthropology was evolved as an alternative to the earlier evolutionary and diffusionist approaches. Malinowski, to whom goes the credit of attempting the first systematic formulation of the approach, felt that the functional method was the only method consistent with the scientific theory of culture. The assumption on which it was based is that like the biological organism, culture can also be conceived as a self-maintaining system and brought within the purview of the scientific method. What the functional theory thus aims to do is to bring socio-cultural phenomena within the unity of the scientific method.

Now, it is one of the basic postulates of scientific enquiry that its method should be adequately suited to the nature of phenomena it aims to describe. In other words, the method of scientific enquiry should be determined by the logical nature of its subject matter. The mistake that the advocates of functionalism commit is that they make the subject matter of their enquiry wholly dependent upon and relative to the method of their study. The functionalist model of culture is nothing but a parabiological model whose only claim to validity is its agreement with the scientific method. But the scientific method itself is relative in the sense that it is validated with reference to the rules of formal logic. Much of the socio-cultural sphere, as we have pointed out, is trans-logical. The method of sociological enquiry, therefore, can be validated only with reference to a trans-logical principle.

Implicit in the functional theory of culture is the idea of a suprasocial purpose which the social structure is supposed to promote through the joint functioning of its individual parts. But this idea is totally incompatible with the fundamental assumptions of the theory. For it is one of its prime concerns to deny the existence of the supreme telos or the final cause. It is for this reason perhaps that contemporary functionalists such as Parsons and Merton have sought to replace the parabiological model of culture by a paramechanical model. The final end in their analysis has been identified with the maintenance or survival of the social structure itself.

The nature of functionalism being what we have shown it to be, the problem of ritual could hardly receive a proper formulation at the hands of its advocates, to say nothing of its solution. In Malinowski's view, all actions right from the routine-end-oriented actions to the holy ritual, must have some bioempirical basis. Adverse life situations such as crises and calamities impose a peculiar psychology on the savage mind. When, for instance, death occurs, the primitive man is caught with a sense of fear and nervous anxiety. Rituals on such occasions give men confidence and allay their anxiety. This may, however, be true. But it is equally true that rituals themselves cause fear and anxiety among men, fears and anxieties from which they are ordinarily free.[4] The drawback of the psychological explanation is that it can be equally cogently put the other way round.

In spite of his commitment to the functional theory, Radcliffe-Brown applies a better perspective on the problem of symbolic action than both Malinowski and Durkheim. "One does not", he observes, "arrive at an understanding of rituals through consideration of their purpose or reason but of their meaning and whatever has a meaning is a symbol and the meaning is expressed by the symbol".[5] Radcliffe-Brown does well again, not to dissociate ritual from its essential mythic background. Since each rite is associated with a myth, its meaning must be understood in the light of cosmology, a body of ideas and beliefs about nature and human society. Durkheim and Malinowski also admit the mythic background of ritual. But they never try to explain the proper relationship between myth and ritual. The fundamental weakness of Radcliffe-Brown's theory, however, is that it is not formulated in terms of a general theory of symbolism. If ritual is symbolic action, then its meaning must be understood in terms of the language in which it is expressed. Radcliffe-Brown fully acknowledges this, but makes an attempt to determine the nature of this language. The theory of meaning implicit in his interpretation is by no means an adequate theory. Myth and rite are not, as he suggests, mere life symbols; they are rather the very source of life and association. The purpose of ritual, then, is ritual itself; partaking in its performance is an end itself and upon the fulfillment of this end, depends the continuity of both the natural and social orders.

Before concluding this review, we would like to reiterate our earlier point that sociological theory, in order to be consistent, must either reject the concept of ritual or it must give up its concept of social order. For in a social order based on rationality, there can be hardly any place for ritual. But if it must insist on retaining the concept, then it must accept it in its true meaning, which as we have shown can be understood only in terms of a sound theory of symbolism.

II

The psycho-analytic theories have their own shortcomings; some of them are inherent in their general conceptual framework and some in the theory of symbolism that they each implicitly or explicitly presuppose. A detailed examination of the conceptual framework of depth psychology will not be attempted here. But, in order to bring out the point that we aim to emphasize, a few general remarks on it will be necessary. A serious limitation on the validity of these theories is imposed by the concept of mind which, as we have shown, constitutes the central point in their explanation of human action. The concept of the unconscious occupies, no doubt, a more pivotal position in their framework, but it is essentially a dimension of the concept of mind.

The concept of mind owes its first explicit formulation, in modern times, to the French philosopher Rene Descartes. Since the Cartesian formulation of the concept has been accepted by almost all schools of modern psychological thought, a brief statement of its main points will be extremely useful in this context. Mind, according to Descartes, is an independent order of existence, but it is indissolubly linked with the body which is another equally independent order of existence. Though independent of each other, the two orders are nevertheless complementary; they are harnessed together always acting with and interacting upon one another. Bodies exist in space which is the domain of the law of mechanical causality; they are linked that is to say by cause-effect relationship. But no such connecting link seems to be present in the realm of the mind. The *modus operandi* of these temporal substances will have to be sought, therefore, in a different principle. This principle must be the law of paramechanical causality because it cannot be essentially different from the law of mechanical causality. One obvious implication of this argument is that since there is no determinable link between the temporal substances (minds), they must be supposed to be leading some kind of ghostly existences in their own insulated fields. For the advocates of this theory are hard put to it to prove that a mind is capable of knowing exactly what is going on in another mind. Even the law of paramechanical causality cannot prove it. Very aptly, therefore, Gilbert Ryle[6] calls this theory the "dogma of the ghost in the machine".

The fatal flaw of the Cartesian doctrine in Ryle's view is that it tries to explain mind in an idiom which is actually appropriate for the description of matter. If mind, as it maintains, is an independent order of existence, then it would be a mistake to interpret it in terms of the causality principle which is applicable to another order of existence. Descartes' initial error was that he treated mind and matter as two independent and ultimate orders of existence. But he further compounded the error when he destroyed the ultimacy of mind by subsuming it under the law of mechanical causality. The prevailing psychological concept of mind is none other than the Cartesian concept. In fact, modern psychology is still desperately trying to become an alter ego of physics; it aims to study the mental phenomena in much the same manner as physics studies the physical phenomena. Psycho-analysis has, no doubt, slightly deviated from the avowed aim of general psychology. It has borrowed its postulates from biology instead of physics, yet there is precious little to distinguish depth psychology from general psychology in respect of fundamental presuppositions. Of course, depth psychology's modified theory of mind has become more blatantly exposed to the Rylian criticism. The mind with its new dimension of the unconscious has a more truly ghostly appearance than the conscious mind of the earlier conception. Depth psychology is vulnerable yet to another attack, the one that was directed against Berkeley's subjective idealism. By reducing all forms of human behaviour to a projection of mind, psycho-analytic theory demolishes the objectivity of social facts in much the same way as subjective idealism destroyed the objectivity of the external world.

Its commitment to a dualistic ontology has placed modern psychology on the horns of a curious dilemma; if it must maintain its paramechanical concept of mind, then it must posit the existence of an absolute mind, a position it will never accept; on the other hand, it must believe in the paramountcy of the causality principle, then it must give up its notion of mind as an independent order of existence and be even prepared to write off its own existence as a science of mind – a still more inconvenient position for it to accept than the former. The dilemma provides the best clue to the fallacies inherent in the psychological interpretation of ritual. Since psychology is not prepared to accept the implications of its theoretical position, it is obliged to treat ritual either as a form of irrationality or at best as a projection of mind. We shall now examine the theories one by one and point out the shortcomings of their specific standpoints.

Freud seems to view life as a process of equilibration of pleasure and pain, rather as a process of avoiding pain and maximizing pleasure. Each bit of life according to him is either a manifestation of Eros (sex or love instinct) or manifestation of Thanatos (death or hate instinct). Underlying the gigantic superstructure of Freud's metapsychology is thus a materialist theory of being and a hedonistic ethics. It will be an unnecessary digression to enter into an examination of materialistic ontology and hedonistic ethics in the present context. Suffice it to say that a materialistic ontology is based on a fallacious disjunction of terms and is wholly unmaintainable. Ethical hedonism stands on the possibility of the idea of pleasure being given a precise meaning and of man being able to stand the burden of infinite pleasure. On both scores, the doctrine has been rejected.

Whatever be the therapeutic value of the Freudian psycho-analysis, its status as a theory of human behaviour is extremely dubious. Let us analyse some of its basic concepts and the meaning theory in terms of which it seeks to interpret taboo, ritual and religious phenomena in general. First, there is the concept of unconscious. Freud arrived at this concept through the study of dreams and neurotic behaviour. MacIntyre has raised a very pertinent question about the status of "the unconscious" in Freudian psychology. He remarks, "either the unconscious is an inaccessible realm of inaccessible entities existing in its own right or it is a theoretical and unobservable entity introduced to explain and relate a number of otherwise inexplicable phenomena. If it is the first, then being a real existent it requires evidence for its existence to be credible. But *ex-hypothesis* it cannot be observed and so we cannot possibly have evidence for its existence. If we dismiss this alternative as too naïve ... Then the other alternative demands that we enquire what precise explanatory role the concept of the unconscious plays. And here I find myself at a loss".[7]

Not only is it difficult to understand the explanatory function of the unconscious (despite Professor John Wisdom's[8] yield defence of the concept), it is difficult even to see how Freud could arrive at through the interpretation of dream material. For, all that dream analysis required is a decoding of the data provided by the dreams. The meaning of these data is determined not by a reference to the unconscious, but by the help primarily of the basic postulates of the Freudian theory, viz., the Oedipus complex and the pleasure-pain principle. The concept of the unconscious seems to be an interpolation; it will not make much difference to the Freudian interpretation whether we make use of the concept or not. Take for instance Freud's interpretation of religion. What is basic to this interpretation is not the concept of the unconscious but the myth of the primeval horde and the Oedipus legend. God is the image of the father and His worship an act of expiation of the guilt of patricide. Exogamy rests on the ambivalence of attraction and repulsion emotions which can be readily explained against the background of the Oedipus situation without bringing in the idea of the unconscious. Freud's major contribution to psychology was perhaps his interpretative method of analysis, of whose importance psychological theory had little awareness at least till the advent of psycho-analysis. For a proper evaluation of his theory, therefore, we had better focus our attention on his method of interpretation rather than on his theory of the unconscious, which as we have just pointed out, has only an indirect bearing on the principal tenor of his argument. But there is one more point.

As such manifestations of behaviour cannot be subsumed under the well-known conscious functions, they must, according to Freud, be considered as expressions of the unconscious. And, the unconscious is nothing but the impulse which is kept off the conscious by the censor operating within the mental process. This repressed impulse is again none other than the libidinal urge, whose satisfaction in Freud's view is the supreme purpose of life. From the point of view of the other who knows that the repressed impulse is verily the sex impulse, there is hardly anything unconscious about it. The individual concerned, say a neurotic, may be thoroughly unaware of the sources of his anxiety, but if he knows that it is the return of the repressed libido in a substitute form, then he is no longer unconscious of what is happening in his mental life: The unconscious then ceases to have any meaning for him. Given, that is to say, the basic postulates of Freudian metapsychology, it would not be difficult to account for the neurotic symptom even without invoking the authority of the unconscious.

Freud considers neurosis as the model of all forms of non-rational conduct. Every symbol, religious, artistic or literary, in the view is a substitute for the repressed sex urge. There is thus in Freud's opinion no meaning in life except the maximization of the gratification of the libido – it is the supreme value of life from which all other values are derived: "Reductive explanations of this type", as Fairboirn observes, "possess the great disadvantage of simply explaining away what they seek to explain".[9] Fairboirn further observes that the Freudian theory involves the implicit assumption that man is not a social animal by nature – an assumption which would seem to be "in complete contradiction of the facts of animal psychology". Levi[10] too criticizes Freud for his Hobbesian view of human life. But these criticisms could be dismissed as pointless if there had been no internal contradictions in the Freudian theory. If sex or pleasure were the supreme value of life, then the super ego, the introjected reality principle, could not be assigned the sovereign status that it occupies in the scheme of human life according to the Freudian view.

There is yet another contradiction in Freud's theory. The superego is treated as a more powerful agency of repression than the ego, but Freud would seem to reject this stand – when he stresses the importance of reason in the overcoming of universal neurosis of mankind, which exists in the form of religion. With the development of reason, Freud believes, man would be able to discard his religious beliefs in the same way as the neurosis produced during one's childhood automatically disappears with the growth of the ego.

Apart from these shortcomings and contradictions which bear an unequivocal testimony to the basically untenable stand taken by Freud, there are two other big fallacies in his theory of ritual. The first is his analogy of neurotic behaviour and ritual and the second, his mistaken notion of the symbol and reality. "Analogy", says Frederick Ferre, "is a relation between objects capable of being classed as a species of likeness". The likeness on which any analogy depends is "reducible to the presence in the similars of an identical abstractible characteristic".[11] One may not accept this definition of analogy, but it is clear that the analogates must share some attribute by virtue of which they can be compared.

Two types of analogy have been generally recognized: analogy of attribution and analogy of proportionality. In the former type, the first analogate possesses the attribute predicated of it in a literal sense while in the latter, it possesses it in a derivative sense. For example, we call both men and mountain resorts "healthy". When "healthy" is predicated of a man, it is predicated in a literal sense but when we say that a place or atmosphere is healthy we are using the predicate in a derived sense: the atmosphere is considered to be healthy because it conduces to the health of men living in it. In the second type of analogy, both the analogates possess the attribute in a literal sense, but the proportion in which they possess it is determined by the nature of each individual analogate. One may draw an analogy between the sky and his wife's eyes because they are both possessed of the attribute blueness. But the blueness of his wife's eyes is appropriate in this case to the female eye, while the blueness of the sky is appropriate to the sky.[12]

Now Freud's analogy of neurosis and ritual is neither an example of the first type nor of the second type. Freud noted, as we have already observed, three main points of similarity be'ween the behaviour of obsessional neurotics and religious ritual: (1) the fear of pangs of conscious following any omission of the neurotic ceremonial or the religious person's rite, (2) the complete isolation of both from all other activities, and (3) the conscientiousness with which the details are carried out. How the compulsion neurotic feels about an omission of his habitual activities, is rather difficult to determine. But one thing is certain and it is that his behaviour is more or less like a conditioned response to the inner stimuli of whose source (according to Freud) he is not aware. But the religious person performs his rituals with full awareness of what he is doing; he is perfectly conscious of the fact that it is not out of addiction that he performs the ceremonial deeds but out of sheer understanding of their transcendentally necessary character. That both the types of practices are extraordinary is no proof that they are similar; the first is a deviation from the normal routine of life, while the second is the norm in terms of which the ordinary routine of life becomes meaningful. It is absolutely wrong to think that ritual is as much an example of deviant behaviour as the conduct of the compulsion neurotic; rational behaviour is not the model of action but simply an imitation of a model which is verily the ceremonial or the ritual deed. As regards the third basis of the analogy, it is too much to say that the neurotic carries out the details of his habitual practice with any touch of conscientiousness. The neurotic, as Freud himself admits, has no awareness of why he indulges in his habits. A conscientious deed, whatever be its real meaning, is always executed with a skill and technique of which the agent has some, if not the full knowledge. The neurotic on the other hand, behaves more or less like a moron; he simply cannot help doing what he does.

This fallacious analogy is responsible for a number of confusions in the Freudian thought about the nature of religious symbolism. Freud seems to believe that the symbol is the same thing as the symptom of a disease. There is no doubt that the symptom reveals the nature of the disease, but the relation between the two is not of the same order as the relation between the symbol and its referent. The symptom is just like the sign whose meaning can be understood by a direct reference to its material counterpart. But the symbolic level of representation lies on a much higher plane than the sign-level of signification; there is no determinable counterpart of a symbol.

The pitfalls of the Freudian theory are thus many and varied. But, the radical source of error in Freud's principal argument is perhaps his wrong interpretation of the Oedipus legend. Not only does he twist the meaning of this legend, but he constructs a fresh legend – that of the primal horde – to justify his prejudices against man and his attitude towards the female sex. Alternative interpretations of the Oedipus legend are available. Fromm[13] has given one. Wheelright[14] has offered a still better one.

One may not agree even with these interpretations, but there cannot be two opinions about the fact that the legend is not an allegory of the immortal man of the Freudian conception. Oedipus is actually the archetype of modern man, ambitious and sex greedy, who is foredoomed to despair and death. Even this view of the legend may be incorrect but the fact would still remain that Freud has made a caricature of every aspect of human life that he has touched.

III

Jung's view comes very much nearer to being correct; at least it is based on sound ontological presuppositions and does not suffer from the disadvantages of a narrow psychological approach. It is entirely appropriate that Jung should not recognize the much emphasized opposition between psychology and metaphysics. Even so, there are certain grave flaws in his theory of ritual. Jung's concept individuation can be regarded as the psychological counterpart of the metaphysical concept of the pure act or the Nishkam as expounded in our introductory chapter. But the difference between the two is perhaps the same as that between the Indian concept of yoga and the Jungian idea of individuation. The former, in our opinion, is the truest psychological counterpart of the metaphysical concept of the Nishkam. Jung, however, rejects yoga as an unnatural attempt at the suppression of the conscious. This is a mistaken view of yoga but since Jung considers the relationship of the whole and the part as a perfect analogue of the relationship between the conscious and the unconscious, he could not have escaped falling into this error.

His conception of the whole-part relationship is quite understandable, but his subordination of the whole to the unconscious leaves one completely mystified. The centre of the psyche, the self which he calls the archetype of wholeness, is located, as he would have us believe, somewhere in the collective unconscious. This would mean that individuation, far from being the process of union of the part with the whole, is the process of merger of the ego or the conscious with the unconscious. In this process of union, the conscious is bound to lose its identity – an implication Jung would never accept. Is he then not advocating a method of integration which in the ultimate analysis involves the suppression of the conscious? Jung's conception of the symbol as emanating from the unconscious, despite his clear recognition of its transcendental character, lends further weight to our criticism of his basic stand. If the symbol has a transcendental character, it can not be derived from the unconscious which being only a part of the whole can not but be a relative concept.

The objection that we raised against the Freudian concept of the unconscious applies with equal force to the Jungian concept of the collective unconscious also. It is not at all difficult to explain the process of psychic development with the help of archetypes without bring in the idea of the unconscious. Then, Jung too, seems anxious to explain the life of the psyche in terms of the paramechanical law of causality. He views the equilibrium of the mental process as the psychic counterpart of the law of entropy, or in other words, as an equilibrium of energy. His effort to distinguish psychic energy from physical energy does not make any difference to the nature of energy as such; it only exposes the contradiction inherent in his theory. Psychic life being different from physical life can not be subsumed under the law of the latter.

There is another fallacy in Jung's theory of psychic evolution. This evolution, in his view, starts from the state of unconscious identity of the subject and object, and is destined to culminate in the ultimate union of the two, on a level much higher than the original state of harmony. The new level of harmony will be produced by the self-operating process of integration of individuation. Jung's theory seems to be a close parallel of the theory of cosmic evolution, expounded by the Samkhya School of Indian Philosophy. The Samkhya School, however, does not commit the mistake of viewing the primordial state of nature (a hierarchic equilibrium of three *gunas: sattva, rajas and tamas*) as a state of unconscious harmony. The unconscious is only a dimension of the mind concept which according to Samkhya is an evolute of Prakriti. An unfortunate implication of the Jungain view is that modern mentality is a direct continuation of primitive mentality. This view is totally inconsistent with

Jung's basic thesis that the unconscious and the conscious must be looked upon as equal partners in the great game of life. For, to suggest that modern mentality is a stage in the evolution of the psyche is to maintain that modernism is an improvement upon primitivism. This is placing the conscious on a higher plane than the unconscious and treating it as superior to the latter.

According to Jung, ritual practices are only a projection of the internal life of the psyche. It may be pertinently asked, why does the psyche project itself outwardly? If the answer is that it does so in conformity with the law of its nature, then it ceases to be the agency of projection. On the other hand, if the answer is that the psyche projects itself of its own free will then it can not be subsumed under a law. But Jung is at pains to demonstrate that psychic life follows a definite law of evolution. The psycho-analytic concept of projection can be maintained no otherwise than by viewing it metaphysically as a reflection of eternity into time or by regarding it what the vedantins call Maya. On this view, everything that man does or everything that happens to the temporal world is simply a repetition of something which happened in eternity, or conversely everything that belongs to this world is an imitation of an archetypal model. This archetypal model, as we suggested earlier, is the Nishkam; all actions are simply an imitation of this model.

It must, however, be said to Jung's credit that he tries to build his concept of ritual upon a fairly sound theory of symbolism. His distinction between the semiotic, allegorical and symbolic levels of interpretation is a most significant contribution to theory of meaning. The difficulty with his view arises only when he equates the "unknown" (the reference point for the symbol) with the unconscious. Unless it is understood on a transcendental plane, the unconscious can not be the reference point for the symbol. For the symbol, on Jung's own view, is of an archetypal character. In our theory of symbolism to which we must now turn, we will see how we can overcome the defects of the Jungian interpretation and explain the significance of ritual in appropriate terms.

Notes

1. Supra, Chapter 1.
2. Durkheim and Fauconnet: Sociology and the Social Sciences". In *Proceedings of the London Sociological Society* (London: MacMill and Co., 1904).
3. More about it in our critique of the psycho-analytic theories which is to follow.
4. A.R. Radcliffe-Brown, op. cit., p. 149.
5. Ibid., p. 143.
6. Gilbert Ryle, *The Concept of Mind* (Penguin Books, 1963, p. 20).
7. A.C. MacIntyre: *The Unconscious* (London: Routledge and Kegan Paul, 1958, p. 71).
8. J.O. Wisdom: "Psycho-analytic Technology". *The British Journal for the Philosophy of Science,* Vol. VII, August 1956, 99. 13–28. Wisdom thinks that the unconscious is not a concept in the sense that it represents something concreted existing. On the other hand, it is simply an explanatory theory as reasonable or unreasonable as Newton's "force at a distance", Maxwell's "displacement vector" and Einstein's "absolute velocity of light", and its only purpose is to facilitate the understanding of the behaviour of a class of phenomena (p. 16).
9. W.R.D. Fairboirn: "Psycho-analytic Conceptions". *The British Journal for the Philosophy of Science,* Vol. VII: 50, 1956.
10. A.W. Levi: *Philosophy and the Modern World* (Bloomington: Indiana University Press, 1959, Chapter V).
11. Quoted by Frederick Ferre: *Language, Logic and God* (New York: Harper and Brothers).
12. Ibid.
13. *The Forgotten Language* (New York: Rinehart & Co. Inc., 1951).
14. Op. cit.

9

Changing Profile of Women in India

*Some Reflections**

"Second sex" is a term which I borrow from Simone de Beauvior who sums up the entire modern exclusionist image of women as the "absolute other". You do not need to be told that much of the postmodern debate on the "politics of inclusion" centres about the triple issues of gender, race and ecology, which makes it all the more fitting that we reflect upon the subject as part of the Golden Jubilee celebrations of our independence. But I crave your indulgence again for presenting my own reflections on the subject as a free sequence of remarks rather than a well-conceived discourse of a commemorative speaker.

Before I come to the issue proper I must dispose of one or two preliminary questions which lurk in the background of the subject. One of these questions relates to the significance of the Golden Jubilee celebrations of our independence for us. For what happened in 1947 in legal terms was a simple transfer of power from colonial hands to our own, the event in itself having little cultural significance for us; not even as much as the foundation of our First Republic in 1950. What we actually achieved in 1947 was liberty – liberation from foreign domination, an indispensable condition of freedom but an event, by no means

* The keynote address presented before the National Seminar on the "Changing Profile of Women in India", held in Allahabad on September 4-6, 1998.

identical with 'freedom' itself. The freedom implied in liberty need not always be positive, for it may lead to rule by a tyrannous majority or by an equally tyrannous minority, not in any case to a true self-rule or *swarajya* as per the Indian tradition or to "no rule" or isonomy according to the Greek tradition, a state in which every one is his own ruler, a faint echo of which we find in Gandhi's utopia of a stateless democracy. But, the question need not detain us. What we have been wanting to suggest is that freedom is an expression of the desire to live together culturally, that is, to live together in an agonistic pursuit of goodness and excellence, a characteristic of the Greek 'polis' or of the traditional Indian 'pur'. Freedom then is the end, of which liberty is the necessary means. The rendezvous where we had promised to meet destiny was not 'liberty', it was 'freedom' which still eludes us. Freedom, let us repeat, is the cornerstone of a true republican living where every one is equal to the other in so far as the availability of opportunity for self-relevation is concerned.

The point which we are hinting at is that for the majority of us Indians these 50 years of free existence have meant nothing much in cultural terms. India for most of us stands for the new India "the nation-state-in-the-making" whose boundaries are limited to a well-defined territorial area. The traditional India whose cultural and spiritual boundaries were coterminous with the cosmic and the eternal, has been completely overshadowed by the new India. There can be no two opinions about the fact that this young nation-state is successor to a civilization which is incredibly old. But even this fact has been politicized; a whole host of historians maintaining the view that Indian culture has always had the same composite, pluralist even secular character as the contemporary nation-state.

Let us not forget that the political language and values of our nation-state like the idea of the nation-state itself have all been borrowed from the West whose polity and culture we have been brain washed for over a century to accept as superior to our own. These imported ideologies and value systems have led to an inevitable disruption of the traditional cultural patterns with the result that what we actually have in India today is not a well-structured society but what Joseph Spengler called a "cultural pseudomorph". No truly creative change can take place till this pseudomorph is dissolved.

This brings us to the question of change in the status of women. We must hear in mind that change cannot be understood without its structural opposite permanence that is, change in the position of women is logically linked with the question of their identity. "What is" we will be led to ask "the woman" whose changing profile is under discussion? Likewise, when we study change in the Indian society we must ask ourselves the question whether the Indian society is constantly losing its identity, its basic form as it is changing? Beauvoir's central thesis in her *Second Sex* is that woman a "free and autonomous being like all human creatures finds herself living in a word where men compel her to assume the status of the other.... to stabilise her as object and to doom her into immanence since her transcendence is to be overshadowed and forever transcended by another ego conscience which is essential and sovereign. The drama of women lies in this conflict between the fundamental aspirations of every subject (ego), who always regards the self as the essential – and the compulsions of a situation in which she is the inessential" (Simone de Beauvoir, *The Second Sex*, trans. by H.M. Parshely, New York: Vintage Books, 1989).

While this is the precise message that Beauvoir's book sends out to its readers, its first chapter reads like the plot of a Greek tragedy in which the human female is the tragic hero whose life is outrolled by fate and whose flaw resides in her autonomy. "What is a woman?" is the question to be answered and Beauvoir writes, "Woman?" very simple, say the fanciers of the simple formula "she is a womb, an ovary, she is a female – this word is sufficient to define her". But, Beauvoir, the philosopher, is not happy with this general description and gives her own definition of women: "She is the other, the relative being, the non essential", she says, and to discover how the nature of woman has been affected in history, what in other words, humanity has made of her is Beauvoir's aim in this work to explore.

The constellation of values – call it modernity – which has changed the "essential" woman into a "non-essential female" as

Beauvoir thinks it has, cannot play a different role in India or any other set-up where it has taken roots. But, the Indian woman is an Indian first and then anything else, like the traditional European woman whose identity has been eclipsed by the modern woman, was woman first and then turned into an "absolute other". In reflecting upon the changes in the status of Indian woman, then, we have to be first clear about what her being Indian means.

In making the distinction between the contemporary nation-state and the Indian civilization, the point we wanted to highlight was that India does not live wholly in the present; on the other hand, it lives in the continuity of it's tradition, maintaining a high degree of stability, permanency of form all through the historical changes which are essential to the keeping of the organicity of her "life" intact. The Indian social organization has preserved, that is to say, a recognizable identity. If things go astray, then they are corrected not so much by revolution but by "reformation", restoring them to "form" by a change of mind metanoia (repentance). It is this continuity of racial life that a woman represents; nor can she desire to be something other than herself; life is so designed for her that she is given the opportunity to be a woman, the essential transcendent feminity of Beauvoir's conception, to realize rather than to express herself.

The transformations that planned changes have brought about in the life of woman in India have in some way distorted her identity. Her perception of herself, at least in its express form, is undergoing a change thanks to the encouragement modernization is providing to the import of concepts and values form the West, in terms of which the human condition in India is being described and evaluated today. Take for instance, the terms "empowerment" and "emancipation" which figure in every description of the situation of woman even in the developing countries. We are not going to suggest that the interpretation of the condition of the Indian woman in these terms which have a typically western origin is a category mistake. But, the context in which they came to be used in Europe and the USA cannot be compared to the one existing in India.

The western society has been appropriately described by Levi-Strauss as a "hot culture", the "slow changing" traditional societies' change in the West from the 16th century onwards has been so rapid and at the same time so radical that it is difficult to determine its secular tendency from any vantage point. But the logocentric society which emerged in the age of Enlightenment which gave rise to the liberal state with universal equality and freedom as its cardinal principles as well as to Practical Reason as an incarnation of the values of impartiality, objectivity and detachment, also spawned serious gender and other contradictions. While it gave the citizen his rightful place in public space of the new republican states, it kept the citizens' wife and her claims to freedom confined to the household.

In the emergent society, the "public realm", the sphere of speech and action, the agonal ground of excellence, as Hannaha Arendt calls it, was invaded by the "social" – a pseudo-space of interaction in which individuals no longer "act" (no longer vie with each other for excellence) but merely "behave" as economic producers, consumers and city dwellers. Public space has thus become a projection of the private space of the household where "labour" and "work" essentially belong. It is not without reason therefore that philosophers from Rosseau to Marx thematize the alienation of the self from the "other" and form "itself" in the social world or the economic world of free exchange of commodities.

In a situation like this, the autonomous citizen whose reasoned judgement was a sine qua non of the public sphere has been transformed into a "citizen consumer" of packaged images and messaged of into "electronic mail target" of large lobbying groups and organizations. It is in this background that Simone de Beauvoir's distinction between the essential and non-essential womanhood is to be understood. The inessential woman is also a package of images and messages, when the private realm occludes the public, functions such as reproduction, child bearing, care for the sick, young and the elderly, reproductive freedom, domestic violence, child abuse, etc., which properly belong to the private realm of the household go public, a Patricia capitalist disciplinary bureaucracy comes to rule. It is this bureaucracy which disempowers women both in the public and the private spheres. By the same process, the administration of needs both in the household and the public sphere gets bureaucratized. What is needed by whom is not decided by the person concerned but by the ruling bureaucracy. This manifest incompatibility between the liberal model of public space including the values of equality and freedom, and the inclusion of women, was rightly noticed by the feminist writers in the West.

The problems that the Indian woman faces are her own and they need not be camouflaged by the idiom into which they are being expressed. The Indian constitution lumps them with the weaker sections of the society. In other words, in Beauvoir's memorable phrase, it calls them the second or the weaker sex which is to be restored to its rightful place in the larger society.

We are not disposed to deconstruct feminist theories, but we do wish to stress the fact that global metatheories of the feminist school can not explain the differentiation within the traditional or developing societies so called. The ascendancy of postmodernism within the social sciences has also gone some way towards undermining the importance of great narratives and globalizing theories as exploration of change. There are concrete studies to show that woman activists in Latin America have forged a political path that bears little resemblance to the way western feminists participate in the public domain. Using their identities as mothers, Latin American women have bypassed conventional political routes and organized mass movements that articulate their political demand. They have created disobedient mothers out of them demanding political and environmental concessions and redefining noticious of the private and the public. The mothers of the disappeared took to streets in their capacity as mothers defending the rights of their children against the state, thus converting human rights into women's rights as mothers. Mothers of diverse backgrounds, many poor, illiterate and previously politically inactive, have found a common cause and fought it successfully where formal politics and its institutions had failed. In India, women in Andhra Pradesh and Haryana who waged a virtual war against alcoholism, were successful not only in compelling the state to ban the sale of arrack, but were able to bring about a change in the habits of their husbands.

The problems and predicaments, urges and aspirations of Indian woman are thus different from those of women in the USA or the West in general. Cross-cultural studies of "women, work and family" conducted by Indian sociologists highlight the fact that there is no undifferentiated category of Asian women and that women's position in the household varies by class, ethnicity, culture, family customs and also by state policy. If the ascendancy of the patriarchal bureaucracy and the ideology of modernity were the determining factors of subordination of women in the West, in traditional South Korea it was the cultural ideology of motherhood. The ideology of motherhood does not grant women rights over the labour of their daughter and daughter-in-law, it also contributes to the establishment of class and gender distinctions.

A very interesting study of trading women in Madras shows patriarchal families to which these women generally belong have a rigid ideology of purity and chastity of women which illassorts with trade ethics. How do they cope with this dilemmatic situation? By extending fictional kinship ties them to their customers in the market. The clash between ideology of patriarchy and capitalist market processes puts women in a disadvantageous position, no doubt but they tackle the situation with characteristic gut and skillfulness.

In view of the culture-specific nature of the subject under discussion it would be a futile exercise to try to explain it in the wider context of the general theory, which is not to say that it does not constitute a problem area. If Indian women are Indian, their development can not be conceived independently of their cultural background – their modernization and history. The question posed by Beauvoir on the seminar "what is woman?" is a literal substitute for the ontological question what is man? de Beauvior's answer is existential, and so in fact is the Greek answer, both men and women in India are regarded as incarnations of a metaphysical principle. The woman according to Markandeya Purana is the collective energy and effulgence of the gods and goddesses. As the myth has it, when the titan Mahishasur triumphed over Indra, the king of Heaven and himself became the lord of the divine kingdom, the gods and goddesses began to starve, as they were deprived of the sacrificial offerings made by men on the earth. In their agony, they approached the lord of lords Vishnu who on hearing their plight went red with anger and then an effulgent light emanated from his body. Simultaneously, similar lights emanated from the bodies of all the gods and goddesses assembled their. All this light collected at one place and became Nari, a female divinity, Shakti or Durga as she is known. The gods and goddesses then armed her with their own weapons with which she overpowered the titan Mahish. This is one image of women in the Hindu tradition. The other is her image as the Ardhangini of Lord Shiva who is sizygy of the male and female principles.

In Plato's *Symposium*, we get an interesting account of how men and women became what they are on this earth today that is, two sexes. In the beginning, we read in the *Symposium* that there were three genders, male, female and the third a joint one called Koinos, an androgynous gender as equal parts of the male and female. The androgynous were similar to gods in strength and energy, therefore, they became arrogant and self-willed. They wanted to ascend Heaven and overpower the gods. The supreme god Zeus then in order to weaken them and control their wantonness split them again into two. So, men and women now miss their other half and only live in their desire to unite with it. This is the genesis of the human instinct for love called Eros.

The purpose of recounting these mythical narratives of the origin of womanhood is to emphasize the point that the identity of the women can not be reduced to her anatomy or her psychophysical characteristics. Nor can her development be conceived in mere social psychological terms of her economic, political and social rights, which of course is not to detract from the effort being made in India since Independence to improve her lot. We cannot close our eyes to the glaring disparities between the status of men and women in India even after full 60 years of planning and development. The social legislations enacted since independence to remedy the situation rising out of the discrimination practiced against them, such as the Hindu Marriage Act 1955, the Hindu Adoption and Maintenance Act 1956, the Hindu Succession Act 1956, the Hindu Minority and Guardianship Act 1956 and the Dowry Prohibition Act 1961 to mention only a few have been long our due measure of social reform.

The Indian Constitution guarantees equality before the law and equal protection of the law and prohibition of discrimination on the ground of sex. It is indeed a depressing state of affairs that the literacy percentage of women as per the 1991 census was only 39.29 per cent. In the Human Development Report 1996, India ranked 103 in the gender-related development index, women-earned income share is partly 24.8 per cent, India ranks at 93 when it comes to gender empowerment measures. A mere 2.3 per cent women are administrators and managers and only 20.5 per cent professional and technical workers, all of whom collectively earn 25 per cent of the shared income. It is good that there was no opposition to one-third reservation for women in the Panchayati Raj Bill.

It is not enough that social legislations to improve the position of women in employment, health and education are enacted, what is more important is that they are implemented effectively. The woman's question should not be politicized as is often done either by the women activists or professional politicians. Slogans such as equality cannot come without power sharing without a political will to implement them, do more harm than good to a cause which is genuine and just in its own right. The other danger is that the problem is being segmenized; what is a problem concerning women in general is politicized into one concerning SCs, STs and OBCs, and minority group women. As academics, it is our duty to steer clear of the politics and the rhetoric of the issue; the question of women's development can be easily delinked with political slogans. In traditional cultures such as Hinduism, Islam and Christianity, women were never disempowered by design. Nor can empowerment as conceived in the western feminist theories can enable women to become what they have in them to become; to realize that is to say their womanhood.

As we said at the outset what we achieved in 1947 was formal independence. Substantive independence or what we call freedom, the essential human condition for the pursuit of excellence is still a distant goal. And, since there are no known parameters of excellence, a real political living can only be imitative of paradigms which only traditions or collective memories of the human race can provide. Hannah Arendt was not unnecessarily worried about women's lack of participation in politics.

References

Cindi Katz and Janice Monk (eds.), *Full Circles Geographies of Women Over the Life Course*. Routledge: London, 1993.

Hannah Arendt, *The Human Condition*. Chicago: University of Chicago Press, 1958.

Janet H. Momsen and Vivian Kinnaird (eds.), *Different Places, Different Voices, Gender and Development in Africa, Asia and Latin America*. Routledge: London, 1993.

Leela Dube and Rajni Palriwala (eds.), *Structures and Strategies, Women Work and Family*. Sage: New Delhi, 1990.

Sarch A. Radicliffe and Sallie Westwood (eds.), *Viva, Women and Popular Protest in Latin America*. Routledge: London, 1993.

Simon de Beauvior, *The Second Sex*, translated and edited by H.M. Parshely. New York: Vintage Books, 1989.

10

Rethinking Development in Relation to the Scheduled Castes*

Caste is no longer the validating principle of privilege in the Indian society. Not only has the traditional distinction between the *dwijas* and the *shudras* or the *savaranas* and *panchaamas* been abolished; untouchability as a basis of exclusion and separation has been banished from at least the public relation. In fact, all exclusionary practices predicated on race, sex, ethnicity, religion, etc., have become untenable in India today. A modern state armed with full panopaly of power has emerged which has conferred a new status on the individual who is first and foremost a 'citizen' and then anything else like a person with a caste or religious name in his private life.

If *homoequalis* is the ideal type of man whose full emergence is awaited in India, then the contours of the social organization are to be redrawn, replacing hierarchy with stratification based on equality. But since the change involves an overturning of the axiological axis, the state cannot be the appropriate instrument to bring it about. What is needed is in fact a transevaluation of values, a change almost total in our *weltanschauung* which law alone is incapable of carrying into effect and more especially

---

* Paper presented at the National Seminar on 'Development of Scheduled Castes in the Emerging Political-Cultural Contest,' held at G.B. Pant Social Science Institute, Allahabad, February 1994.

when change in India tends towards the maintenance of permanence.[1] For social mobility in India *down the ages* has taken the form of *sanskritization* or *brahmanization* – tribes getting *Hinduized* by adopting a caste name and the lower castes climbing on the social scale by rituals of the upper castes, both raising their status within the same hierarchy.[2]

All through the fusion and fission that castes have undergone, the Indian society has not sloughed off its basic form; there has been a change in the society, but not of the society. Even the induced social changes being brought about through the instrumentality of law have so far not touched the axiological axis – the value – system, in substance. Caste has been excluded from public discourse, but the exclusion has only taken the form of repression.[3] Like all taboos, the public taboo on caste conceals behind it an ambivalence of emotions; the repulsion against caste is as strong as the attraction for it. The attraction is unconscious, the repulsion is conscious. Also, like all repressed desires, caste invades the conscious or the public space in numerous disguised or surrogate forms like a parapolitical community.[4]

Take the Indian Constitution which makes a two-fold distinction between backward and non-backward (high-class citizens) and between casteless citizens and those called Scheduled Castes (SCs) including the Scheduled Tribes (STs), as if even for describing the secular self of India we have do not have a more appropriate category than caste. The schimsm in the traditional non-secular self of India was understandable. It was a reflection of the bipartite division of the Indian society into the *dwijas* and *shudras*, and *savaranas* and *panchamas*, a division whose archaeology has not been adequately explored. But it is not easy to understand the schism in the secular self of India, reflecting again the division of the citizenary into casteless citizens and the SCs. If the grand narrative to rationalize the traditional schism in India's self was borrowed from myths, the narrative to justify the split in her secular self is borrowed from the rational legal code. The typical argument to justify the retention of the word 'caste' for a particular class of citizens who deserve special consideration in the form of compensatory discrimination is that since caste was the basis of discrimination between the privileged and the underprivileged in the traditional Indian society, there can be no other basis of selecting the citizens of the modern state for positive action other than caste. Granting that there can be no better substitute for the category of caste for social identification in the contemporary India, be it only for marking out the underdogs, we can not afford to shut our eyes to the sinister fall outs of this separation.

In the prevailing distinction between the private and public realms, public realm has come to be associated with urbanity, caste-neutrality, secularism, rationality and sophistication, and by the same token the private realm has become associated with casteism, boorishness, non-secularism and sub-rationality. The public realm is again coterminus with urban social space and elitist discourse based on English, and the private realm with rural social space, and the commoners discourse based on vernacular. The SCs and STs are naturally located in the caste-based rural space, irrespective of their actual location. This partly explains the elitist attitude of pity and commiseration usually deployed by the *savarna* or even non-*savarna* planners and administrators in dispensing social justice to the SCs and STs. And this also explains the growing distance between the elites and the masses or commoners even among the SCs.

A truly secular self will never look upon the 'other' in casteist terms except when it is under the influence of its darner side, its 'shadows', i.e., the non-secular self which constantly baulks his normal development as if in a dream.[5] Secularization through a repression of non-secular faces, such as caste and religion, cannot lead to a normal growth of a secular self. Nor is a more positive method of secularization possible within the framework of social change through state action. A set of bureaucrats sitting around a table and drawing up plans for the development of the SCs or for that matter for any kind of community development can not come up with anything more than new versions of failed plans or programmes. This is no place to examine the archaeology of knowledge in relation to the

Indian bureaucracy. Suffice is to say that like its counterpart in the other parts of the world, bureaucracy in India is totally alienated from the people. And as a part of the ruling class, it has to follow a particular method of validating statements and to call it truth. It is not without reason then that Weber could foresee the emergence of the dictatorship of bureaucracy in formalized organizations rather than that the dictatorship of the proletariat.

Nor again can democratic actions initiated by the so-called people's representatives for the people and on behalf of the people can play any better role in getting any developmental plan for the SCs or the STs effectively implemented. For, to reduce 'people' to an 'abstract quantifiable mass', democratically approving or disapproving a pre-constituted agenda or voting for candidates or parties which have no organic roots is not democracy but manipulation.

It is against this background that the impact of the ongoing programmes for the development of the SCs and the STs should be examined. There is no dearth of appropriate constitutional provisions or civil or penal laws to safeguard the interests of the SCs and to protect their fundamental rights or the compensatory discrimination in their furon. The ongoing programmes initiated by the government are again good enough to enable them to raise themselves by their boot straps. What is in fact lacking is a real political well backed by an equally deep concern for their upliftment.

The term scheduled caste in fact is the homogenized name of the erstwhile class for the untouchables which comprised a large number of castes or sub-castes which were discriminated against in the traditional Hindu society, whose touch was considered polluting and who were thus called 'shudras', 'antyaja', 'panchamas' and not unoften 'chanals'. At one stage in India's contemporary history, they came to be known as 'depressed classes' for a variety of reasons; but mainly because they followed an occupation which was considered degrading, but for which they would not be subjected to any disability. Gandhiji called them 'asprishya' but eventually gave them the respectable name of 'Harijans', meaning the 'chosen men of God'.

It was after 1901 that the depressed classes started receiving political attention. J.H. Hutton, the 1931 Census Commissioner had proposed a series of tests for determining whether a particular caste could be identified as an untouchable caste. However, till 1936, there was no unanimity about the number of groups to be included under the category of the depressed classes when for the first time a number of castes were listed to give effect to the provisions of special electoral representation in the Government of India Act, 1936, although there was no unanimity about this list also.

This then is the genesis of the term scheduled caste. The Constitution empowers the President to specify after consulting the Governor of the state the castes, races, or tribes or parts of or groups within castes, races and tribes which shall for the purposes of this Constitution be deemed to be SCs in relation to that state (Article 341[2]). Accordingly, an SC order was promulgated by the President in 1950, which was basically a reenactment of the 1936 list. The only noteworthy changes in the list since 1936 were the addition of a million persons each in Rajasthan and UP, and the inclusion of the Sikh untouchables also. The total population of the SC in 1951 was 55.3 millions, which in 1971 rose to 80 millions, i.e., 14.6 per cent of the total population. According to the 1991 census, the total population of the SCs was 13.82 crores, constituting 16.48 per cent of the population showing a slight increase over the SC population in 1981 (15.75%) of the total population.

Although positive action in favour of the SC had started during the 30s, it remained mostly confined to the political and legal spheres. It was however during the Sixth Five-Year Plan that the SCs and STs were made a target group for the economic development and certain strategies were adopted to implement the plan for their development. These included: (i) protective measures, (ii) developmental measures, and (iii) positive discrimination in employment and other facilities. The protective measures include the provision in the Constitution ensuring their equality before law and equal protection of the laws, Articles 15(1), 15(2), 15(4), 16(1), 16(2), 16(4): Article (17) abolishes untouchability and Article (19) protects rights considered as basic to all citizens.

The developmental measures consist of (i) the Special Component Plan, (ii) Special Central Assistance, and (iii) Creation of Scheduled Castes Development Corporation. In February 1989, the National Scheduled Castes and Scheduled Tribes Finance and Development Corporation was constituted as an apex body to speed up the economic development of the SCs. The developmental measures also include the instrument of positive discrimination consisting in a policy of reservation in public services for SCs to the extent of 15 per cent, besides other concessions in the economic sphere such as priority in the distribution of surplus land, housing, dealership, etc. The SCPs aim at proper channelization of the plan outlays and benefits from the general sectors of the plans of the states and the Central Ministries for the development of the SCs. The SCPs of the states are supplemented by Special Central Assistance to create a booster effect on the developmental impact of the SCPs.

The Scheduled Castes Development Corporations in the states are designed to act as an agency of interface between the poor SC entrepreneurs and the financial institutions where bankable schemes of economic development are involved. The SCP outlay which stood at Rs 3614.66 crores in the VI Plan (1980–85) rose to Rs 7385.42 with VII Plan (1985–90), then to Rs 2377.82 in 1990–91 to Rs 3066.33 in 1991–92 and to Rs 3315.48 crores in 1992–93 comprising, respectively, 7.66 per cent and 8.27 per cent diverted to other heads, states have been asked to provide separate budget heads of account for these funds. Norms for providing Special Central Assistance include the SC population of the state/UT and the relative backwardness of the state/UT.

The aim of the National Scheduled Castes and Scheduled Tribes Finance and Developmental Corporation is to accelerate the economic development of the SC/ST families below the poverty line by sanctioning special projects to these SC/ST. Its role is basically supportive as it operates through the State Scheduled Caste Development Corporation. The NSFDC has to date an authorized capital of Rs 125 crores (paid up Rs 61.67

crores) entirely provided by the Central Government. The criteria for selecting the projects are: (i) high reliance to SC/ST families and high employment generating potential, (ii) high viability and quick return, and (iii) moderate capital investment. The NSFDC has so far sanctioned 312 schemes costing Rs 277.63 crores, benefiting 140,472 SC/ST entrepreneurs. During the VII Plan, Rs 1,200 crore SC families were assisted as against the target of Rs 1.04 crore amounting to 115.05 per cent achievement. During the financial year 1990–91 against a target of 2,230,608 families, 2,239,927 families were assisted the percentage of achievement being 100.40.

There is yet another centrally sponsored scheme called the Post-Matric Scholarships for SCs and STs. For the year 1992–93, there was an allocation of Rs 46 crores. The scheme which started with a meagre 144 scholarships in 1944–45 increased to 14.92 lakhs in 1991–92. The prematric scholarships to the children of those engaged in unclean occupations were started in 1977–78 through central assistance provided to the states on a 50:50 basis. There are then centrally sponsored schemes of providing book banks for SC/ST children, girls/boys hostels, coaching and allied schemes through grants provided to the State Governments. The government has also been promoting a National Scheme for the liberation and rehabilitation of scavengers. Provision also exists for overseas scholarships for SC/ST children for higher studies abroad.

The Government of India also gives special grants to voluntary organizations engaged in the development of the SCs. The schemes which the voluntary organizations are encouraged to take up are: Ashrams, Schools, Hostels, Maternity and Child Welfare Centres, etc. During 1992–93, these organizations were given grants to the extent of Rs 2.27 crores.[6]

A central law called the Untouchability (Offences) Act was passed in 1955 to provide punishment for offences regarding the practice of untouchability was enacted in pursuance of Article 17 of the Constitution. The Act was subsequently amended and renamed as The Protection of the Civil Rights Act, 1955. The states are requested under the Act to set up 'special courts' to try offences committed in violation of the above Act. It must be noted that the measures adopted by the government to raise the status of the SCs are only an external index of their development. Even if it is agreed that their development consists, as in the case of development of the country as a whole, as part of the nation-building programme, in modernization, the steps taken by the state for their upliftment cannot exhaust its meaning. In fact, what constitutes their true development can not be determined by others. Given the external parameters of development, it is they who should decide how they would like to develop themselves.

But to lift them upto a level where they can participate meaningfully in national as of course in their own development, is one of the major prerequisites as envisages with the constitution of establishing an egalitarian social order in the country. It is of utmost importance therefore that at least the government-sponsored schemes for their development are implemented as part of a crash programme. There can be no excuse for instance for the delay in raising the level of their literacy which has not gone beyond 50 per cent of the total literacy achieved for the population as a whole. For instance, as against 27.86 per cent literacy for the total population in 1961, literacy among the SCs was only 10.27 per cent and in 1981, only 21.38 per cent as against the total literacy rate of 41.32 per cent. Even behind this average there are regional variations and invariably the lowest female literacy. Likewise, the target as regards implementation of the reservation quota in appointments always remains unfulfilled on one plea or another. In report after report, the Commission for Scheduled Castes and Scheduled Tribes has been converging its displeasure to the government over the woefully poor performance of the Ministries and the PSUs, nationalized banks, etc., as regards the implementation of the reservation quota for the SCs in services. Nor is there any abatement of the atrocities being committed day in and day out against the SCs. In fact, the overall number of cases of atrocities against the SCs, which as per the report of the Commission had declined from 15,051 in 1982 to 14,847 in 1983, recorded an increase to 16,586 in 1984. In this year, the highest number of such cases were reported from MP, UP, Bihar and Rajasthan.

Thanks to the implementation of the various poverty alleviating schemes, there has been a steady decline in the poverty, both rural and urban, but the decline in the case of SC families is only to the extent of 19.5 per cent as against the total decline of 22.6 per cent, which is not a happy trend. The delay in raising their literacy level and reducing their poverty has been responsible for their growing exploitation by vested interests both outside and in their own ranks.

Besides ensuring greater involvement of non-governmental agencies in the implementation of the welfare for the SCs, the government must devise a more effective method of monitoring the SC programmes. However, more than the Government efforts what is required is a new social consciousness which should recognize the virtues of freedom, equality, non-discrimination and social justice. Such social consciousness can be created only by well-organized social movements against discriminatory ethics and manipulative democracy. Social scientists have to play their own role in exposing the vested interests and power-relation behind the social taxonomy inherited from the part and in its replacement by an appropriate taxonomy. In any case, the solution to the problem cannot be political.

Notes

1. See, especially, Dumont Louis: *Homo-Hierarchicus*, Chicago (USA): Univesity of Chicago Press, 1980.
2. See Srinivas, M.N.: *Social Change in India and other Essays*, California: University of California Press, 1966. Even Dr B.R. Ambedkar considers the Shudras as Kshatriyas who had nothing to do with the untouchables. The latter according to him who on account of their conversion to Buddhism had broken off from the village, had started catering beef and had been declared as untouchables by the upper castes. Dr Ambedkar's own interpretation of the Vedic literature thus confers a status on the Shudras as high as that of the Kshatriyas. There is nothing new even in Dr Ambedkar's interpre-

tation of the Hindu tradition, as the social taxonomy validated by the Vedic episteme which had created the distinction between the *Dwijas* and Shudras remains intact in form. Dr Ambedkar only tempers with its contents. See *Who were the Shudras?* B.R. Ambedkar, Thacker and Co., Bombay, 1996.

3. See Dhareshwar Vivek: *Journal of Art and Ideas,* 'Caste and the Secular Self' pp. 115–127, New Delhi: Tulika Print Communication Series, Issue No. 25–26, 1993.
4. The role of castes as pressure groups or what Rudolfs call the panpolitical comments is increasingly being emphasized in even by serious-minded political scientists. The behaviour of caste as a pressure group in the limited context of an election or as mobilized at the local- or national-level political group to extract or bargain a concersious or favour from or with the Government, is its role as a surrogate of caste and not as caste qua caste.
5. We owe this term of C.G. Jung. The 'shadow' according to him is the dark half of the conscious which always thwarts its plan even in his dreams. Man's darker side or shadow is the female 'anima' and the women's darker side or shadow, the 'animus'.
6. Source: Annual Report 1992–93, Ministry of Welfare, Government of India.

11

Eradication of Poverty

*Rhetoric and Reality**

Elimination of poverty has been high on the agenda of the national government ever since its inception; to start with as part of the constitutional obligation of the state to establish a just and egalitarian society and subsequently, since the late seventies to be exact, as a measure of government policy to improve the lot of a targeted cross-section of the population living below the subsistence level.

Removal of social inequality and poverty has been uppermost in the mind of the leaders of the nationalist movement even before independence. In his famous 'Tryst with Destiny' speech delivered by Jawaharlal Nehru in the Constituent Assembly on the night of 14 August, 1947, he had stated in no uncertain terms that the "service of India means the service of the millions who suffer. It means the ending of poverty, ignorance and disease and inequality of opportunity. The ambition of the greatest man of the generation (Gandhiji) has been to wipe out every tear from every eye".

However, the government under Nehru's stewardship never felt it expedient to dilute its constitutional obligation to promote social justice and equality into a political programme like 'Garibi Hatao'. Which is not to suggest that Jawaharlal Nehru

---

* National Workshop on Attacking Rural Poverty, University-NGO Partnership (February 19–21, 1999)

was not conscious of the gap between the formal legitimacy of his government as reflected in the massive popular mandate he used to receive in general elections and its substantive legitimacy, the solid moral backing of the people that his government needed in order to rule effectively. This is not the occasion to enter into the question of how Nehru managed to fill this gap between the legal and moral bases of his government's legitimacy and how in the post-Nehru era the popular mandate became the basis of both legal as well as moral legitimacy of the government; duly elected governments needing to do little or nothing substantive to justify their continuance in office.

Delinked from the constitutional obligation of the state to promote the welfare of the people the poverty alleviation programme became more of a rhetoric than a meaningful economic programme. This largely explains why poverty has survived all attempts to eradicate it all through these 50 years of planned development. The Five-Year Plans which, had been launched for purposes much larger than economic development "to open to our people opportunities for a richer and more varied life" as the First Five-Year Plan put it, or to "expand the community's production power to provide the environment in which there is scope for expression and application of diverse faculties and urges" as the Second Five-Year Plan document said, have steadily turned away from their avowed purpose to become bland economic policy statements of the government of the day.

Thus, while poverty, say rural poverty, still continues to be government's major preoccupation, the state is gradually lapsing into amnesia as regards the fulfilment of its constitutional obligations. In the wake of "globalization" and "liberalization" it seems to have virtually forgotten about its constitutional responsibility to establish a just economic order "in which the ownership and control of the material resources of the community are so distributed as best to subserve the common good" and wherein "the operation of the economic system does not result in concentration of wealth and means of production to the common detriment".

We specifically refer to this point because elimination of poverty is no guarantee that inequality will also disappear and if inequality does not disappear poverty will return in new garbs; it may not be absolute poverty in the sense of physical destitution; but poverty in a more excruciating form, as obtains in affluent countries of the west. Under the "market socialism" in China inequalities of a worse order giving rise the unique forms of poverty and destitution surfaced. "The rural cadres who were "commanders" in a command economy are now indispensable brokers who obtain for the farmers state procurement contracts and ensure supply of needed inputs at especially reduced prices". The end-result is new forms of impoverishment and resource networking lubricated by corruption. Reduction of poverty is undoubtedly a positive step towards equality, but if inequality, as we said above, does not disappear, poverty will persist.

That reduction in poverty need not ensure reduction of economic inequality can be clearly seen from comparative percentages of population below poverty line and those of distribution of household and assets over a period of time. The Seventh Five-Year Plan had claimed that percentage of people below poverty line had declined from 48.3 in 1978–79 to 36.9 in 1984–85 and was projected to decline further to 25.8 by 1989–90 (Volume I, p. 33). However, the available evidence in regard to inequality measured in terms of ownership of assets or consumer expenditure had shown that inequality had persisted and was likely to increase. The Nehruvian model of a mixed economy with the public sector occupying the commanding heights, with comprehensive planning alongwith the use of market mechanism, land reforms, emphasis on science and technology and self-reliance, of which there are not money takers today, in fact provided a much better socio-economic framework for tackling the problems of poverty and inequality than Deng's market socialism. India's path to socialism under Nehru, was not communist, not market-unfriendly either. There was a human purpose behind Nehru's economic policies which were framed and formulated within the four corners of the Constitution. He never allowed expediency to guide him in his choice of strategy and method of development.

This should bring us to the practical problems involved in the implementation of the programme of poverty alleviation in what form it has been launched. But, the context calls for reference to yet another relevant point about the issue. Let us not forget the fact that removal of poverty is no longer a national issue; it has become by now the affluent "West's burden" as was "civilization of barbarians" the burden of the "imperial West" in colonial times. It is worth recalling that soon after the Second World war US President Harry S. Truman in one of his policy announcements had underlined the need for making the benefits of the wests' wisdom and experience available to the poor and under-developed countries for their own progress. "We must embark" he had said "on a bold new programme for making the benefits of our scientific advances and industrial progress available for the improvement and growth of the underdeveloped areas. More than half the people in the world are living in conditions approaching misery. Their food is inadequate. They are victims of disease. Their economic life is primitive and stagnant. Their poverty is a handicap and a threat both to them and to more prosperous areas".

This the background to the involvement of the affluent west, specially the UN agencies like the World Bank, International Monetary Fund, UNDP etc., in the anti-poverty programmes initiated by national governments in developing Asian and South African countries. We will be making use of UNDP's 1997 report on poverty later in this address to highlight our own achievement in combating poverty in India. Because of the vested interest of international funding agencies in the anti-poverty programmes of developing countries, national governments and their own agencies have also developed vested interest in these programmes. There is no systematic record of the money spent on the new bureaucracy created for the implementation of poverty alleviation programmes. There are hundreds and thousands of voluntary organizations and NGOs funded by foreign agencies which are engaged in development projects relating to poverty and other areas. Can there be a better explanation of the reason why only 15 naya paise out of every rupee spent on poverty alleviation reaches the target groups and the remaining 85 paise is spent on the upkeep of the bureaucracy and other agencies meant for the implementation of the programme.

Definition of poverty in India was attempted for the first time in 1962 by a group of economists basing on the recommendations of the Nutrition Advisory Committee of the Indian Council of Medical Research on balanced diet. The cut-off point for drawing the poverty line was determined by the calorie requirement of rural and urban population for physical subsistence. This was more or less an academic exercise with little practical value. But, the Task Force on Minimum Needs and Effective Consumption Demand constituted by the Planning Commission in 1979 proposed a more operational definition translating the earlier definition based on calorie requirements into monetary terms. The poverty line thus come to be identified with per capita monthly expenditure of Rs 49.09 in rural areas and Rs 64.64 in urban areas at 1973–74 prices, corresponding to per capita daily calorie requirement of 2,400 in rural and 2100 in urban areas. It is this definition of poverty which the Planning Commission still uses with necessary modifications from time to time.

According to estimates based on the aforesaid calorie intake concept as translated into monetary terms, the highest percentage of population below poverty line in 1972–73 was living in Orissa 68.6, Tamil Nadu 59.7, Madhya Pradesh 58.6, West Bengal 56.8, Kerala 56.9, Bihar 54.5, and UP 52.8. The corresponding figures for 1977–78 were Orissa 65.1, Tamil Nadu 52.8, MP 58.9, West Bengal 52.2, Kerala 48.4, Bihar 56.3 and UP 49.7 and for 1983–84, Orissa 92.9, Tamil Nadu, 39.6, MP 46.2, West Bengal 39.2, Kerala 26.8, Bihar 49.5 and UP 45.3; again, the figures in respect of the year 1987–88 were Orissa 44.7, Tamil Nadu 32.8, MP 36.7, West Bengal 27.6, Kerala 17, Bihar 40.8 and UP 35.1. Respective figures for the whole of India during this period were 51.5, 48.3, 37.4 and 29.4. These figures suggest that poverty has declined during this period of 15 years since 1973 in all these states, but the comparative decline has been slow in Orissa, Bihar, MP and UP. The state to which we belong has been a laggard in this respect, being still above the all-India level by about 6 per cent. The per capita income of the state in 1995–96 stood at Rs 5,983 as against the all-India figure of Rs 9,321, the short fall being 35.8 per cent.

The occupational structure of the state showed a preponderance of workers in primary over secondary industry, 72.9 per cent being engaged in agriculture and only 9 per cent in non-agricultural occupations. The all-India figures for the same period (1991 census) were 66.9 and 17.8 per cent. UP in this respect is better than Bihar, MP and Orissa only.

The state has 8.96 per cent of the country's land area and 15.44 per cent of its population and 19.84 per cent urbanization as against all-India percentage of 25.73. Eastern UP (19 districts) has 29.16 per cent of UP's land area and 37.9 per cent of its population 526.61 lakhs as per 1991 census. The average size of holdings in eastern UP is only 0.68 hectares as against 0.93 hectares for the state, bulk of the holdings, i.e., 82.42 per cent being marginal. The average yield per hect. of land is 13.69 quintals as against 17.65 quintals in western UP, and 14.61 quintals in UP as a whole. Literacy in UP is 41.60 per cent while it is only 35.12 in eastern UP, Bahraich having the lowest percentage, i.e., 24.29.

The picture that average of UP and eastern UP from these figures is one of extreme backwardness and underdevelopment, and since this workshop is a joint venture of the university and NGOs eastern UP must be a matter of understandable concern for it.

The poverty line for the Government of India and the Planning Commission as we have said above is defined in terms of economic poverty or what is called 'income poverty'. The 1997 UNDP (United Nations Development Programme) report, however, introduces a new concept of poverty, what it calls the Human Poverty Index (HPI) which provides a country by country measure of poverty from a human development perspective. It looks at basic choices of opportunities available in the developing world for the people to lead a long and healthy life. As per this report, among the 78 countries in the index, Trinidad, Tobago, Cuba, Chile, Singapore and Costa Rica rank the best as they have reduced human poverty to less than 10 per cent of their population. Select HDI figures for India are: Kerala 15, Punjab 38, Orissa 41, Rajasthan 51, and Bihar 52.

The HPI is made up of three factors, viz., life span (percentage expected to live till 40 years), access to public and private resources (health services, safe water) and reasonable nutrition. Other critical dimensions of the HPI are political freedom, ability to participate in decision making etc.

Space will not permit us to refer to the successes and factures of the anti-poverty programmes introduced in India since the late seventies, their failures being more pronounced than their success. To give a list of only the more important measures, they include the Integrated Rural Development Programme (IRDP), National Rural Employment Programme, (NREP), Training for Self-Employment of Rural Youth (TRYSEM), and Development of Women and Children in Rural Areas (DWCRA). Some other newly started programmes are National Social Assistance Programme (NSAP), Intensive Jawahar Rozgar Yojana (IJRY), Employment Assurance Scheme (now both merged) Indira Avas Yojana (IAY) and so on.

Government functionaries associated with the implementation of these programmes know it full well that hardly 20 per cent of the money allotted for the beneficiaries reaches them. The partners of this workshop the university and the NGOs therefore can best play their role in the implementation rather than the formulation and coordination of these programmes. They can be better and more effective agencies of their supervision and evaluation. Experience shows that despite so much wastage and pilferage of the funds allotted to these programmes there is no proper monitoring and coordination of the activities of the government and panchayat functionaries. Perhaps not even one per cent of the funds is spent on monitoring. It is also found that there is considerable overlap in the contents and objectives of some of these programmes which are generally devised to suit the political convenience of political leaders. Economists, sociologists, and statisticians from the universities can play an important part in the entire process of formulation, implementation and monitoring of a programme.

One of the most useful insights offered by Amartya Sen into the understanding of poverty, is that it is not so much the non-availability of material resources but the non-availability of opportunity to use them, which lies at the root of poverty. The other insight Sen offers is the improved level of literacy of the population, as a measure of poverty alleviation. And facts stand in support of Prof. Sen. There are 500 to 1,000 area-based pockets in the country (not only in Kerala or Dakshina Karnad or Kolar district (Malur taluka) in Karnataka where the total fertility rate is equal to or less than one, where in other words the population is not increasing but might even be decreasing. In these areas, both better education of the girl or literacy of the woman and availability of clean drinking water, and a reasonably decent level of nutrition for the mother as well as better health services, have played their part. The university-NGO partnership can be of great help in educating women in the use of family planning techniques and better delivery of health services to prospective mothers.

12

A Sociological Perspective on the Development of Eastern UP*

In a status report[1] on UP's economy, the State Government, Department of Planning has attributed the backwardness of the state mainly to what they call 'the iniquitous distribution of investments in the country,' or in other words, to the denial of the state's legitimate share in the national cake, by the powers that we. If statistics are any guide, the State Government has a point, to which we will return a little later. But, the blame that the State Government lay at the door of the Central Government and the Planning Commission for the chronic sickness of UP's economy can be laid equally justifiably at their own door, when it comes to identifying the causes of the continued backwardness of eastern UP.

It is worth recalling how eastern UP came into sharp focus way back in 1962, when the socialist leader Sri Vishwanath Gahmari narrated the plight of the villagers of eastern UP, of those of his own district Ghazipur in particular, in the Lok Sabha with tears in his eyes. Moved by Sri Gahmari's tears Pandit. Nehru, the then Prime Minister of India, suggested to the Deputy

---

* Paper presented at the National Seminar on 'Economic Inequality and Backwardness in the Context of UP,' held at Banaras Hindu University, Varanasi, 1999.

Chairman of Planning Commission that the question of accelerated development of eastern UP and similar other districts elsewhere, might be gone into by the Planning Commission. The Deputy Chairman then wrote to the Chief Minister of UP advising him to arrange for an intensive study of the social and economic conditions of at least three districts of eastern UP and also of the impact of the development programmes launched in the Third Five-Year Plan on these districts by a Joint Study Team consisting of experts from both the Planning Commission and the Government of UP. The Chief Minister welcomed the move of the Planning Commission and proposed that a Joint Study Team take up for study the districts of Ghazipur, Jaunpur and Deoria. Accordingly, a Joint Study Team was appointed by the Planning Commission with Sri B.P. Patel, the then Chairman of the state Trading Corporation, as Chairman and nine other members representing the Planning Commission as well as the Government of UP. The Joint Study Team held its first meeting in January, 1963 and decided to include Azamgarh district also in the scope of the study.

These four districts[2] had together a population of 72.38 lakhs as per the 1961 census, of which 96 per cent lived in the villages as against 87.1 per cent of UP's population which lived in the villages. The density of population per square mile in these four districts was 1,094 as against 649 per square mile in UP as a whole. The population engaged in cultivation or worked as agricultural labourers was 84.5 per cent as against 75.4 per cent of the population depending on cultivation and allied activities in UP. The per capita income of these districts was Rs 172 in 1960–61 (as per the 1960–61 prices), which was much lower than that of UP's Rs 261.33 and that of the country's Rs 330. Again, these four districts had among them about 10 per cent of the population of UP with only 4.6 per cent of UP's total area. Twenty-two per cent of the total number of holdings were below one acre, and out of the 78 lakhs population only a little over 2 lakhs worked in industrial occupations. The road mileage in the area compared favourably with that in the rest of the state when related to area but was deficient in relation to population. The per capita indebtedness in Deoria stood at more than three months' per capita consumption expenditure in the district. In Ghazipur, it was more than two months' per capita consumption expenditure, in Azamgarh, a little more and in Jaunpur a little less than the per capita consumption expenditure in these districts.

While the per capita consumption expenditure in Deoria was Rs 16.95, in Ghazipur it was Rs 16.80, the same in Jaunpur and Rs 16.69 in Azamgarh. The prevailing wage rate varied from Rs 0.66 to 0.98; precisely, it stood at Rs 0.69 in Azamgarh, at Rs 0.98 in Deoria, at Rs 0.66 in Ghazipur and at Rs 0.69 in Jaunpur. In Mathura and Sitapur districts (now in the central and western regions of UP), the per capita consumption expenditure was Rs 22.62 and Rs 24.30, respectively; the wage rate being Rs 1.49 in Mathura and Rs 1.18 in Sitapur in the same period. This low-wage rate was obviously due to both lower investment for development and an abundant supply of labour in these districts. The per capita outlay in these four districts in the First Five-Year Plan was Rs 14 only as against Rs 26 for the state as a whole. Only 534 tube wells were constructed in the entire area during the First Plan. But it was during this period that the Rihand Dam Project was started in Mirzapur. While no tangible headway could be made in the Second Plan over what had been done earlier, some concrete steps were taken in the Third Five-Year Plan to give a spurt to developmental activities in the area.

Incidentally, it was in the Third Plan Period that UP was recognized as a backward state and a substantial step was taken to raise the plan outlay and the quantum of central assistance for the state. Meanwhile, UP had been divided into five economic regions for purposes of investment and development, viz., the Hills, the Western, the Central, the Eastern and Bundelkhand regions, of which the Eastern region, the Hills and Bundelkhand region were recognized as backward regions needing special assistance for development. Also, an additional assistance of Rs 4 crores was sanctioned to UP during 1959–61 for special programmes to be implemented in these backward regions.

The total population of the area was estimated to go up to 1 crore in 1975–76 and the annual per capita income expected to touch Rs 330 figure, the per capita income of India in 1960–61 (as per the 1960–61 prices). The total population of these four districts is now over 1 crore and 30 lakhs, India's per capita income is Rs 7,060, and of UP is Rs 4,787, which means that the gap between the per capita income of eastern UP, of UP as a whole and that of India has further widened over these 20 years since 1975.

In the above background, we can look at the problem of eastern UP in perspective. This region of UP which initially comprised 15 districts, namely, Allahabad, Azamgarh, Bahraich, Ballia, Basti, Deoria, Faizabad, Ghazipur, Gonda, Gorakhpur, Jaunpur, Mirzapur. Pratapgarh, Sultanpur and Varanasi, now consists of 27 districts with the addition of 12 more districts, although its geographical area remains the same. It covers an area of about 85,844 sq. km. which is 29.16 per cent of the total geographical area of UP. The total population of the area as per the 1991 census is 5.27 crores and the density of its population is 614 per sq. km. as against the density of UP's population, which stands at 473, the density of population of the Western, Central, Hill and Bundelkhand regions standing at 603, 528, 116 and 229, respectively.

The observation of the Joint Study Team that agriculture is the mainstay of the economy of these four districts holds good for the entire region. While 84.5 per cent of the working population in these four districts was engaged in cultivation as against 74.5 per cent of UP's population being engaged in cultivation in the 60s when the study was actually conducted, 77.2 per cent of the working population of the larger chunk of eastern UP, now consisting of 22 districts, still remains dependent upon agriculture and allied activities. The corresponding figures for UP are 71.72 per cent; for western UP, 66.4 per cent; for central UP, 72.9 per cent; for Bundelkhand, 78.5 per cent and for the hills, 64.6 per cent.

As against the 25 per cent urbanization in the country as a whole, it is 19.8 per cent in UP; 23 per cent in western UP, 11.6 per cent in eastern UP. Low urbanization and inadequate diversification of the occupational structure are symptomatic of under underdevelopment and backwardness. However, the little urbanization that eastern UP has achieved all through the long years of planned development is more *parasitic* than *generative*. If the growth of towns and cities does not lead to an increasing diversification of their occupational structure, that is, to a larger percentage of the working population shifting from primary to secondary industry, urban growth becomes parasitic. Urban growth in eastern UP, in fact in UP as a whole, is largely ungenerative or parasitic in this sense, being largely the result of migration from the villages to the cities on account of the rural push, i.e., the increasing pressure of land in the villages due to population growth.

No attempt has been made by the planners in UP to exploit the development potential of the cities and small towns which have come up in no small number in eastern UP. There are over 170 urban settlements in eastern UP, which can be made to play a major role in the development of the region.

The average size of holdings in eastern UP is only 0.68 hectare as against 0.93 hectare in the state, 82.42 per cent of which are marginal or sub-marginal, i.e., below 1 hectare. The average yield per hectare of land is 13.69 quintals as compared to 17.85 quintals in western UP and 14.61 quintals in UP. The total area under irrigation in eastern UP is 55.26 per cent as against the 73.84 per cent in western UP and 57.19 per cent in UP as a whole. The number of dispensaries per 1 lakh population in eastern UP is 3.2 as against 3.1 in western, 3.5 in central, 4.6 in Bundelkhand, 11.8 in hills and 3.68 in UP as a whole.[3]

Literary percentage in eastern UP (1991 census)[4] is 38.6 as against 42 in western UP, 42.6 in central UP, 42.3 in Bundelkhand, 59.6 in hills and 41.8 in UP. Literacy percentage (female) in eastern UP is 20.9 as compared to 26.6 in western UP, 28.3 in central UP, 23.9 in Bundelkhand, 42.9 in the hills and 25.3 in UP. The number of schools (Junior Basic and Senior Basic) is 48+9 as against 50+9 in western UP, 58+12 in central UP, 70+13 in Bundelkhand, 143+3 in hills and 53+11 in UP as a whole. Likewise, the number of colleges in eastern UP as on March 31, 1994 was 165, that of higher secondary schools was

2,088, that of senior basic schools was 5,173 and of junior basic schools was 26,484.

The number of persons engaged in working in factories per lakh of population in eastern UP (1988–89) was 242 as against 704 in western UP, 631 in central UP, 235 in Bundelkhand, 655 in the hills and 492 in UP. The per capita gross value of the industrial produce in eastern UP (1988–89) was 604 as against 2,028 in western UP, 1,140 in central UP, 331 in Bundelkhand, 1,611 in the hills and 1,235 in UP. The number of working factories per lakh of population in eastern UP (1988–89) was 1.6, in western UP it was 9.2, in central UP it was 5.9, in Bundelkhand it was 1.9, in the hills it was 7.7 and in UP it was 5.4.

As regards the infrastructural facilities, eastern UP again trails behind all the regions – the length of PWD roads per lakh population (1994–95) in the region being 47 km. as against 50.7 km. in western UP, 50 km. in central UP, 85.8 in Bundelkhand, 200 km. in the hills and 57.2 km. in UP. The situation is equally unfortunate when the road transport facilities are considered per 1,000 sq. km. of area. The percentage of electrified villages to total number of villages in eastern UP is 74 as against 84.8 in western UP, 66.8 in central UP, 64 in Bundelkhand, 76.1 in the hills and 75.3 in UP.

The above figures speak loudly of the eastern UP's plight, but they do not reveal its exact nature. For instance, it is not easy to believe that with barely 11 per cent urbanization, eastern UP will be facing problems which generally go with high urbanization, viz., those of cultural decay and degradation. The cities of eastern UP, howsoever small, are becoming pockets of poverty, misery and filth. While the quality of life is a little better around their central business destructs, their zones of decay are gradually widening in area. There is a marked change, no doubt, in the outward appearance of the villages – Kharanja roads, semi-*pucca* dwellings in place of the old mud houses with thatched roofs, tubewells, tractors and so forth. There are no longer any lean months in the year even for the landless labourers as far as provision for two square meals is concerned. 'Gobari'[5] has long ceased to be an important point in the concept of rural economy of eastern UP. But is that development? An area where 80 per cent of the female population is illiterate and where even primary education is still voluntary cannot be called civilized, much less developed. No serious attempt was ever made to study the unintended consequences of the Panchayati Raj Institutions (PRIs), nor was the government ever keen to profit from the findings of such studies conducted by the non-government agencies. The Panchayati Raj in its functioning has spawned much unnecessary conflict and violence in the villages, which have proved detrimental for the development of the latter. We have no complete official data on how the small bureaucracy associated with the work of land redistribution at the village level, in the initial stages of land reforms in eastern UP, tilted the whole programme against the landless and in favour of the influential people, or how it again bungled the programme of redistribution of the ceiling land.

It is not without justification that UP has been put at the bottom among all the 14 major states of India in respect of Human Development Index (HDI); its index being 0.07 as against Bihar's, MP's, Rajasthan's and Orissa's, which stand at 0.11, 0.14, 0.19 and 0.21, respectively with the national average standing at 0.37. Bihar and MP have a lower per capita state domestic product, but they still rank above UP in this respect because of their higher life expectancy and higher literacy percentage. Similarly, Orissa has almost the same per capita domestic product as UP, but stands above it in life expectancy and literacy rates. Rajasthan has a lower literary rate but a higher life expectancy and therefore it ranks above UP. Uttar Pradesh has the highest infant mortality rate and has the largest concentration of people living below the poverty line. According to the State Annual Plan 1997–98, the absolute number of people below the poverty line increased from 506 lakhs in 1977–78 to 530.6 lakhs 1983–84. Figures for 1987–88 however show a decline both in the absolute number and the percentage of people below the poverty line. But figures as, we said above, do not speak the whole truth about the reality. The so-called poverty line is essentially the subsistence line, its dropping down and further down does not mean much in terms of development, for it does not actually show that poverty has declined; what it shows is that the people have risen above the subsistence level. The Patel Study Team in 1964 had identified 80 per cent households in Azamgarh, 82 per cent in Deoria, 84 per cent in Ghazipur as against 78 per cent households in Sitapur and 73 per cent in Mathura, which did not possess any consumer durables such as cycles, sewing machines, gramophones, radios, wrist watches, etc. The situation even today is none too rosy, at least for the bulk of the landless labourers, sub-marginal (owing 0–1 acre) and marginal (owing 1–2 acres) farmers.[6]

It should be clear from what has been said above that the gap between UP and India and that between eastern UP and UP in respect of development is widening rather than shrinking in spite of relentless planned efforts since independence to lessen it. As we pointed out above, till the end of the Second Plan, UP was not considered a backward state, Bihar up until then was on the top of the list of laggard states needing special attention of the Planning Commission, MP came next and then came Orissa and Kerala. Since the Third Plan when it was recognized as a laggard state, UP has consistently gone down hill and is perhaps the most sick among the BIMARU states.

This brings us to the point we made earlier, viz., that the UP government has a core when it says that it has been taken for a ride by the Central Government ever since the launching of the Five-Year Plans in the country. When everything has been said in favour of UP, the point that its smart economic advisers forget is that development is not an exclusive function of investment and also that it is not a value-neutral process. The point was well taken by the Patel Study Team which observed in its report that 'the study of the four districts has thrown up data on the basis of which it is possible to state that mere investment and application of other inputs can achieve only partial progress. A fuller development is possible only through a change in the basic structure of the economy in the area and orientation in the approach of the people of the area towards life and social values'.[7]

It would be an oversimplification to say that UP's backwardness is the result of 'inequitous distribution of investment in the country.' This is not the place to enter into a detailed discussion of the factors responsible for the stagnation and slow growth of UP's economy. The states which have a higher HDI than that of UP do not claim a proportionately higher share in central assistance, nor can their demand be conceded even if they claim it. Uttar Pradesh's grouse is not genuine. But the fact remains that the Planning Commission has failed to honour its initial commitment to provide special assistance to backward and poor areas in UP. The Patel Committee's recommendations were never fully implemented by the Government of UP and the Planning Commission. In the meanwhile, life has continued to deteriorate in eastern UP and its backwardness has reached a point where it threatens to resist all efforts to undo it.

As things stand today, massive planning efforts will be needed to effect even a semblance of development in eastern UP. First, what will be the target of development planning in Eastern UP? To catch up with the level of underdevelopment reached in UP or with the one achieved in western UP, which is generally higher than that of UP? In the short run, we cannot but think of selected areas whose development could play the role of a catalyst in triggering off developmental change in the region as a whole. However, we will come to this point shortly. But it must be emphasized that separate five-year plans as sub-plans of the major state plan have to be drawn up and launched in eastern UP. The state cannot take adequate care of eastern UP within its projected target of 7 per cent economic growth in the Ninth Plan, which is lower than the growth expected to reduce to disparity between the per capita income of the state and that of the country. One very encouraging message received through the states' Annual Plan 1997–98 (Volume I) is that 'increasing dependence of the state on central assistance is perilous for future planning and a sound financial management' (p. 69). Allocater of an outlay of Rs 460 crores to the Poorvanchal Vikas Nidhi in the Ninth Plan, howsoever limited the states' resources may be, is much too meagre an amount considering the developmental needs of the 22 districts of eastern UP. It is indeed unfortunate that the state pleads its helplessness when it comes to raising the level of investment in eastern UP, but it has no difficulty in finding resources to raise the level of investment in western UP. On the basis of the 1991 census, the per capita investment in Ghaziabad has been about seven times as high as that in Eastern UP barring Sonebhadra and Sultanpur and in Nainital about five times as high as in eastern UP (Rs 4,877, Rs 3,947, Rs 800). With the limited resources of the state notwithstanding if the government had been fair and important in dealing with the backward regions, the situation would not have deteriorated to the extent it has in eastern UP. It is a flood-prone area, also over populated having the highest density of population in the country. But these physical drawbacks of the region should not be allowed to become a factor in discouraging effective human intervention to raise its economic level.

We will leave it to the economists to work out the quantum of investment that will be needed over a period of time to facilitate a speedy take off of the region to the stage of self-propelling development. As it concerns us, we will continue our attention mainly to the non-economic variables relevant to the purpose in hand.

First and foremost, the Patel Study Team had recommended the creation of a special Areas Cell by the State Planning Board to be entrusted with the overall supervision, watch and control at the district, sub-divisional and tehsil levels in backward areas. Besides, this cell which may have a pre-eminently monitoring function, a separate authority for planning and development of eastern UP may be set up, which may be charged with the responsibility of formulating plans in terms of the genuine needs of the people and negotiable with both the State Government and to Planning Commission for funds. This will be a much needed measure for the decentralization of power and democratization of planning.

Secondly, as the status report of the State Government has pointed out, much distortion in the planning process may take place because of lack of proper institutionalization of the administrative framework of planning. To depersonalize the working of the administrative framework and to make it fully transparent are the preserving needs of the hour, which must be attended to by the government.

The third problem which calls for special attention of the government, concerns what Gunnar Myrdal has aptly called 'softness' the general tendency on the part of the people in general in developing countries, to resist the rule of laws. Laxity and arbitrariness in dealing with matters can be and are exploited for personal gain by men in high places who have the backing of economic, social and political power. It is this softness which breeds corruption and provides the due to the understanding of why benefit work only 20 paise out of every rupee spent for development reaches the targeted beneficiary. The problem has to be dealt with and effectively.

As directly relevant to eastern UP, the top priority has to be given to the education and empowerment of women. If growth of population is to be effectively controlled, for without an effective birth control there is no change in the pressure on land being reduced, then the involvement of women in the process becomes crucial. The consensus that has emerged among population experts after the International Conference on Population and Development held in Cairo in 1994 is that there should now be an increasing focus on 'promoting the health of mothers and children through an emphasis on individual reproductive choice, access to information and health services and empowerment of women' for success in any policy of population management. Women's education therefore deserves top priority in a backward region faced with the twin problem of high birth rate and illiteracy with concomitant misery and poverty. Investment in women's health and education should be the first charge on the allocation provided for the regions in the State plans. The urban centres in the region as we have suggested above should be made to play an effective role in the development of the region. Strategies could be worked out in consultation with the experts, demographers and urban sociologists.

Full advantage should be taken of the presence of universities and hundreds of colleges in the region to improve our understanding of the socio-economic conditions and its cultural traditions. In fact, the universities should be actively involved in the process of developmental planning in the region. They may be entrusted with the responsibility of conducting the necessary research studies which might enable us to better understand their problems and devise methods to tackle them.

Notes

1. See *Backwardness of Uttar Pradesh: Some Reasons,* Government of Uttar Pradesh, State Planning Commission, 1996.
2. See *Report on Joint-Study Team Uttar Pradesh (Eastern Districts) Ghazipur, Azamgarh, Deoria, Jaunpur,* Government of India, Planning Commission, 1964.
3. See Draft Ninth Five-Year Plan, 1997–2000 and Annual Plan 1997–98, Vol. I.
4. See *Backwardness of Uttar Pradesh: Some Reasons,* Government of Uttar Pradesh, State Planning Commission, 1996.
5. Gobari was the dried excreta discharged by the cattle which during the harvesting season ate the standing wheat or barley crops or the harvested crops stored in the farmyards and were unable to digest the grains, so the chewed and swallowed grains discharged as faecal matter which when dried up was collected by the landless and the abjectly poor in the villages for separating the wheat or barley grains present in the dung for consumption. The grains packed up from such animal excreta were called 'gobari.'
6. See K. Shanker, *Economic Weekly,* October 20–27, 1990.
7. See *Report on Joint-Study Team Uttar Pradesh (Eastern Districts) Ghazipur, Azamgarh, Deoria, Jaunpur,* Government of India, Planning Commission, 1964.

13

The Traditional Theory of Caste

The modern sociological theory regards the caste system as a variant of the ascriptive system of stratification in which the allocation of role and status is governed by non-rational principles such as age, kinship, birth, etc. Not much, however, is known about the actual mode of the working of these principles, but the assumption behind the view seems to be that caste system is anything but a normal form of social organization. The traditional theory or what is disdainfully called the Hindu theory of caste is a radical anti-thesis of this view; it considers the system as a model of just and healthy society in which the distribution of privileges and responsibilities is based on the law of one's nature. According to this theory, then, the caste system is the most truly natural or normal form of social stratification. It must be remarked at the very outset that the theory like all traditional doctrines is an enunciation of certain metaphysical principles which can not be justified on sociological grounds. In what follows, no attempt will, therefore, be made to prove the theory; our aim, instead, will be to show that it is based on the consistency procedure and requires no additional proofs for its validation.

The texture of the theory is made up of a number of principles, all penetrating into one another and centring around the supreme principle of what the Hindus call dharma.

Dharma is a difficult word to define. The root 'dhri' (sans) from which it is derived means 'to hold', 'to sustain', 'to support', 'to keep'. Following this meaning, Dr Bhagwan Das has offered the definition of the term, which considering its extremely subtle and indeterminate nature is perhaps the best ever attempted. It is as follows:

> That which holds a thing together, makes it what is, prevents it from breaking up and changing it into something else, its characteristic function, its peculiar property, its fundamental attribute, its essential nature, is its dharma, the law of its being primarily. That which makes the world process what it is, holds its parts together as one whole in a breakless all binding chain of cause and effect is the law of nature or nature's god, dharma, in the largest sense the world order. That scheme or code of laws which binds together human beings in the bonds of mutual rights and duties, of causes and consequences of actions arising out of their temperamental characters in relation to each other and thus maintains society is human law Manava dharma.[1]

The definition makes it clear that dharma is the principle of being par excellence; viewed from the microcosmic standpoint, it is the law of one's nature; viewed from the macrocosmic standpoint, it is nature's law or the law of cosmic being. Now, to say that the caste system is based on the law of one's nature is actually to say that it is based on dharma. In a dharmic system, each individual will exist in his naturally ordained place or in other words the allocation of privileges and responsibilities in a dharmic system will be determined by the specific requirements of each individual's nature. It will, that to say, be a fixed or more appropriately 'an irrevocable' system of stratification. But it must be borne in mind that every fixed order of relationships would not constitute a dharmic system. The latter must be understood as a metaphysically determined system and in this sense, distinguished from a logically closed homoestatic system in which the position of each part is determined by the structural requirements of the system as much and in which no part is supposed to share the existence of other parts or to exist independently of its relationship with the whole. In a metaphysically determined system, the part whole relationship assumes a different significance. Hence, the part is cosubstantial with the whole, which means that the former does not derive its existence from its relationship with the latter even though in certain respects it may be subordinate to it. The nearest example of a dharmic or metaphysically determined system is a hierarchy (GK hieros = sacred + arkho = rule), a ritually closed system of stratification within which the position of each individual is ritually fixed, predetermined that is to say. In distinguishing between a dharmic and homoestatic system, we are not reiterating, however, the sociological distinction between atonism and holism; the latter distinction, we maintain, is based on a reductionist fallacy. Nor do we intend to suggest that the dharmic system is a model of the psycho-social world and the homoestatic system, a model of the biophysical world. The dichotomy of nature and man is also based on a wrong ontology. Both man and nature are included within the unity of the dharmic system; they do not represent two disparate realms of determination and freedom, but are two different though cosubstantial levels of being. In fact on the metaphysical level of reference, there can be no opposition between determination and freedom; they would both appear as aspects of Manava Dharma. In conforming to the law of one's nature, man is essentially asserting his freedom and in asserting his freedom he is essentially sacrificing it (more about this point later on).

If a dharmic system is a natural system, it follows that a dharmic system is also a normal system because in their essential meaning nature and norm are identical terms. What we have to demonstrate now is that a dharmic system is bound to assume a caste like form. Let us see what the term caste actually represents. Of all the definitions of the concept, the one which seems most appropriate is that given by Rene Guenon. He says 'caste which the Hindus describe indifferently by one or other of the two words Jati and Varna is a social function determined by the particular nature of each human being'.[2] Though somewhat unusual, the definition is nevertheless in perfect accord with the orthodox view on the nature of caste. According to the Gita, for instance, the functions of each of the four castes are born of their nature (swabhava). 'The function of the Brahman, Kshatriya, Vaishya and Shudras, O Parantap have been allocated according to the qualities born of their nature'.[3] The suggestion implicit in this statement is that the caste system is a naturally determined organization of social functions. And this is also the implication of Rene Guenon's definition. We have been using the term 'nature' over and over again without saying anything about its actual connotation. The term ordinarily refers to the sum total of habits and despositions acquired by man in the course of his adjustment with the external environment. At least this is what it means in current psychological usage. But it is essentially a metaphysical concept: its meaning cannot be determined in psychological terms. The 'nature' of a thing is its essential attribute, a characteristic property which makes the thing what it is. One of the implications of this statement is that the nature of a thing is something 'given' to it, something which it has not acquired but got readymade.

In terms of the above meaning of the concept, a naturally determined organization of functions can be interpreted to mean a 'given' or 'unalterable' system of functional differentiation, a system to be taken for granted. And this precisely is the point that the traditional theory of caste aims to emphasize. If there is any unmistakable thread of identity running through the diverse versions of the theory, it is that the caste system is not a man-made order but a primordial model of social organization within which to quote Commaraswamy 'every one shall be enabled to become and by no misdirection prevented from becoming what he has in him to become'.[4]

It would seem that we have been arguing in a circle; the statements that we have made about the traditional theory are all tautological. But if this is any shortcoming of our exposition, it is inherent in the theory itself. It can be expressed either in tautological statements or in the hortatory language of the myth. There are thus two principle versions of the theory: Metaphysical and mythical. But since it was primarily addressed to the faithful, in the traditionally available accounts of the theory, the mythical version stands in sharper relief than the metaphysical. We shall soon return to the Purusha Sukta and other myths concerning the origin of caste. But before we do so, we must show the relationship between the model of the caste system and it's concretely existing form. The question that we have to examine in this connection is: How can a natural model of human society assume the form of a social stratification based on birth and ritual? We said above that the nature of a thing is it's 'characteristic property'. From this, it would follow that human nature consists of qualities which are exclusively man's own, which, in other words, make for the humanness of man. According to the Hindu view, the swabhava (nature) of an individual comprises two sets of qualities: gotrika and namika.[5] Gotrika refers to those qualities and despositions which the individual inherits from his gotra or lineage; these he shares with all the members of his family. But besides these hereditary qualities, there are certain other attributes of his nature which are specifically his own; which he does not share with any other member of his family, but which rather mark him off from the other members of his family. Of any two brothers for instance who have inherited the same set of gotrika qualities, one may be a prodigy, while the other may be a fool. These unique qualities of the individual are what individual names are meant to express. They have been, accordingly, called namika. Thus, the metaphysical concept of swabhava or nature becomes the principle of birth and ascription on the sociological plane. But it must be borne in mind that jati comprises both gotrika and namic qualities. It would be a mistake to think as many sociologists do that it simply refers to biological birth or hereditary qualities. The latter is only an index and a very sure index at that, of one's swabhava, the tendencies and qualities that will be manifested in the course of one's existence and that will entitle him to a role in the society. This explains the significance of the statement that everyone is a shudra by birth; one becomes a dwija (twice-born) by virtue of samskaras (ritual training).[6] In order to eliminate the possibility of a misdirection by which an individual might be prevented from developing his individuality, the Hindu society had devised a well-planned system of ritual training aimed at perfecting his natural abilities. Both the so-called elements of 'nature' and 'nurture' are thus included within the meaning of the Jati concept. But 'nature' in this context does not mean biological upbringing; it refers, instead, to the ritual training or transformation.

The Indian caste system (Jati Vyavastha) then, with its characteristic emphasis on hereditary occupation and ritual observance is the nearest approximation to the model of natural social hierarchy. But as is well known, the caste system is a four-fold hierarchy with each hierarchical division comprising innumerable sub-castes. There are some other features of the system also: endogamy, restricted commensality and connubium, for instance. In the traditional theory, there is no direct reference to these features; the theory only suggests that there can be four main types of swabhavas and four types of functions corresponding to these swabhavas. But if the theory is based on a normal view of life, then it would be possible to show that the human nature would normally tend to be differentiated into four forms and human action likewise would tend to be organized into four principal types. Again, if the Indian caste system is the nearest approximation to the Chaturvarnya model of the Gita and other traditional sources, then it should also be possible to deduce the general features of the caste system from its basic principle. Let us see if it is possible to do so. The natural tendency of functions, in very social system normally organized, would be to divide into two fundamental categories: ordinary and extraordinary. Functions which require no special skills for their performance will fall into the former category, while those requiring highly specialized knowledge and training for their execution will fall into the latter. The extraordinary functions would again tend to be differentiated into three main types: technic-economic, political-legal and cultural-religious. A logical analysis of the concept of action would readily suggest this typology. Such an analysis, for obvious reasons, can not be attempted here. It would suffice to say that action will generally have three principal modes of orientation: end-oriented, means oriented and agent-oriented. There may be one more mode of orientation: situational, but since it cannot assume any meaningful form, we can easily exclude it from the category of action. The organizational form of agent-oriented action we call cultural-religious, that of end-oriented action, political-legal and that of means-oriented action, technic-economic. It can also be shown that these three types of actions will inevitably tend to be organized in a hierarchy, that is, a natural order of super- and sub-ordination. The cultural-religious by virtue of being oriented to the agent (the ultimate end of life) will be the superior-most action and occupy the top position in the hierarchy. The technic-economic action by virtue of its mode of orientation will be inferior to both cultural-religious and political-legal actions, and will be placed lower to them. But, the ordinary actions will have to be placed lower still in the hierarchy just because they are ordinary. This four-fold organization of function has a very close resemblance with the natural division of karmas as suggested in the Gita. The cultural-religious function belongs to the Brahmans who constitute the spiritual and intellectual authority. The political-legal comprising the royal, administrative and military functions belongs to the Kshatriyas. The technic-economic including the varied range of technical, commercial and economic functions belong to the Vaishyas and the ordinary functions which do not require any special skill for their execution belong to the Shudras. The first three classes are, therefore, rightly called dwija (twice-born), for the dwija is actually the initiated one, he who has undergone an esoteric training. The Shudras were not considered fit for this training for the simple reason that it did not accord with their natural disposition. But it will be wrong to conclude from this that the functions assigned to the Shudras were none the less important than those assigned to the dwijas.

In fact, every society has its dwijas and Shudras, even the secular societies of the modern West have not been able to dispense with the necessity of distinguishing between the ordinary and extraordinary spheres of life. The continuing dichotomy of the elite and the mass in the modern societies only shows how meaningful is the distinction between dwijas and Shudras.

In a hierarchical organization based on a clear-cut differentiation of functions, restrictions such as those associated with commensality and connubium are bound to exist. Much has been said by western scholars about the origin of these restrictions. But the important point that they have failed to see is that in every society organized on the basis of a bipartite division of life into sacred and profane, there must be a set or rituals aimed at maintaining and preserving the discontinuity of the two spheres. If the two spheres are allowed to encroach upon on another the very purpose of their division would be defeated. A number of ritual interdictions exist in the primitive societies whose primary object is to realize the state of natural separation between the sacred and profane spheres of life. The commensal and connubial restrictions prevailing in the caste society of India are thus simply an application of the metaphysical principle of differentiation of functions. Their aim is to prevent any undue mixing or confusion of functions and to minimize the chances of an individual deviating from his duties and engaging in pursuits which do not accord with his natural disposition.

In order to demonstrate finally that the Indian caste system is a contingent form of the dharmic model of the human society, we must show that it is also consistent with the principle of individual freedom. For as we said above in the dharmic system, the part though in certain respects subordinate to the whole is yet quite independent of it. On the face of it, the caste system, however, seems a complete negation of the idea of individual freedom; it does not permit any freedom of choice either in regard to private matters such as marriage or public matters such as vocation. In what sense then, is it compatible with human freedom? To answer this question would entail a review of the entire philosophy of life as understood by the Hindu. That will not be possible here. But a few general remarks will be in order. The paramount (param) aim (artha) of life according to the Hindu is the attainment of Moksha. Moksha literally means 'liberation'. Hence, the attainment of Moksha literally means the liberation of the jiva (life monad) from the chain of actions (karma bandhanat). More positively it means the attainment of a state of pure being (sat), pure consciousness (hit) and pure bliss (ananda), a state of perfect identity between the jiva and Brahman 'wherein all qualifying attributes are transcended, a state of intelligence beyond the pairs of opposites wherein all ideas of separation and variety are effected'.[7] Karmabandhan is actually the dynamic counterpart of what we earlier called the principle of metaphysical determination. The paramount aim of life according to the Hindu, then, is the overcoming of this determination. It is a curious paradox of Hindu thought that while man is supposed to be totally governed by the law of karamic determinations, the ultimate end of life is supposed to be freedom from determination. But for all that it is a paradox it is a most meaningful paradox. In the concept of the ultimate end, also grounded is the possibility of its attainment. And it is this possibility that constitutes the essential basis of human freedom – the freedom to choose to be or not to be. Despite all the limitations of this nature, man is always free to decide whether to shake off the burden of life and enjoy everlasting happiness and freedom or to suffer perpetual pain and bondage under its dead weight. Of the three kinds of karmas, Sancita, Agami and Prarabdha, the force of the first two can always be destroyed by Vidya (genesis). It is only the third, the Prarabdha over which man has absolutely no control. It consists of karmas accumulated in the past which have started showing results. The Sancita are those accumulated karmas which have yet not started bearing fruit but which are sure to bear the fruit if they are not destroyed. The Agami comprise those karmas which are accumulating and which will become the seeds of destiny if one were to continue on the path of ignorance (Avidya). It is possible for man to prevent the accumulation of Agami karmas, equally possible it is for him to destroy the potentiality of the Sancita karmas, but to undo the Prarabdha is entirely beyond man's power. One can not change his jati once he is born into it, but it is within one's means to escape the cycle of birth and rebirth should one choose to escape it. Now to the extent to which it is possible for man to transcend the law of his nature in spite of being determined by it, he is free even within the frameworks of the karmic law of determination.

So far, our discussion has been confined mainly to the metaphysical aspect of the traditional theory. It is time we turned our attention to its mythical aspect. To show the link between the two aspects of the theory, it would be necessary, however to make a few more observations abut the concept of Moksha. There are two accepted ways of realizing Moksha, the way of renunciation and the way of action, Pravritti[8] Marga and Nirvitti Marga as they are called in the Hindu tradition. The Gita calls them Samkhya Yoga and Karma Yoga, respectively. The Samkhya Yoga or the Yoga of Knowledge is the way of total renunciation of action. Accordingly therefore, it is also called Samnyas Yoga. The second too is a way of renunciation, but unlike the first it involves no abstention from work but is based, on the contrary, on a complete affirmation of life. It requires everyone to carry out his duties in a spirit of total non-involvement, disregarding completely the consequences thereof, the gains and losses that they will entail. To do one's duties in this spirit of detachment (anasakti) is to do them skillfully and a skilful performance of work is true yoga (yogah karmsu kausalma). This is the essence of Karma Yoga or Nishkarma Karma Yoga as enunciated in the Gita. The Nishkarma Karma is also the highest form of sacrifice, for all sacrificial operations according to the Gita are in essence a sacrifice of desires. Now the emphasis, in the caste system, on everyone sticking to and skillfully executing his natural duties irrespective of whether they are externally good or bad, is a clear indication of the fact that the system has been designed to facilitate each individual's fullest participation in the sacrificial operation through which the ultimate end of life can be realized. Thus what was earlier defined as a system based on dharma would now appear to be a system determined by the requirements of the sacrifice. And this brings us direct to the mythical aspect of the theory. There are several myths concerning the origin of caste. In the Vishnu Purana, we get the following statements: 'Brahma made this four-fold system for the performance of sacrifice'.[9] And 'when true to his design, Brahma became desirous to create the world, creatures in whom harmony and goodness (sattva) prevailed sprang from his mouth; others in whom passion (rajas) predominated came from his breast; others in whom both passion and ignorant darkness (tamas) were strong proceeded from his thighs: others he created from feet whose chief characteristic was ignorant darkness, of there was composed the system of the four varnas, Brahmanas, Kshatriyas, Vaishyas and Shudras, who had respectively issued form his mouth, breast, thighs and feet'.[10] There is a similar statement in the Gita also. It is like this: 'The four-fold system (chaturvarnya) was created by Me according to the division of qualities (gunas) and functions (karmas)'.[11] And according to the Purusha Sukta of the Rig Veda, 'His mouth became a priest (Brahman), his arm was made a nobleman (Rajanya), his thigh was transformed into a farmer (Vaishya), from his feet sprang the serirb man (Shudra). The moon was produced from his mind, the sun sprang from his eye, air and fire proceeded from his mouth and wind came from his breath. The intermediate region was produced from his navel, the sky from his head, the earth from his feet and space (lit. the quarters of the sky) from his ear; thus did he frame the world'.[12] The suggestion implicit in all the three myths is that the caste system has been created by a super-human agency for the performance of sacrifice. Now anyone familiar with the anagogic nature of the mythical language would agree that there is nothing personal or anthropomorphic about any of three figures occurring in these myths. Brahma, Me and Purusha do not refer to divine persons; they are rather the archaetype of man the maker. 'Creation' and 'sacrifice' likewise should not be taken to mean deeds accomplished by a personal agency. They are on the other hand, archaetypes of human action. Similarly, the relationship of mouth, arms, thighs and feet in the body of the Purusha (Universal or Cosmic man) is the archaetype of the organic relationship.

All that the above myths seem to suggest is that the caste system is a reproduction of an archaetypal model, the chaturvarnya or the natural hierarchy. The Purusha Sukta for instance, which is perhaps the completest Vedic myth of creation clearly suggests that the four-fold varna hierarchy is a reproduction of the Cosmic Man. The implied meaning of the statements in the Gita and Vishnu Purana is that all works irrespective of whether they belong to the Brahman, or the Kshatriya, the Vaishya or the Shudras, are an imitation of or are born of creation (sacrifice). Understood in anagogic terms, sacrifice and creation are identical operations. With sacrifice the Lord of Creatures of old created creatures and said 'By this you shall bring forth (fruits and offsprings), let this be your milker of desires. Foster by this the gods and let the gods foster you, fostering each other, you shall attain to the supreme good. Fostered by sacrifice the gods shall give you desired enjoyments; who enjoys their given enjoyments and has not given to them, he is a thief'.[13] And again 'sacrifice is born from work, work from Brahman, Brahman from Akshara and therefore the all pervading Brahman sarvagatam brahma is established in the sacrifice'.[14] In the Gita, thus, not only is sacrifice shown to be identical with 'creation' and 'work', but sacrifice, creation and work are all shown to be cosubstantial with Brahman. The archaetypal character of the sacrificial operation is further emphasized in the following passage 'brahman is the offering, Brahman is the material of the offering, by Brahman is material poured into the fire of the Brahman'.[15] There is, however, a close resemblance between the view of sacrifice taken by the Gita and that taken by the Vedic tradition. The Satpatha Brahman thus says 'the sacrifice is the other self of good ... therefore the sacrificer having made the sacrifice his other self takes his place in the sky, this heavenly world'.[16]

It is curious that certain castes of south India are still called 'Balija' born of the sacrifice[17] and both in the India and Ceylon, the position of each caste in the social hierarchy is determined by its part in the sacrifice. Take for instance the barber and washerman. The barber is ordinarily supposed to be a man who shaves and the washerman likewise a man who washes dirty clothes. But these popular notions about the service castes are true neither in the modern context nor were they true in the traditional context. The barber is actually the man who does the ritual shaving and so is the washerman, the man who does the ritual washing. The status of the barber and the washerman in the caste system is determined thus by the respective position of each in the sacrifice. The first holy tonsure (Chaula Karma) which is a ceremony of removing the profane hair from the head of the child is to be done by the barber. This he does in a number of ways, especially by removing the polluted hair from the heads of all the male members of the family. No ceremony in the household will be completed without the part played by the barber. The washerman's role is equally important. Besides washing the polluted clothes – there are several occasions of pollution in the Hindu household but birth and death are the well-known ones – he (strictly speaking the washer woman) offers blessings to the bride at the marriage ceremony for her happy and prosperous conjugal life. At a Tamil wedding, the washerman spreads cloth for the bridegroom (who for the time being is god Shiva) to walk upon.[18] And 'in the rear other washerman assisted by barbers sing or howl blessings and praises of which he (the bridegroom) is the subject'.[19] The barber carries the tali or marriage necklace and the cloth called Kurrai for the bride.[20] At funeral, the barber, the washerman and the drummer are sent for not the musicians. The barber prepares the fire for the cremation and conducts the person who lights the fire three times round the pyre.[21] The barber and the washerman are thus looked upon even till this day as low-order priests performing rites which the high-order priest can not touch.

It is clear from what has been said above that there is absolutely no difference between the metaphysical and the mythical aspects of the traditional theory. They are just two ways of stating the same truth. Whether we say that the caste system is a metaphysically determined organization of social functions or that it is an organization determined by the requirements of sacrifice, we are making substantially the same statement. If the traditional theory does not find favour with modern sociologists – the reason is not that it is intrinsically unsound but that it is wholly out of tune with the prejudices of modern sociology. It is, no doubt, meaningless in the modern context to say that the caste system is a sacrificial organization. But the fact that despite the increasing secularization of life in modern India, people have yet not ceased to believe it to be so and tenaciously cling to this belief, is evidence enough that at one time or another the system must have corresponded to a sacrificial organization.

Notes

1. *The Science of Social Organisation*, Vol. I, Second edition, pp. 49–50.
2. Renè Guènon, *Introduction to the Study of Hindu Doctrines*, London: Luzac & Co., 1945, p. 216.
3. Gita, Chapter XVIII–41.
4. *Hinduism and Buddhism*, Ananda Kentish Coomaraswamy, New York: Philosophical Library, p. 26.
5. Renè Guènon, op. cit., p. 218.
6. Janmana jayate shudro samskaradwijuchyate.
7. Heinrich Robert Zimmer, *Philosophies of India*, USA: Princeton University Press, 1969, p. 448.
8. Manusmriti.
9. *Caste*, A. Hocart UK: Russel and Russel Bolton, 1968, p. 18.
10. Mees: *Dharma and Society*, Gualtherus Hendrik Mees, New Delhi: Seema Publication, 1935.
11. Gita; Chapter IV–13.
12. Mees, op. cit., p. 65.
13. Aurobindo: *Lectures on the Gita*, p. 154.
14. Ibid., p. 157.
15. Gita, Chapter IV–24.
16. A. Hocart, op. cit., p. 18.
17. Ibid., p. 21.
18. Ibid., p. 10.
19. Ibid.
20. Ibid.
21. Ibid., p. 11.

14

Dimensions of Development

Development is the preoccupation of social sciences in the Third World, now struggling hard to retain its political identity, and since this world has always been at the receiving end in relation to the First and Second Worlds, the concepts and theories of development in terms of which it has been used to perceiving its situation have all been borrowed from the latter two worlds. In this respect the only change that has come about in the wake of the collapse of the Second World is the final exclusion of the left perspective from the main corpus of these theories. If the poverty and sluggish growth of the Third World was earlier attributed to mutually two sets of antogonistic causes, it is now the single cause theory which has come to prevail and to which intellectual opinion has willy-nilly reconciled itself.

If, earlier, the "dependency theory" existed as a strong contestant of the "lag theory" within the same corpus of the imported theories of development, the former has finally been ousted by the latter now. The dependency theory which considers the underdevelopment of the Third World as an overflow of the inequitous distribution of resources between the affluent North and the impoverished South inherent in the

---

Text of lecture delivered by Prof. S.P. Nagendra at XVI National Conference of ISSA on *Dimensions of Development* held from February 10 to 12, 1995 at Kashi Vidyapeeth, Varanasi.

structure of global, and which was popularized by left intellectuals, such as Gunder Frank and others, was basically inspired by Lenin's theory of imperialism. As is well-known, Lenin's thesis it was that when capitalism reaches its highest stage, i.e., when it becomes imperialism it begins to export exploitation to the colonies where native, labour and raw materials can absorb "surplus capital". It means that the contradiction which would bring down capitalism was not the class struggle within the developed world, but the conflict between the developed world and the "global proletariat" in the underdeveloped world.

There were not many takers of the lag theory in the Third World which explained development and underdevelopment in terms of a country willingness or reluctance to participate in the global market economy. There was nothing like satellitic or dependent development according to this theory; if a country was poor or underdeveloped, it was largely because it did not want to be wealthy or developed.

If as we said Lenin writing on imperialism provided the intellectual scaffolding to the "dependency theory", it is Francis Fukuyama who emerges as the true philosopher of the lag theory. The stand that Fukuyama takes in his much talked of recent publication, *The End of History and the Last Man* (1992), is that with the final triumph of capitalism and liberal democracy over communism and all other economic and political formations the parabolic movement of history has ceased, humanity having become what it had in it to become, or universal history having arrived at its destination. Liberal democracy and capitalism are then the only choice before man in the underdeveloped South or the erstwhile Third World if he wants to get out of his impoverished state and if he wants to realize his aspirations. Fukuyama is not the only social scientist to have said this; in fact all advocates of modernization as the goal of induced change in the developing countries have each in his own way been saying the same thing. The beauty of Fukuyama's philosophy however consists in the analogy which he uses to describe the end of history. In the parabolic movement of history, as he says, man who began as an inferior animal, the slave of nature, who was bound to a ready made environment, ends up as the most superior animal whose nearest example is the dog. "A dog", in Fukuyama's words, "is content to sleep in the sun all day, provided he is fed, because he is not dissatisfied with what he is. He does not worry that other dogs are not doing better than him, or that his career as a dog has stagnated, or that dogs are being oppressed in a distant part of the world. If man reaches a society in which he has succeeded in abolishing injustice, his life will come to resemble that of the dog. Human life, then, involves a curious paradox, it seems to require injustice, for the struggle against injustice is what calls forth what is the highest in man" (p. 311).

Whether or not Fukuyama has improved upon the performance of Kant, Hegel or Toynbee, is not the concern of this discussion. But neither Kant nor Hegel much less Toynbee thought in terms in which Fukuyama has conceived the ultimate stage of man's development. The motive force behind man's evolution to a higher level of rationality in Kant's view is, no doubt, his urge to give up the war or all against all and join together in a civil society where everyone could pursue the higher forms of life such as beauty, truth and goodness as in Hegel's view it was to realize the highest level of consciousness or the ideal of absolute freedom as exemplified in the constitutional state. But, the well-fed dog's life was the examples neither of Kant's higher form of civic life, nor of Hegel's highest form of rationality. But, to the extent to which Fukuyama's Eldorado promises to be the consumerist paradise, its best examples will definitely be the contested life of a dog.

After declaring God dead man had to establish a new centre of ultimate authority, invent a new totality of truth, goodness and beauty. Nietzsche, however, thought that such a fictional entity was not needed. Given his power of creativity or his "will to power" as he calls it, he will locate the *ubermench,* the superman in him. Fukuyama on the other hand not only considers such an entity necessary, he even invents one; his liberal democratic utopia represents this new visible totality in place of the invisible God. But Fukuyama forgets that the dog does not do anything else than to keep repeating his cycle of eating and sleeping throughout his short life. The traditional Greeks, Indians, Chinese all thought that man had a more superior purpose in life to realize than merely combining his labour power with nature to keep alive. No known civilization has approved of futile labour which Fukuyama considers the supreme preoccupation of man in his promised land. We say "futile" because repeating the same exercise day in and day out is life – Sisyphus rolling ceaselessly a stone to the top of a mountain and rolling it back when it fell down. Homer's Sisyphus is the archetype of the hardworking man who has no other occupation in life except hard work. But, then, Sisyphus had been cursed to this kind of uncreative life by the gods whose command he had violated, who, in other words, had forgotten virtue. Fukuyama cannot convince even the modern godless world of the wisdom of his thought.

But the New World Order, coming in the wake of the end of the Cold War in which a "peace dividend" is supposed to be an additional human resource to promote enhanced human welfare, social equality and environmental protection, is essentially the translation into practice of Fukuyama's utopia. The fascination exercised by the free global market on the minds of intellectuals in the Third World is so great that they overlook even its patent welfare losses, such as overexploitation of the existing natural resources for the consumption needs of the present generation ignoring completely the claims of the future generations, not to speak of the degradation of life caused by excessive consumerism. Whether structural adjustment policies have a human or a non-human face, some of their consequences will be culturally disastrous.

We do not want to touch upon the cases of the "little tigers" of the South, viz., Taiwan, South Africa and also the dark tiger Thailand often cited as examples of low consumption countries achieving development targets over the past few decades. If we go by empirical evidence it is both in favour of and against the policy of globalization and structural adjustment. The highly critical noises being made by the environmentalists in the developed North are only a reflection of the increasing distress being felt by the people in these countries as a premium for development.

Technology's major achievement in sociological terms is the development of *reified institutions* within which the human soul is made to languish. What has actually collapsed in the form of the Second World is not the Russian community of humans but only a part the refied structure of the West. The other part which is still intact has also become lifeless. Its tendency to become formal and lifeless had been noticed as early as the beginning of the twentieth century by Joseph Spengler. We have come to live in a world today, where in our neighbourhood philosophers are busy demolishing all arguments in favour of the existence of man as an individual.

15

Social Vision with Reference to Gandhi

To Albert Schweitzer whose credentials to speak about the western civilization can never be in doubt, the modern civilized world is not civilized at all; it is on the contrary a world of epigoni, inheritors, rather than creators of any positive good. In other words, according to Schweitzer, we stand today in the West close to the Nadir rather than the zenith of the Christian civilization, and modern science and technology – the two ruling signs of this civilization represent the decline rather than the ascent of the creative spirit of the West.

There would not be many takers of Schweitzer's view, nor would there be many to share the vision life implicit in his assertion. But it would be apropos to begin with Schweitzer while remembering Gandhi on his birthday; for he is among the few good men, known for his good work in the West, who comes close to Gandhi, at least in his thinking about modern civilization.

That Gandhi rejected modern civilization and all that it stood for, lock, stock and barrel is not quite important; what is important is that India had the option to choose between Gandhi and what he thought she should not choose and she finally chose what Gandhi did not want her to choose, and rejected him. What

---

Radio talk delivered on 2 October 1991 at All India Radio, Allahabad.

India had in fact contributed to world civilization was her Indianness which still remains the hallmark of her identity and without which she would appear before the world empty-handed. But, painfully it was her Indianness which India was called upon to surrender in exchange for her independence and everything it brought in its train.

In her encounter with the Christian West India had really a decadent civilization to imitate, as a kingly model, a civilization with an extremely feeble creative elan consisting, as Schweitzer would have us believe, of epigones rather than a genuine creative intellegentsia. Those who differ with us on this point may look at the progressive impoverishment of life in the West beginning from the thirteenth century as evidenced in progressive increase of material prosperity to the exclusion of spiritual values.

The wider human consequences of West's material progress accompanied by man's increasing mastery over nature are a subject of continuing debate. Today, the civilizing mission upon which it had ironically embarked during the eighteenth and nineteenth centuries, had, in the meanwhile, its desired effect, viz., that of uprooting generations of Asians, South Africans and other hapless victims of European imperialism from their traditional moorings. This impact of modern education through the imperial languages particularly English can be seen writ large on the faces of the young university graduates in India today. And it is not without justification that Ananda K. Coomaraswamy describes the present-day India as a land of cultivated peasants and uncultivated leaders. The peasants are more cultured to the extent that they are less exposed to the influence of modern education.

Modern West's most proud contribution to the world is her industrial civilization based on notions of social advancement, climbing free enterprise and production in quantity. "The one considers man's needs (which are but little here below); the other considers his wants, to which no limit can be set, and of which the number is artificially multiplied by advertisement". What Weber calls acquisitive or profit-oriented economy is set to spawn an ever-expanding multinational market for the surplus produced by its "over-occupied men" as Schweitzer would like to call them or by the "human labourans" as Hannah Arndt would like to describe them. It is this ever-expanding multinational trade that makes the modern industrial civilization a curse for humanity and from whose womb have arisen and will arise all wars.

In her progress towards modernization, young India has now reached a point where it must look back, particularly on an occasion like the birthday of Gandhi. For it was Gandhi among the leaders of resurgent India who had a clear vision of how India could retain her identity, and at the same time refashion her social institutions according to her genius and tradition and also liquidate the British legacy. Again, it was Gandhi who had the courage to attempt a redefinition of the primordial values of truth, non-violence, non-acquisition, cooperation, sacrifice, trusteeship and villagism, to establish their contemporary relevance – values which modernizing young India either disparages or offers only lip-service to.

Shall we then not take a closer look at Gandhi's vision and see if we can still own it and try to disown what cannot be legitimately our own. Gandhi outlines the basic principles of what to him constitutes a true civilization in the following words:

> "It is a society based on moral duty rather than on individual rights. It is based on the principle of limited wants and easy contentment. It is non-competitive. It places a premium on the use of hands and facet. It shuns the evil cities and flourishes in small villages. It is based on a belief in God and subscribes to the principle of non-violence and moral force of the soul ... It has a simple technology and a closed economy".

Gandhi rejects the state of things denoted by "civilization" because it is a complete negation of the normal state of things. In pursuit of its supreme goal of maximizing "bodily welfare", civilization has built as Gandhi says a whole host of artifacts and amenities: better houses, better clothing, generation of greater wealth through machine and technology, printing and publication, faster communication, postal system and what not of the same species. People trapped in the labyrinth of this civilization are "half-mad", lack physical strength and courage, and keep up energy by intoxication. In fact, it is this civilization which should be called Satanic by the Muslims and Kaliyuga by the Hindus.

India's slavery, to Gandhi's mind, was not on account of any superior strength of England, but due to India's own weakness. Indians, Gandhi said, have been lured by money and luxury and in this process forgotten their morality and religion and also their internal strength as a nation. Swaraj therefore cannot mean the political legacy of the British rule minus the rule. For it would be a substitution of the "tiger by the tiger's nature" and not the real replacement of the tiger, as Gandhi put it. Gandhi, in other words, did not equate Swaraj with mere political independence; for him it meant a total abandonment of the British system taken as a lamp post of civilization. This also explains Gandhi's aversion to parliamentary democracy. "That which you consider to be the mother of Parliament", he writes in *Hind Swaraj,* "is like a sterile woman and a prostitute". A sterile woman because it has not done a single good thing of its own accord and a prostitute inasmuch as it has to work under different kinds of pressure groups and different Prime Ministers. It is therefore no better than their mistress. "If India copies England", Gandhi further writes, "it is my firm conviction that she will be ruined".

Nor is democracy for Gandhi a mere formal participation in the ritual of general election; it is, on the other hand, the freeing of man from political and social bondage and from economic exploitation. It is equally a striving to realize one's identity with all beings. We have real Swaraj "when we learn to rule ourselves", and it is this Swaraj which Gandhi calls Ramraj. Ramraj to him is the kingdom of righteousness. By Ramraj he says, "I do not mean Hindu Raj, I mean by Ramraj divine raj, the Kingdom of God; the ancient Ramraj is one of true democracy".

Gandhi's vision of India, once wrote M. Chelapathi Rau, the illustrious editor of *The National Herald,* then, was one of "pastoral paradise". What Chelapathi meant by this phrase is that in the social set-up that Gandhi visualized for India, agriculture would be the mainstay of the economy and the village the basic unit of society integrated into vocational groups, which will be internally democratic and outwardly responsible to other groups only for the fulfilment of their own functions. Since the village was to be the cornerstone of both the economy and society in this set-up, the cities would not be allowed to ride roughshod over the destinies of the villages. Rather than functioning as agencies of economic exploitation of the villages, cities will serve as emporia for village products, they will be centres for the disposal of the surplus produced in the villages. A symbiotic relationship between the villages and cities will thus be the bedrock of villagism which Gandhi wanted to be revived in India.

It would be cruel to remember Gandhi to deify him or to reduce him to the rifle of a doctrine or to a paradigm of action to be prescribed to others. For in a age of broken lights and dying culture like ours, doctrines and paradigms of action have a tendency to endless ramification like the legendry monster, every drop of whose blood gave rise to another monster like him. Gandhi's rejection of modern civilization was essentially a repudiation of its false metaphysics. Let us then see how far we can go in reliving the experience already lived by him rather than trying to fit him into this or that philosophical moulds.

16

Human Resource and Industrial Development

Industrial development is listed high on the agenda of the Third World countries, which have all opted for modernization as a long-term goal of development planning. So powerful has been the hold of modernization on the minds of the intelligentsia in these countries that even its worst detractors who outright reject its economic implications, particularly its inherent tendency to promote industrial capitalism, do not reject its cultural connotation. Nor has modernization meant different things to the different people who have opted for it; on the contrary it has conveyed the same meaning to them all. What it has basically meant to them is following the same path in respect of economic development and social change, as the affluent West has traversed all through the centuries to become a modern economy and polity.

In other words, their pattern of development has been throughout satellitic rather than autonomous. In the name of development they have been trying to relive the experience of the modern West (including both Europe and the USA) which in effect has come to mean (i) rejection of religion as a guiding principle of life from the public realm or short of it, its total secularization; (ii) cultivation of the scientific spirit and acceptance of the sovereignty of reason in human life; and (iii) promotion of industrial capitalism by the state.

In no way is India's case different from that of other countries; all the ideals enshrined in her constitution – democracy secularism and socialism – are an essential component of modernization. But even after full four decades of sustained planning effort she has not been able to implement the modernizing ideals with any tangible degree of success. How slow has been the pace of industrial development in India for all the effort that has gone into it, can be judged from the fact that bulk of the country's total workforce is still engaged in primary industry, i.e., agriculture, animal husbandry, poultry farming, dairying etc. As per 1981 Census, the percentage of the workforce engaged in agriculture was as high as 66.6 as against 10 to 15 in Europe. Likewise, urbanization, an equally important index of development, as a major factor in industrialization, was only 73 per cent as against 80 to 90 per cent in Europe and the USA. So, even if we were to forget about the more sinister consequences of modernization such as increasing globalization of industrial capitalism, trade imperialism etc., and go the whole hog for industrial modernization, we would not be sure how much time we will take to join the club of developed nations.

From poverty to affluence through modernization will be a long and tedious journey; nor are there any short cuts to it. What, however, is a matter of serious concern to us is that despite a sizeable increase in saving and investment from 1950 to 1980, the pace of industrial development has not registered any meaningful increase. This probably explains the emphasis in the Seventh Plan on human resource development which in effect means expansion of education, health care, water supply, sanitation etc. The fact of human capital formation being a basic ingredient of industrial development should have been realized by our planners much earlier than the Seventh Plan. Manpower planning, in order to be appropriately linked with our developmental needs, should have been made part of a wider institutional planning, a component which our plans still woefully lack.

It is a pity indeed that India spends only 2.7 per cent of its total expenditure on education while South Korea spends 18.5 per cent and Singapore 19 per cent. A comparison of our case with South Korea and Singapore will be odious, but we often cite the good example of these countries, when we try to make out a case for privatizing our economy. Reduction of the plan allocation for education from 7.6 per cent in the First Plan to 2.6 per cent in the Sixth Plan only shows what priority do we accord to human capital formation in our plans. It is not only education which has been a low priority item in our plans; scientific research, sanitation, health, water supply etc., essential components of human resource development whose improvement will definitely mean a better quality of life, have also received scant attention in our plan priorities.

As a result, the overall literacy rate which stood at 43.46 per cent in 1981 has increased only to 52.11 per cent in 1991. Female literacy which in 1981 was 29.75 per cent has increased to 39.42 per cent only. There are any number of studies to show that a positive correlation exists between literacy and smaller family size, increasing achievement motivation and better entrepreneurial skill.

Therefore, if we are keen on showing better results in our programmes of alleviation of poverty, improvement of quality of life and accelerated industrial development, we have to integrate human capital formation with both population control and industrial development. Man is both the agent and patient of planned development. As an agent he has to be clear about the goal of planning, as also of the appropriate means to achieve it. He has also to ensure that the human material which is to be transformed through planning does not become deformed. It is human resource development which is the real key to success in all planning and development.

17

Enrichment of Life through Science and Religion

In the logical order of thought, religion is prior to science. It may precede science even in the chronological order, which is not to say that the two orders always coincide. What the logical priority of religion over science implies is that the relationship between the two is hierarchical: one of opposition and complementarity; within a graded whole; it always being the case that while the latter cannot subsist without the former, the former need not presuppose the latter. What Aristotle calls "first philosophy" stands in a similar relationship to second philosophies, including science, whose primary aim is rationalization; to interpret or to analyse, that is to say, the raw materials of experience, to make sense out of them, which they do either by subsuming particulars under universals or by deriving particulars from universals, according to their nature as theoretical or practical philosophies.

Unlike these, metaphysics or the first philosophy is not about any particular domain of thought, but about the ultimate reference of thought. In other words, metaphysics is about the first principles with reference to which the second philosophies validate their own principles or laws and which they try analogically to explain or demonstrate. The first principles are, then,

Radio talk delivered on 20 January 1993 on All India Radio, Allahabad.

self-validating or are valid a priori, needing no reference to "facts" or "second principles" for their authentication. But all second philosophies, be they theology, logic, epistemology, ethics, or mathematics, are in constant need for their formal validation and correction, which they cannot accomplish without reference to metaphysics. Religion is the enactment, the lived experience of metaphysics, or conversely metaphysics is the defining principle of the "religio", which constitutes the essence of religion. Revelation and gnosis are two names of the same unnamable.

On this normal view of the relationship between religion and science, no question as to their reconciliation or respective role in the enrichment of life should arise. They have both been equally trustworthy aides of man in his quest of himself. Before the dawn of modern age, any divorce between religion and science was unthinkable. Any number of studies can be cited to show the close historical link between magic, mysticism and science. Whether we take the case of traditional China and India or of the Islamic Middle East, religion has everywhere been the directive principle in the pursuit of science. Taoist temples were the early centres of observation of nature in China; all Indian and Islamic sciences of antiquity as well as middle ages, such as astronomy, mathematics, geology, mineralogy, medicine, music, etc., were steeped in religion and mysticism.

And this explains, what has been called the "stationary" nature of science and technology in the societies east of Athens as against their "hyper-dynamism" in western societies. Tribal technology, for anything we know of it, is still more "static". The slow growth of these technologies, as contrasted with the exponential growth of modern, is essentially an aspect of their self-balancing nature: their inbuilt capacity to resist wanton growth. What constitutes a check on their limitless expansion is their heteronomous character, that is, their dependence on something higher than themselves for their legitimation. Traditional science can likewise never aspire to be independent of the source from which it derives its authenticity and meaning. However, it is the peculiar situation of modern science that it not only asserts its uniqueness, but declares its total autonomy in the domain of knowledge and it is the same value-free science which refuses to be hostage to extra-scientific values. What scientific values are, we are never told; although we are clearly told what they are not. Metaphysical commitments on the part of the scientist, we are told, are all extra-scientific values.

Autonomy of modern science is only one facet of its discontinuity with tradition, its other facet being the former's overweening ambition to become a complete substitute for religion. And so fast has been the replacement of deism by reason, at least in the modern West, that even Bishops today are respectfully distancing away from God and trying to profess and preach their faith in a non-theological language. Atheistic theology is no longer a contradiction in terms, nor is a non-revelationary concept of God – a blasphemy. Not only has God been finally dislodged from his Kingdom; He has been declared dead and Reason crowned in his place as his successor.

If religion was the language through which God spoke to his subjects, the language of the new sovereign is verily science. It is not without reason, then, that those like Feuerbach, Karl Marx, Freud, Bertrand Russell and others, who reject religion as a series of intellectual mistakes or as a contrivance to legitimize social power by masking the real character of class relations, or as a universal neurosis of mankind, pin their hopes on science to transform society, so that man could do without religion in coping with the day-to-day difficulties of life.

If this be the meaning of religion, can it be credited with a positive role in the enrichment of life? The answer is a plain "no" and cannot be expressed more beautifully than in the words of the late Lord Keynes, who, while speculating on the "economic possibilities for our grandchildren" during the great depression of 1930, warned the coming generations against "valuing ends over means and preferring the good over the useful", if they wanted continued prosperity. Keynes wrote, "For at least another hundred years we must pretend to ourselves and to everyone that fair is foul and foul is fair; for foul is useful and fair is not. Avarice, usury and precaution must be our gods for a little longer still." If the road to prosperity is paved with bad intentions, as Lord Keynes would have believed, then religion, ethics and traditional wisdom must be suspended till at least we have attained full prosperity. Is not this the real face of rationality which the philosophers of European Enlightenment had been extolling over religion and metaphysics?

But granting that full material prosperity can be attained by a pursuit of unprincipled economics and amoral politics, are we sure that it can be universalized and that it will be lasting? If the affluent West, the exemplar of material prosperity, is any guide, both the possibilities are remote. Concealed behind the egalitarian exterior of the modern West lie gross inequalities of income and rank. Not all income groups are prosperous and rich; in fact it is in the very nature of modern technology to promote miserly in the midst of plenty. Lord Keynes, in his zeal to reject the economics of socialism as a universal remedy against business cycles, ended up with an economics worse than Karl Marx's.

There is yet another side to affluence-based prosperity. The affluent society, let us not forget, worships at the shrine of production; in its economic system needs are created in the same process in which they are satisfied. In an economic system like this, needs are bound to get the better of means. No human contrivance, much less technology, can keep the gap between the two at the minimum. Life in an environment, created by affluent society, therefore, cannot be rich; for man in such an environment cannot enjoy the fruits of this own labour, nor need they be of much use to him. If the best environment, which man can ever think of making for himself, is the one which, as Karl Jaspers puts it, auguments his being, then the environment in which he finds himself at the moment is just the antithesis of it, as it both kills his instinct of workmanship and destroys his aesthetic sensibility.

True, commodification is no longer the central concept in the understanding of a good life; the alternative concept is that of an ever-improving quality of life whose parameters extend far beyond gross hedonism. What is of essence to this alternative concept of good life, is leisure-based creative freedom that will lift man above the level of *human labourons* to which he has been reduced in the bureaucratic organization of work, and transform

him into a human being. There is no disputing the concept of a good life understood as an ever-improving quality of life. But, the trouble with all such alternative concepts – be they of development, progress, or good life – is that they are basically crisis concepts born of the failure of earlier concepts to click with reality. In other words, they are the new conceptual categories in terms of which science, in its self-expanding odyssey, has been trying to express the non-conceptual. The more and more has science become institutionalized, the greater the confidence with which it has tended to subsume reality under its own concepts.

It would be folly then to think that the requisite conditions of a good life can be created by succumbing to the labyrinthine logic of modernity. Poverty of life is only a softer name of dehumanization which simply cannot be overcome by a mere reproduction of modernity in whatever form and by whatever manner of means, we may choose to do so. To believe that modernity will accept any pre-existent value as an essential ground of a good life is again to labour under an illusion. Equally naive it will be to believe that its technology will ever agree to subserve any such value, as traditional and archaic technologies do.

Nor are we hinting at a post-modernist solution to the crisis of modernity. Both modernity and post-modernity are philosophies of an age of crisis. If the former arose in the background of the "death of God" the latter was born of the experience of the "death of Reason". As a child of Enlightenment reason was expected to do better than simply ensuring economic and technical progress. For instance, it was expected to play a more positive role in the eradication of poverty and ignorance and through it, in the abolition of tyranny and totalitarianism. The least that was expected of it was to become an instrument of domination. Therefore, to the extent that post-modernism is a project aimed at unmasking reason or making it aware of its mistakes and misadventures, we have no quarrel with this philosophy. But its hope that reason can be chastened and made to behave by debunking or exploding it, is just not going to be confirmed.

In fact, no project short of putting reason in its place, i.e., of making science aware of its limitations which may involve dismantling at least part of the superstructure of modern society, can take man out of his predicament. There is much point in what Gandhi has to say in his *Hind Swaraj* and what Schumacher has to say in his *Small is Beautiful*. Intermediate technology which Schumacher suggests as a replacement for the modern gargantuan technology, is intermediate not only in the sense that it is neither wholly primitive nor modern, but primarily because instead of being self-serving like its modern counterpart it will be subservient to the ends of life. After the manner of Gandhi, Schumacher likewise, talks of production by the masses as an alternative to mass production, and similarly "of an optimal pattern of consumption which means producing a high degree of satisfaction by means of a relatively low rate of consumption, instead of consumption by an optimal pattern of production".

We would be laughed out of court, if we were to talk of a religious science conscious of its moral responsibility and equally aware of the higher extra-scientific ends it has to serve. Instead of trying to dislodge religion from the scheme of life, science would do well to understand its own limitations and derive the maximum strength from ethics and religion to make human life nobler and richer.

18

Value Crisis and We

Value crisis in India is basically a crisis of transition, the outcome, or in other words, of an unduly prolonged rigour mortis of a civilization gasping for breath and of an equally inordinate delay in the birth of a new civilization. In the result, what we have in India today, is not a society but an "as if society", a "cultural pseudomorph" as Josepth Spengler would like to call it; a historical reality which not only lives in two social spaces but speaks in two voices simultaneously. One of these social spaces belongs to the traditional world, in which India lived before her encounter with the West and the other, to the modern world which the West had brought with it and which had been ushered in Europe in the wake of Enlightenment.

Life in the traditional world was considered sub-species enternitatis, a reflection, that is say, of eternity. Eternity, then, was the ultima ratio of life, the supreme goal to be realized. Plato had precisely this meaning of eternity in mind, when he defined man as a rational animal and equated rationality with the "logos" or "telos" which man was directed by nature to attain. To have anything else as a goal of life, was to know not, or to have only an imperfect knowledge of our nature. And to know this was to know wisely and also to love the order of nature or to look at

---

Radio talk delivered on 19 October 1994 on All India Radio, Allahabad.

everything as good and valuable. The renowned orientalist Paul Deussen could not appreciate the full meaning of the Biblical saying "love thy neighbour as thyself" until he read the philosophy of the *Upanishads* which equates the "I" with the par Brahman or Godhead. In the traditional world, nothing is devoid of meaning and value, which says that there is a perfect identity of knowledge, action and love in this world.

In the order of things that characterize modernity, things are primarily viewed as objects of manipulation and control and without any intrinsic value or significance, and life is considered a mode of temporality, sub-specie temporis, a teleology without telos, an arrangement without a design. In this order scientific knowledge is the only knowledge from which all other forms of knowledge are derived and with reference to which all other forms of knowledge are validated. Scientificity or scientific rationality is the only legitimate source of morality and goodness in this order. Bacon, the father of the modern empirical method, thought that to see reality without error or confusion, that is, to see it through the method of science, was to put oneself in tune with God in the truest sense of the word. Bacon in fact considered the traditional view of the universe as a meaningful order, as a positive hindrance in the way of scientific understanding of reality. Science demanded a discipline, an ascesis on our part, which could train us to see things as they are and not as we can see them in our own subjective way as things of value and significance.

It is the co-existence of these mutually opposed world views which is the source of our inauthentic existence in contemporary India and the breeding ground of all crisis in values. Reverting to the idea of the cultural pseudomorph, it is not giving any indication of early dissolution. On the contrary, every passing day it is creating an impression that it has come to stay. How it becomes a cause of confusion and crisis in our value-judgements can be illustrated by an example. Western societies, which went through an early and quick transition from tradition to modernity in the seventeenth and eighteenth centuries, have no need of the term "secularism" to express their sense of

commitment to rationality. Nor do they have any need to espouse the cause of rationality or to reject religion publically. But we need to do both, because even though we are secular according to the letter of law, we are religious in spirit, while in the West they may be religious according to the letter of law but are deeply rational and secular in spirit. Thanks to our divided existence, we often try to express tradition in the idiom of rationality and rationality in the idiom of tradition, to wriggle out of the embarrassing situations that we often face in our public life.

For instance, we have our own idea of symbolic activities such as observation of protocols as part of statecraft, appreciation of excellence through award of prizes and conferment of distinctions on individuals or groups, or performance of ceremonies like flag hoisting or singing of the national anthem. Their purpose, according to our thinking, is purely expressive. We do not sincerely believe that strict observance of these ceremonies will be really efficacious, and this largely explains our cavalier attitude to the secular ceremonies. A breach of procedure in their case does not constitute a sin as it does in the case of the religious rites. In the traditional order of things there is nothing symbolic; to the traditional man, the *yajna* (sacrificial operation) is not mere symbolic offering to gods, to him the gods literally accept the offerings and ensure a continuous flow of wealth and prosperity in the life of the sacrificer.

But our idea of religion is different. For us, it is the same kind of activity as our stylized social protocols which have no meaning beyond their execution. We, therefore, consider it as a private affair of the citizen for whom it supposedly means the same thing as it means to us. We, then, define secularism which is a cardinal value of modernity, as equidistant from religion, and under the cover of this play upon words, we exploit religion to promote our secular ends and take advantage of our formal secular status to honour our religious commitments at state cost and things go on like this.

We may take another example to bring home the point we want to stress. Exclusivist institutions in any form are inconsistent with the egalitarian character of our social polity.

We accordingly dispensed with the institution of caste, in fact with all kinds of discrimination. But as we had to minimize social distance, as a first step towards achieving social equality, we had to take recourse to a policy of protective or positive discrimination. Alongside of equality of opportunity and equality before law, we had therefore to provide in our Constitution for reservation of public space for certain sections of citizens to quicken the process of social levelling, which is to say, to bring them on a par with the other socially better off sections. We can now see for ourselves how this policy of protective discrimination is threatening to become a process of reverse discrimination because of the growing vested interest of political parties in the matter. A modern open society cannot afford to be discriminative for a long time, if it has to promote the values of merit and excellence.

Again, far from ensuring distributive justice, positive discrimination itself becomes exclusivist, if not implemented prudently, as experience has shown, leading as it does to the formation of "elite groups" within the discriminated and underprivileged themselves. While the principle of positive discrimination is succeeding in the West, yielding good results, in India it is threatening to become a disvalue.

Another aspect of our contemporary existence that needs to be touched upon in a discussion like this is the clash of values of what Aristotle calls "life" and "good life". Life means only biological survival and catering only for the needs of the body – be it hunger, sex or security. A career devoted exclusively to the pursuit of consumerist values is, therefore, not a human career but animal living. Good life, on the other hand, is centred around the virtue of excellence. The needs of the body, man shares with the animals, but what puts him in class different from and above the animals is "dharma" or virtue. The Indian saying which goes like this is only an endorsement of the Greek idea of a good life. This "good" or "virtuous life" is now under heavy inroads of consumerist values. The unabashed display of sex and violence on the screen and through the media is not only robbing the younger generations in India, of all sense of privacy as a virtue, it is also making them highly insensitive to universal values of temperance and self-control. There is nothing spiritual to them that does not inebriate.

Yet another aspect of the situation we are in. Violence cannot go with democracy, if democracy stands for a way of life or a form of government based on speech, argument and discussion. Violence is not necessarily physical always; it consists in an arbitrary exercise of power or enforcement of one's will over others. The so-called criminalization of politics consists essentially in the increasing area of social space that violence is being allowed to occupy in the public as well as private lives of individuals. The game of power has its own rules which if always honoured in breach will gradually convert it into an exercise in violence. Politics becomes the last refuge of scoundrels and criminals because it ceases to be good and moral, that is, when it ceases to be a value. Gandhi considered politics as a part of his religion to serve his compatriots, and linked it with the virtues of non-violence and *satyagraha*. To delink politics from religion is to delink it from goodness and morality, in other words, to make it value-neutral and this willy-nilly we are doing with vengeance in India today and facing the music produced by it. Reinhold Neibuhr, who thought that the individual was intrinsically good and moral as Gandhi also believed, and immorality belonged to institutions, was voicing the opinion expressed by all great thinkers who prized character over the role of social institutions that one's crime cannot be determined in the abstract way as is being done under the modern legal set-up. Overrationalized or formal justice is only a reification of substantive or living justice.

However, we are not suggesting that the dissolution of the pseudomorph or a quicker change over to modernity will lead to a solution of the value crisis. The western societies, which had rejected metaphysics, myth and religion long back in favour of rationality and humanitarianism, are faced with an equally deeper crisis.

19

Cultural Deprivation and Community Dynamics

Culture is the art of life. But much more than prudence, it is the pursuit of goodness and excellence; and since there are no known parameters of goodness and excellence, a cultured life can be lived only in imitation of an exemplary model, for that life will be verily uncultured which is unparadigmatic or without a pratirupa; such life will be equally ugly and deformed. If it be asked what is the model, which it is given to us to imitate, to be cultured, the answer would be "a life of suffering and sacrifice" as exemplified in the life of the Purusha or Prajapati of the Hindu mythology who is both the lord as well as the victim of the sacrifice which he himself performed to create the primordial norm "rita", primordial truth, "satya" and the primordial virtues "dharmanis" including the sacrificial act itself. Another approximation to the model of sacrificial life is the life of the suffering Christ and that of the suffering Buddha. Truly and consistently therefore good and excellent life in the Christian tradition is the imitation of "imago christi".

To imitate the life of suffering and sacrifice is to participate in life divine or to enjoy the companionship of the gods, indeed to translate oneself into godhood. Culture, in other words, is

---

Radio talk delivered on 2 September 1995 on All India Radio, Allahabad.

transubstantiation, an act of transformation of the lower self into the higher or of the symbol into the reality. The cultic origin of culture is an insight, modern man is wont to forget and disparage, as he has come to belong to a world where culture has been reduced to an object or worse still, a commodity with an exchange value, which can be acquired, purchased or even pirated and hence the pathetic relevance of the phrase "culture-vultures" men who are ever eager and who have the wherewithals, to acquire culture. Culture as a form of participation in sacrifice means a life based on competition in giving; in a sacrificial organization of work every one is a giver and no one an acquirer; where every one is trying to excel every one else in the art of giving or sacrificing and where all work is a loving service to humanity.

Equally as culture is the celebration of a rite, it is cultivation of the self. Cultivation of one's self or consciousness is the process of becoming firmly fixed in consciousness or to become "dhir" or "isthir buddhi". Such a state of mind is the result of total self-control. A self-cultivated, cultured-man is a picture of kindness, love, humility and commiseration – qualities which alone can enable one to true membership of the community.

The principal ingredient of the human situation which has become the breeding ground of cultural deprivation today and to which we may now turn, is the "overproletarianized" and "overmediated" life of modern man. Life in the modern industrial society is all work and no play and no leisure. Huizinga traced culture to the play element in life which in his opinion constituted an area of freedom and leisure. It is in play and leisure, according to him, that the spirit of competitive excellence, the basis of all civilized living, is rooted. Man for Huizinga is basically a playing animal, Homo Ludens as he calls him. If the Greeks could promote a culture of excellence in every walk of life including politics, it was mainly on account of their agonistic spirit of competing for the best and the excellent without any display of rancour or ill-will.

The link between culture and leisure has been still more thoughtfully worked out by Josef Pieper, who is of the view that denial of leisure to modern man is the real source of his cultural impoverishment. The modern proletarian man has no doubt ample leisure at his disposal in the form of vicarious free time, that is, free time in which he is occupied in a manner more conducive to hard work. His leisure is actually not a break *in* time but *of* time. Leisure as Pieper says is a form of silence in which we not only do not speak and do not exert but enjoy an extraordinary moment out of our overly busy work-a-day life when our mind is at complete rest, the kind of rest which was the bliss of solitude for poets like Wordsworth.

If man becomes a total labourer to which he has been reduced in the modern world, he looses his creativity both as maker and creator. Living in a community imposes on men the obligation to enjoy the fellowship of others, which he can do by displaying his excellence over others, i.e., by initiating deeds which will make him immortal or by which he can carve out a permanent place for himself in the memory of the coming generations. It is this striving immortality that lifts him above the labourer and the worker in him, or in other words makes him cultured. In the Indian tradition also perfect performance of one's vocational duties which is called "skill in works" or "Karmasu Kaushalam" is the way to the attainment of immortality. To do well, is given only to cultivated men.

In modern West, culture has become an industry and a vested interest in the hands of a class of elites which holds the monopoly of cultural goods or the symbolic capital as Pierre Bourdieu calls it, such capital comprising honour, prestige, recognition, titles and all, which is not open to the uncultivated, howsoever cultivated otherwise they may be.

Another source of disturbance to community life in the present-day world is the reified culture being offered for general consumption through the media. So powerful is the impact of the media blitz on the tastes and preferences of the common man that it is the images of life as projected on the TV by vested industrial interests that have become a substitute for reality rather than the other way around. However, as things stand, there seems no way out of the predicament in which modern man finds himself. His life has become totally unparadigmatic as we said above even though we are supposed to live in an age of paradigms.

20

Indian Social Diversity

A Boon or Bane

What reveals the true nature of Indian society even today is the deep diversity of its culture; and it is a remarkable testimony to her resilience that India has been able to preserve it, despite being hit by successive waves of cultural homogenization all through her long history of encounter with alien cultures. As is well-known, the first major cultural onslaught on her identity came from the modern western civilization with which it had come into contact through an imperial hegemony, viz., the colonial rule in India, which in the name of civilizing the barbaric races of India, as it then called the Indian people, tried to expose them to modern western ideas such as the homogeneous culture of a civil society, a liberal democratic state, a bureaucratic form of administration, a system of higher education in which a university degree rather than one's birth was the hallmark of one's identity and status, a middle class as bearer of this homogenized culture and so on.

However, it was not without resistance that the western ideas found acceptance from the people; may be that the resistance in the case of Anglicized nationalist Indians was more in the form of opposition to the agency which propagated them rather than to the ideas themselves. But for the generality of the

Radio talk delivered on 19 February 1996 on All India Radio, Allahabad.

people, none of the two – neither the ideas nor the agency – through which was spreading them was authentic, and hence they rejected them both. Still, by the time India won her independence, in fact long before it, western ideas had taken firm roots in the Indian soil so much so that a westernized modern India had already come into existence as an overlayer of traditional India. But, as we said, there was a tough resistance to homogenization if it threatened in anyway to detract from the richness of the Indian cultural heritage. Nor, did the British rule overtly plan to destroy the customs and traditions of the Indian communities; in fact it was none of its missions to westernize its colonies. To say so, may be an oversimplification of facts, as it was largely the modern system of education through a foreign language introduced by the colonial rule that was instrumental in cutting off and alienating generations of young Indians from their tradition and culture, in a word, in smudging their collective memory of what they were.

But, the threat to her cultural identity that India faces now after independence emanates not from any imperial hegemony, but from auto-imperialism: India's own easy and willing acceptance of westernizing ideals. What was an imposed westernization becomes a voluntary participation in the project of nation-building and development after independence. In fact, all the western ideas which were sought to be transplanted in India by the colonial rule were consolidated into this project of nation-building.

The idea of the nation or of the nation-state, we may point out, was carved out of the urban culture of anonymity which came in the wake of the Industrial Revolution and the Age of Enlightenment in Europe, as a replacement for the conventional ideas of the state which rested its claim to legitimacy on mythic origins of kingship and rituals associated with the coronation of kings. The nation-state, on the other hand, claims legitimacy on the identification of the people with the nation, on the promise, that is to say, of delivery of welfare services to the former. It is thus not the real but an imagined community.

But it is a bitter irony of history that while the nation-state is in process of erosion in the West where it arose – and its erosion has come in the aftermath of dissolution of the "information society", it is still in the nascent stage in Asia, and in India in particular. In the new information society in the West the individual is no longer tied down to a territory, he is no longer a citizen of a state, but a world citizen, a free floating individual being drifted to a destination which he does not know. In Europe, thanks to information explosion, national boundaries have ceased to be sacred or sacrosanct.

To revert to what we said above about Indian culture variety and heterogeneity are not the unique features of Indian culture alone. All normal cultures are characterized by variety; it is only when their variety is destroyed by an imposition of uniformity or systematicity on them that they lose their vitality and become moribund. What has surfaced as "ethnic upsurge" in overhomogenized societies of the West, is essentially the manifestation or assertion of the unreified part of the human spirit which resists undue regimentation. Ethnicity itself is a reified idea carved out of the vast pool of cultural anonymity of the urban West and is set in contrast with all that is global and universal.

Diversity is the natural expression of the human spirit, of the human will to creativity. Cross-cutting the natural diversity that the traditional cultures of India, Hindu, Muslim, Sikh, Parsi, Christians and others possess. We have a cultural pluralism created by the colonial rule which it had done by changing the ontology of the Indian people, through their decadal enumeration and their re-classification. The Hindus who were already divided into numerous religions, sects and culture groups were again classified as depressed classes and upper castes, and the majority community. The Muslims, likewise, who have their own religious sects, were again classified as a religious minority and so also were the other communities. It was this pluralism criss-crossing the natural diversity of Indian cultures on which Gandhi and Nehru wanted to base the Indian project of nation-building.

The Indian Constitution abolishes caste and untouchability and introduces a new social taxonomy conferring the status of an abstract citizen on every individual with fundamental rights, and re-classifying the people into Scheduled Castes, backward classes, religious minorities and so on. It thus also tries to create the twin imagined communities of the nation-state and civil society both based on secular law and cultural pluralism and throws the challenge to integrate them with the rest of India – the traditional, vibrant and living India.

How to do is the problem but a delicate one – delicate, because if we try to homogenize the rest of India with the secular nation-state in total disregard of the non-secular social space in which the large majority of the Indian people – we will be creating more intractable problems than we have had so far. We simply cannot whisk away the problem by relegating religion to a private enclave in an imagined secular social space. Nor will it help us to read secular meanings into the customs and traditions of the cultural groups just because it may suit our rhetoric of integration. What we are trying to suggest is that secular integration of traditional India, with the civil society or the nation-state in the making, will be the like old wine in a new bottle, of uniformization.

Likewise, the opposite ideology of integration of cultural groups with the so-called "mainstream culture" thought of as resting on a pre-fabricated unity of Indian culture is equally misconceived and sinister as it repeats the same mistake of imposing the cultural ideology of a particular group on other groups.

It is not necessary to borrow everything from the West in the name of nation-building and development, much less to mortgage our individuality and identity to global cultural hegemons in the name of participation in the information revolution. At the same time, we have to resist every internal attempt at cultural regimentation – be it in the form of promotion of secularism or glorification of the religion of nationalism. Our pluralist culture is an asset which we can ill-afford to fritter away.

Index